心繫今古，筆匯東西：

中華民國筆會季刊五十周年精選集

Bridging Past and Present, East and West

Celebrating 50 Years of Translating Chinese Literature

from Taiwan at the Taipei Chinese PEN

廖咸浩　主編

THE TAIPEI CHINESE **PEN**

CONTENTS

散文

小說

Editor's Preface

The publication of the English quarterly journal by the Taipei Chinese PEN proudly enters its fifty-first year. Reflecting on the history that led up to this historical milestone, I cannot help but appreciate the dedication of our predecessors who blazed a trail. It is hard to imagine how, without visionary guidance and unwavering determination, a non-governmental organization like The Taipei Chinese PEN could take on the tremendous cultural responsibility of translating local literary works for overseas readership and moreover managed to persist beyond fifty years even as it has consistently produced innovative content and published without interruption.

The quarterly, which was first inaugurated fifty-one years ago by Mrs. Nancy Chang Ing, has consistently invited exceptional translators proficient in both Chinese and English to translate masterpieces of contemporary literature from Taiwan and distribute them globally. This quarterly stands as the only publication of its kind among all PEN branches worldwide, others being primarily member newsletters. The translated works of poetry, prose, and fiction in the quarterly now exceed 2789, all of which are exemplary works of contemporary literature from Taiwan. With its distribution covering all corners of the world, the quarterly has gained increasingly widespread recognition. If one were to designate the quarterly as Taiwan's most crucial channel for translation of local literary works and cultural export over the past fifty years, it would be well-deserved.

On the occasion of the fiftieth anniversary of the quarterly, we have compiled this bilingual anthology to allow readers to witness, on the one hand, an overview of the evolution of contemporary literature from Taiwan over the past fifty years and, on the other hand, to appreciate the unique flavor these masterpieces have acquired through artful translation. Due to page restrictions, we unfortunately could not include every outstanding work, and thus, many exceptional ones had to be left out. However, we welcome interested readers to explore our previous quarterly issues for a comprehensive overview of literature from Taiwan compiled and translated in our journal.

Last but not least, I would like to express our special thanks to Mr. Tzu-hsien Tung, chairman of Pegatron Corporation, for his generous support that has revitalized the Taipei Chinese PEN and propelled us towards continuous improvement. Our gratitude is also extended to Mr. Winston Shen, CEO of Hotel Royal Group, for his kind contribution toward the timely publication of this commemorative book as a testament to history.

President: Sebastian Hsien-hao Liao 廖咸浩
at "Floating Boat on Starry River" on Qingtian Street
Friday, November 17, 2023

Yu Kwang-chung 余光中

A Pine Cone Falls
空山松子*

A pine cone comes stealing down
With no notice at all.
Who's there to catch it?
The needles or roots upon the ground?
The rocks or moonlight all around?
Or by chance a passing wind?
　　But it's sooner
　　Done than said:
A pine cone comes down, caught
By the vastness and naught
Of the whole mountain.

Translated by YU Kwang-chung 余光中

---

* From Yu Kwang-chung 余光中, *Yu Kwang-chung youmo shixuan*《余光中幽默詩選》
  (*Selected Humorous Poems by Yu Kwang-chung*), Taipei: Commonwealth Publishing Co.,
  2008, 60-61.

Pai Chiu 白萩

The Square
廣場[*]

The crowd noisily disperse back to bed
    to embrace sweet smelling women

Still the bronze statue upholds its principles
Arms raised in a call to action
Facing the empty square

But the wind
Impishly scatters the leaves
Laughingly erases the footprints

Translated by John J. S. BALCOM 陶忘機

---

[*] From Pai Chiu 白萩, *Shi guangchang* 《詩廣場》 (*The Square of Poems*), Taichung: Hotspot Publishing Co., 1984, 25.

Lo Fu 洛夫

Mailing a Pair of Shoes*
寄鞋**

From one-thousand miles away
I've mailed you a pair of cloth shoes
A letter
With no words
Containing more than forty years of things to say
That were only thought but never said
One sentence after another
Closely stitched into the soles

What I have to say I've kept hidden for so long
Some of it hidden beside the well
Some of it hidden in the kitchen
Some of it hidden beneath my pillow
Some of it hidden in the flickering lamp at midnight
Some of it has been dried by the wind
Some of it has grown moldy
Some of it has lost its teeth
Some of it has sprouted moss
Now I gather them all together
And closely stitch them into the soles

**From Lo Fu 洛夫, *Yinwei feng de yuangu*《因為風的緣故》 (*Because of The Wind*), Taipei: Linking Publishing Co., 2005, 64-67.

The shoes may perhaps be too small
I measured them with my heart, with our childhood
With dreams deep in the night
Whether they fit or not is another matter
Please never throw them away
As if something trivial
Forty years of thought
Forty years of loneliness
Are all stitched into the soles

Translated by John J. S. BALCOM 陶忘機

Bai Ling 白靈

Kite
風箏*

Rising steeply,
How high can a small hope soar?
Isn't a long, long lifetime just such a game?
One thin thread
Straining in a tug of war with the sky
Higher and higher, nearly out of sight
I run along the riverbank
Pulling the sky behind me

Translated by Nancy CHANG ING 殷張蘭熙

---

* From Bai Ling 白靈, *Wuhangshi ji chi shougao*《五行詩及其手稿》(*Cinquain and Their Manuscripts*), Taipei: Showwe Information Co., 2010, 27.

Shang Qin 商禽

The Electronic Lock
電鎖[*]

THAT NIGHT the street lights in the area where I
live again suffered a power cut just at midnight.

While I was groping for the keys in my pocket, the
considerate taxi driver saw to it that he turned the
car in such a way that it pointed straight at me; the
pitiless glare of the headlights threw the dark shadow of a middle-aged man on the iron gate. It
wasn't until I had selected the right key from the
bunch and inserted it in the lock of my heart that
the considerate taxi driver drove away.

Only then did I carefully turn the key which was
inserted in my heart and—click—at once pulled
out the ingenious piece of metal from my heart,
pushed open the door and entered resolutely. It
didn't take me long to get accustomed to the darkness inside.

Translated by N. G. D. MALMQVIST 馬悦然

---

* From Shang Qin 商禽, *Yongjiao sixiang*《用腳思想》(*Thinking with Feet*), Taipei: Hilit
Publishing Co., 1988, 12-13.

Lomen 羅門

Fort McKinley
麥堅利堡*

> What is beyond greatness,
> Is Man's sense of 'loss' in the presence of greatness.
> Lomen

Here War sits and weeps for the dead,
Seventy thousand souls sink to a realm deeper than sleep.

Cold is the sun, cold the stars and the moon,
Cold lies the Pacific, once seething and sizzling with plunging
    shells.

Smith, Williams, even glory stretches no arms to welcome you
    home.

Your names, telegraphed home, were colder than the wintry sea.

Betrayed by death, God is helpless about your helplessness.

The negative of greatness was developed in blood.
Here even War himself cries and Greatness smiles not.

Thousands of crosses bloom into an orchard, a lily lane, unshaken
    against the wind, against the rain.

---

* From Lomen 羅門, *McKinley bao*《麥堅利堡》(*Fort McKinley*), Taipei: The Liberal Arts
  Press Co., 1995, 3-5.

Silent to the gaze of Manila Bay and pale,

To the tourists' lenses. Smith, Williams,
On the confused lense of death, Where is the landscape often
    visited by youthful eyes?

Where were kept the records and slides of spring?
McKinley Fort, where birds have no heart to sing

And leaves, no heart to dance around.
Any sound will stab the silence and make it bleed.

Here is a space beyond space, time beyond clock.
Here even the speechless gray horizon speaks more than the dead.

Sound-proof garden of the dead scenery of the living.

Here. where God comes and also come the motorcars and the
    town,

Smith and Williams will neither come nor leave.
Motionless as a dial without a clock, sightless as the face of years.

In the darkness of high noon, in the starlessness of the night,

Their eyes are shut upon the seasons and the years,

Upon a world that never dies a complete death,
And a green lawn, green beyond my grief.
Here death reaps a rich harvest in the marble fields,

Where gaze the stars and stripes, timelessness and clouds.
McKinley Fort, where white crosses dash on white crosses

As dash the white surfs against the Pacific coast,
Where a great bas-relief of compassion is silhouetted

Against the blackest background of black doom,
Seventy thousand stories are burning in white restlessness,

Smith, Williams, when sunset sets the mango groves on wildfire,

(Even God is ready to depart, and stars fall in a downpour)

You cannot go anywhere, anywhere.
There is no door to the grim bottom of the Pacific.

Translated by YU Kwang-chung 余光中

Mei Hsin 梅新

Curriculum Vitae
履歷表*

Place of Origin:
I'll leave this space blank for the moment
Because I can't remember it
But I'm sure I have a place of origin
I just can't remember where right now

Date of Birth (Month, Day, Year):
That was the year China's lunar calendar
    had an intercalary month
An extra tenth month
That's when I was born
The weather that year . . .
Mother's words are legend
She said that no sooner was the umbilical cord cut
Than it froze solid
And when dropped onto the floor it gave off an icy gleam

Education:
My certificate from the old style private school
Is still being held beneath the teacher's rod

---

* From Mei Hsin 梅新, *Liulibiao*《履歷表》(*Curriculum Vitae*), Taipei: Unitas Publishing Co., 1997, 91-93.

Experience:
Shouldering a gun and holding a pair of binoculars
Sitting in a big old banyan tree
As a lookout for a new luxurious gambling house
Out of loneliness
I fired a shot into the air
Scaring everyone in the house
And so I lost my job

I haven't pasted a photo
On this CV yet
You can have it if you like

Translated by John J. S. BALCOM 陶忘機

Hsiang Ming 向明

Embroidered Quilt Cover
from Sister in Hunan (1987)

湘繡被面*
——寄細毛妹

Several days ago, I received from my sister, who was separated
from me for 40-odd years during the Nationalist-Communist
antagonism, an embroidered quilt cover. She did not include a
letter.

Four darting purple swallows
Two clusters of budding branches
In simple, plain strokes
Have captured all you want to tell me, all
Neatly and tightly embroidered on this thin silk.

This is a letter that one never gets tired of reading,
A letter without words,
When folded, it measures less than a foot,
One fold, the drifting heart would sink,
Another fold, forty years of separation time is stayed.

Hesitating for a long time, shall I open the envelope?
Fearing that opening it, a blood-dripping heart will jump out.
As I spread it out in display

---

* From Hsiang Ming 向明, *Hsianghui de shui*《想回的水》(*Water That Longs to Return*),
  Taipei: Chiu Ko Publishing Co., 1988, 165-167.

A whole bed of broad bright beautiful silk
Transforms itself into a road flanked by birds and flowers
As if one can walk on it leading to home.

If I could return home just like that!
Beautiful is this island; my floating roots lack soil.
Eyes that have been dulled for years
Must be released again into hometown's rimless sky,
But the folds and folds upon the silk
Are rugged as life.
The end of the road, the sea
The face of the sea, still
Turbidly hideous.

Translated by Wai-lim YIP 葉維廉

I-Chih CHEN 陳義芝

In Search of a Poet Recluse[*]
尋淵明[*]

Legend has it that he wrapped a cloth around his head
Picked up a cane, plunged into the wild forest
And vanished into god knows where
I have seen people search the tall grass and make their way
    through the mulberries and the hemp field
I hear the barking of dogs and the cock-a-doodle-doo of the rooster
See the elms, pagoda trees, pears and peaches
But not the door that some say he purposely left half open

I run into someone who stocks firewood and ask
He used to live in his hometown there
After his house burned down, he moved to South Village
I run into a fisherman and ask
He hid his drinks in his poetry tomes and his life in the lute strings
Boated on the full lake and paddled in the clear streams

Rumor has it that he planted willows and mended the fence
Donned a formal cap and an official robe
Single-heartedly planted glutinous rice to brew his own drinks
He hankered for the crop, but refused to bend his knees to the
    harvest

---

* Tao Yuanming (365-427 AD), a Chinese poet of reclusion, famously abandoned his offcial
  career as a gentleman scholar for a simple agrarian life in the countryside.

**From the Literary Supplement of *Lianhe Bao*《聯合報》(United Daily News), December 5,
  2014.

Autumn arrived with a telltale leaf falling down to the stone steps
    in the yard
That muted the words he wanted but could not bring himself to
    say

He dined on dew-glazed chrysanthemum petals
Looked up to meet the familiar glance of the southern ridge
Nearby there were people talking, in the distance he saw smoke
    disperse in the wind
Farther away he heard the muffled sound of a cruel, raging war
A boundless red glow illumined the dark yellow sky
Lighting up the trenches of humanity twisted

Legend says he dreamed of an unknown river
Flowing from nowhere, that had never greeted visitors
Some place as yet unborn, perchance the same setting
Where he, heavy-hearted, would pace back and forth in the middle
    of a sleepless night
Where a thousand peaks shone in the fog
And ten thousand peach trees blossomed in unison

I stretch my eyes to look far into the unknown distance
A lone hawk shrieks loudly in the sky
An aged pine bends down as if to till the land like the poet recluse
The penniless gent who once begged for food, a scholar
    nevertheless
Whom I call an anarchist in times of chaos
One who prefers to live without a government

Alas! Is there anyone in this modern age who can
Dialog with him, pour him a glass of wine?
Where can one find the fishermen on
Wuling Brook now

Or the reclusive herbalist Liu Ziji?
The Taoyuan hamlet of the Taiyuan era vanished a thousand years
    ago
Where in this world does one find a curious inquirer now?

Translated by Yanwing LEUNG 梁欣榮

CHEN Yu-hong 陳育虹

I Call Thee Syria
—*to Aylan Kurdi, the Little Boy Who Perished on the Beach*

我叫你叙利亞*
——給Aylan Kurdi，沙灘上的小男孩

Like a good boy you just lie down and sleep on your tummy
Your puckered lips may suggest thirsty
Your bulging behind may perchance indicate a wet diaper
You sleep on the sand in your red tee and blue shorts
Grains of sand stick to the bottom of your running shoes
Are you running tired?
Are you listening to the sound of the waves?

(As you set out
For Ithaca, says the Greek poet**
May you have a long journey
Filled with adventure, filled with discovery . . . .)

You are heading for Ithaca
And yet the beach is cold, this is not
Your home. The waves are cold
You can't find your bed here

---

* From Li Chin-wen 李進文 ed., *Chuangshiji shi zazhi*《創世紀詩雜誌》(*The Epoch Poetry Quarterly*), No. 185, Taipei: Epoch Poetry Society, 2015, 29.
**A loose quote from "Ithaca" by the Greek poet C. P. Cavafy.

Someone picks you up
Like a sacrificial lamb
Your 3-year-old body stiff and motionless

(On your way to Ithaca. Someone
Spots your drifting body
Bobbing in the waves
To arrive in Bodrum a tourist attraction)

At least there is no fighting and killing on the beach
You gently close your eyes, Ithaca is still
A long way from here, but nearby heaven takes down
Its borders. My child
I call you Syria
At this moment, you lie in the arms of Jehovah
Or rush to meet Allah

Translated by Yanwing LEUNG 梁欣榮

Hung Hung 鴻鴻

I Am Running Out of Time

—To the workers fasting in protest of the labor
 protection laws revised for the worse

我現在沒有時間了[*]

I am running out of time
Time is on your side
Eight days a week, six seasons a year
You are the Almighty, and all my ribs and my spine
Have been repossessed by you

I am running out of time
I fall asleep behind the wheel
Sleepwalk when tending to someone
Eat my bento when sitting on the toilet
Pick up a child when I smoke
And you
Get paid to attend meetings
Count your money while vacationing
Count your money while having sex
Truth is, you don't even need to count
A brass pipe will siphon what's in the juice machine
All the way to the safe box hidden in your home

---

* From Ling Hsing-chieh 凌性傑 ed., 2018 *Taiwan shixuan*《2018臺灣詩選》(*The Best Taiwanese Poetry 2018*), Taipei: Fish & Fish, 2018, 169.

I am running out of time
You have the alarm clock
But I do not intend to surrender the battery in my hand
Nor do I want to forfeit my spine
Or the precious moments of time when my child and I
Lift our heads to look at the sky
I have no intention to surrender my own sky

The soil will turn fertile given time
Time will change a caterpillar into a butterfly
I need time to be able to breathe
And you also need time
To come to terms with yourself in the mirror

Translated by Yanwing LEUNG 梁欣榮

Hsu Hui-chih 許悔之

A Flea Hearkening to the Buddha's Teachings
跳蚤聽法*

My Buddha, when You sit there in Your meditation posture, back
  straight,
With the raw force of a roaring ocean and the serene poise of a
  huge mountain
All I hear is the noise of chirping cicadas, filling my ears
Swallowing all other sounds like breaking waves, drowning out the
  sound of
Me calling out to You
Calling You, my Buddha
I've been following You, listening to You expounding the Dharma
  for
Forty years
And I've realized long ago that You've got no Dharma to talk about
And that there's no Enlightenment for me to attain
Yet You are the boat that's supposed to ferry me across the river
How can I burn the boat when I've not reached the other shore
  yet?

For forty years, I've been smelling Your scent
Observing Your shape, and watching the Dharma grow bigger like
  an

---

* From Hsu Hui-chih 許悔之, *Buyao wenxundi duoru naye youshang*《不要溫馴地踱入，那夜
憂傷》[Do Not Go Gentle into That Sorrowful Night], Taipei: ECUS Publishing House, 2020,
103-105.

Abandoned infant
Yet You, my Buddha, You've been growing thinner with every
    passing day
I can hear the gaunt bones coming apart within Your emaciated
    form

I, too, know happiness, though not preoccupied with the joy of it
I'm a little flea, graciously tolerated
In the folds of Your robe, living in Your generous embrace
They are still listening to You expounding the Dharma
Some are crying tears of shame and humility
Others are rejoicing, awed as they grasp Your message
But only I, I alone, know that
You already have nothing left to say

For the first time in forty years,
I will—sadly, but without fear—
Bite You and drink Your blood
Now I exult in the Dharma, for I alone in the whole world
Have sucked Your precious blood
Now I am stricken with terrible Dharmic grief, for what I'm
    imbibing is
The very last teardrop of this world

Translated by David VAN DER PEET 范德培

Yang Mu 楊牧

MSS Sealed in a Bottle
瓶中稿[*]

Now the sun sinks where it is the west
Beyond the cypress. The waves are
On this shore. I know, of course, each of them
Sets off from Hualien. I was inspired once
When I was a child to ask the ocean whether
There was another shore beyond its faraway edge—
And now the other shore is this, here, with
Stars scattered around

And there are just the scattered stars
Shining on my exhausted sentiments
Tenderly asking the surging waves
If they remember the beach of Hualien

I wonder if it takes ten years, too
For the wave, which roars up to the Hualien beach
and ebbs orderly, to travel to this place. I wonder
But I suppose it takes just a determination
To participate: as the wave turns back to the ocean
It assumes the permanent form, as it always does
And, immediately, it flows on this solitary shore

* From Yang Mu 楊牧, *Yangmu shiji yi: 1956-1974*《楊牧詩集・壹：一九五六——九七四》
(*Collected Poems of Yang Mu I: 1956-1974*), Taipei: Hong Fan, 1978, 467-470.

Suppose I sit down quietly and listen to it
And suppose I am observing its form
To figure out a portrait of myself:
Can the little one on the left
Be a fry of fish?
The other one, bigger and rather exquisite
Is probably a blade of sea weed. And farther
There is a sizable one, which may very well be
A skipjack rushing the fisherman's light in the summer night

I wonder what I should choose to be
Now, when there is a wave surging near
Toward this solitary shore
Maybe I should just become a wave
Turning back and merge, presently
In the peaceful ocean
And flowing up to the beach of
Hualien

But, if I do walk toward the ocean
The waters will rise, due to the law of conservation of mass
And the sand on the other shore will be wetted a little more than
    usual
And if I keep on walking and even submerge
Seven feet west of the solitary shore
I suspect there will be a rumor in Hualien
Now when it is June, that a tidal wave will engulf the town

Translated by Mu Yang 楊牧

LUO Chih-Cheng 羅智成

Father
父親*

I have always wished to write you a poem,
But the secret of our mutual love
Is a family possession, not to be wastefully expended

We will walk one day along the big lake's shore
As his spirit counts the shoal of fish
We will help him check the fragrant flowers and water fowls
As the stars appear after their daily ablution
We, with our vagrant spirit
Help him measure the soil;
Then we squat on the field
Our eyes, filled with abundance
And in quietude, the murmuring of wind with rustling grass
Peaceful smiling faces relaxing with the night
One day we will rise from the paddy fields of our posterity
Never again singing pessimistically of our bodies
We will bequeath our blessings to the stubborn strong heads
Of our next generation—
If we had not obstructed the blazing sun
The blazing sun would mold their shoulders
If we had not stopped the flood

* From Luo Chih-Cheng 羅智成, *Guang zhi shu*《光之書》(*Book of Light*), Taipei: Commonwealth Publishing Co., 2000, 172-173.

The flood would give them trunkfuls of wisdom
Deeply locked within their brows

One day, we will rise to the sky
To reclaim
Staking out our fields on the constellations of the stars
Cultivating our vegetable fields
Compiling the records of our locality
This moment, please look at me
My silver brow due to my deep slumber, melting
The farm animals drink beside my pillow
The village women knit fish nets with the shimmering light of the
    waves
Along the big lake's shore
Stretching ever tightly the curtain of night, yet unable to cover
This vast rich land, Look
The distant dawn,

Father, and our family
Will flourish like the forest
Like the tall mast raised up high in the sea of time.

Translated by Nancy CHANG ING 殷張蘭熙

LIN Wen-yueh 林文月

From Wen-chou Street to Wen-chou Street
溫州街到溫州街[*]

Between Professor Cheng's home on Lane 74, Wen-chou Street and Professor Tai's on Lane 18, there was only Hsin-hai Road.[1] At a brisk pace, it took only seven to eight minutes to go between the two, and strolling, it wouldn't take more than fifteen minutes. The cars, however, racing along that street had frightened the two aged scholars from visiting each other for some years. In earlier years, before Wen-chou Street was cut into two by Hsin-hai Road, faculty housing for National Taiwan University was scattered throughout the area. Many of our teachers lived there. They used to take walks through the less frequently traveled lanes to visit each other and talk about everything under the sun. As time rapidly passed by, the population of Taipei greatly increased, and the face of the city became terribly altered. Our teachers became old men over eighty. Hsin-hai Road became a line of demarcation of two worlds hard to cross, and Professors Cheng and Tai would keep in touch and exchange information by telephone. On the rare occasions they would meet, it would be in restaurants some distance from each other's home. They would be driven and escorted there by their students and, sitting next to each other, would be seen laughing and

---

[*] From *A Collection of Prose Works of 1991*, Ed, by Lin Hsi-chia, Chiu Ko Publishing co. Taipei, 1991.

1 Tai Ching-nung（臺靜農）and Cheng Chien（鄭騫）were two distinguished professors of Chinese Literature at the National Taiwan University for about forty years since 1946.

talking jovially.

One spring afternoon three years ago, I went to see Professor Cheng after teaching my class. It was when *The Poetry of Ch'ing-chou-t'ang*[2] had just been published. Professor Cheng could hardly conceal his joy and told me to wait in the parlor, saying he wanted to get a copy for me that he had already signed. As he rose slowly from the sofa, he mumbled, "My legs have become weaker and feebler recently." Then, he carefully fumbled along in his own hallway. Looking at this frail figure in a blue Chinese long gown, I could not help feeling once more the sorrow and helplessness of someone being left behind by time.

The *Poetry of Ch'ing-chou-t'ang* was a collection of more than one thousand poems that Professor Cheng had written before he was eighty-two years old. He had done the annotations himself. With 488 pages in all, it was a weighty volume.

Receiving the elegantly-designed volume from his slightly shaking hand, I shared with my teacher's joy at seeing his poems published. I knew quite well how much time had been spent on the editing and copying to the proof-reading and publication. My teacher greatly valued the publication of this collection and hoped through it to leave something for posterity.

Seeing me excitedly paging through the book, Professor Cheng asked as if in consultation, "I want to present a copy to Professor Tai personally. When you have some time, would you drive me there?" The title on the cover of the book was written in Professor Tai's very regular *li* script,[3] and Professor Cheng concludes his Preface to the collection, "My old friend Mr. Tai Ching-nung long ago in his *Lung-po* essay 'Calligraphy and Me'[4] declared that he would do no more calligraphy for the public, so I am especially grateful that he

---

2　The Poetry of Ch'ing-chou-t'ang（清晝堂詩集）, published by Tung Ta Publishing Co., 1988.

3　Li (official) script is a style of calligraphy developed in the Han Dynasty.

4　"Calligraphy and Me"（我與書藝）an essay in Tai Ching-nung's *Lung-po Essays*（龍坡雜文）, published by Hung Fan Publishing Co., 1988.

has made an exception for me." Of course I also understood that his wanting to place his new collection of poetry in Professor Tai's hands personally was not just out of gratitude. A couplet from T 'ao Ch'ien [5] goes:

Sharing the delight of unusual masterpieces,

Together we try to interpret their ambiguities.

Moreover, since this collection was the crystallization of over half his life time, he must have been very anxious to share the results with his respected, old friend.

We called Professor Tai and made an appointment for the next Sunday morning at ten o'clock for me to take Professor Cheng to Professor Tai's residence. We decided on Sunday morning because the traffic on holidays is lighter, and his daughter would be at home to watch the house.

It was a sunny, warm Sunday morning. I called Professor Cheng before starting out so that he could get ready. I arrived at 74 Wen-chou Street and parked the car. With the help of his son-in-law, Mr. Ku Chung-hou, I seated him in the car, and returned to the driver's seat. He was, as usual, in his long blue gown, and carefully holding a copy of his new book. Though he wore very thick glasses for near-sightedness, he had a very good memory. As soon as we got on the way, he began to give me instructions where to turn left and right to get out of the narrow Wen-chou Street labyrinth. Actually, those lanes and alleys were familiar to me, too. At the south side of Hsin-hai Road, I stopped, waiting for the traffic light to turn green so that I could go straight across to the other section of Wen-chou Street. But Professor Cheng asked, "Have we passed Hsin-hai Road?" He then told me, "After Hsin-hai Road, you have to turn right, go to the end of the lane and turn left, continuing on to Professor Tai's house." I hesitated. It was not the route I would usually take. My teacher's tone, however, was very firm, just as when he had taught us

---

5 This two lines are taken from Tao Ching (365-427)'s poem "Moving"（移居）.

many years ago. So I followed his instructions, until I ended up on a lane with a "NO LEFT TURN" sign, and was forced to turn back and go the way I knew. When Professor Cheng realized his instructions were in error, he repeatedly apologized. I tried to console him by saying, "It's not that your memory has gone wrong, but that the roads in Taipei have changed too drastically. What you remember is the way we went in the past. Many roads and lanes are restricted now, and do not permit right- or left-hand turns." "It has been some years since I last visited Professor Tai. Now I can't even find the way," he said with a touch of melancholy, habitually rubbing his bald head with his right' hand.

"The fact is that you have such a good memory that you still remember the way it was in the past," I said, trying to cheer him up, but I felt a surge of sadness and was not sure whether it helped to comfort him.

After seeing us off, Chung-hou had given Professor Tai a call to let him know we were on our way. When my car entered Lane 18 of Wen-chou Street, we could see from a distance that Professor Tai was already standing at his gate waiting for us. Since I had driven quite slowly and had gone the wrong way, ever-anxious Professor Tai must have been waiting for a long time. Lane 18 had cars parked on both sides, allowing only one car to pass through. I could not get out, so Professor Tai had to help Professor Cheng get out of his seat. I drove further down the lane to find a parking space. As the car slowly moved forward, I saw the tall dignified Professor Tai carefully supporting the frail and slightly hunched over Professor Cheng as they stepped over the threshold. It was such an interesting contrast of images as well as a memorable, heart-warming scene. Professor Cheng was four years younger than Professor Tai, now, with his waddling foot steps, he looked older and weaker.

When I finally had the car parked and entered Professor Tai's study through the half-opened door, my two teachers were already seated in their customary seats—Professor Tai calmly seated in his rattan chair, with Professor Cheng lightly perched on the seat opposite him. Facing each other, the two were talking across the large desk. In the middle of the desk, amid books, inkstands, brushes, tea-cups and ashtrays, was the opened volume of Professor Cheng's poems. Professor Tai was already flipping through the book, eagerly reading some lines, and then would turn to the front or back cover, saying, "Ahh! This is a good expression. This is good!" Professor Cheng would lean forward, slightly bending over, and look at Professor Tai through his thick, near-sighted glasses. He would not say much, only responding with a muffled exclamation. It was his way of expressing approval or concentration when he was reading a student's good report or listening to people talk of something interesting. And such was the way he listened to his old friend's opinion of his new book. It was then that I suddenly realized how it must have looked when the ancients were "appreciating a masterpiece together."

I sat quietly at a distance by the wall, sipping the lukewarm tea, trying to watch this meeting from an objective and detached perspective. However, I could not help becoming involved in their emotional world and partaking of their joy and friendship. Tears began to gather in my eyes.

A few days later, Professor Tai wrote a poem eulogizing *The Poetry of Ch'ing-chou-t'ang*:

Thousands of poems composed after crossing to the south,

Exquisite and elegant, worthy as models for posterity.

More admirable still is the poet's unique effort,

That there is no need for a more authoritative Cheng's Commentary.

There can be no argument regarding Professor Cheng's poetic exquisiteness; however, Professor Tai's allusions to the "Cheng's Commentary"[6] is like a Heaven-sent stroke, marvelously surpassing

---

6 Cheng's Commentary（鄭箋）: Cheng Hsuan（鄭玄）(127-200) was the last Han scholar whose commentaries on the *Shih Ching and the Li Chi* supplanted earlies commentaries on these classics and were considered by early scholars as the primary and orthodox commentaries. It has also been a model of its kind. Prof. Tai's allusion to Cheng's commentaries here is a most

time and space. Could it be that they often call each other on the phone so that now when face to face they seem not to have any worthy news to talk about? Or could it be that the profound understanding between them cultivated through the years had made words unnecessary so that their silence was even more eloquent than words?

About half an hour passed as they visited. Then Professor Cheng said, "Well, I'm going back." "Alright," was Professor Tai's equally brief reply.

Our method for getting back to Professor Cheng's house was the same as coming to Professor Tai's. First, I asked Professor Tai to call the daughter and son-in-law of Professor Cheng, Ping-shu and Chung-hou, so that when we reached Lane 74, Wen-chou Street, they would be waiting in front of the house. This time, however, I did not get out of the car. After I saw that Professor Cheng was safely escorted back to his home, I drove to my home at full speed. Once back home, I broke out into a sweat. I realized then what a risk I had taken to have driven an old man over eighty years old who had very poor eyesight and great difficulty in walking through the nerve-testing traffic of metropolitan Taipei. Nonetheless, I felt as if I had completed a great mission and a feeling of joy and satisfaction arose within me.

That was the last meeting of Professor Cheng and Professor Tai. The condition of Professor Cheng's legs worsened; and the usually robust Professor Tai was unexpectedly found to have a malignant tumor. After being bedridden for nine miserable months, he passed away last autumn.

On the day of Professor Tai's funeral, supported by his daughter and son-in-law, one on each side, Professor Cheng came to the funeral hall early in the morning and sat mournfully in a front-

---

remarkable literary pun, because Prof. Cheng has the same surname, and he has written the most authoritative commentaries of his own poetry.

row seat. He was the first to pay public respect to the deceased. His frail figure looked even thinner. His long put-aside suit seemed to be dangling on a hanger. Supported by his daughter and her husband, his feet hardly touched the ground. He cried while moving tremulously toward the platform, tears streaming down the front of his suit. This sight saddened everyone present in the hall. I looked around at the elegiac scrolls hanging throughout the hall. The one contributed by Professor Cheng read as follows:

Friendship of sixty years made profound by literature and wine and now facing your portrait I am left alone.

Homeland eight thousand Li away grows dearer in the sorrow of knowing we are both doomed not to return.

Ever since then, the memory of that spring morning still remains vivid in my mind. It is hard to believe it was not a dream.

Following Professor Tai's death, Professor Cheng grew more and more forlorn. Once, during my visit, he said, "With his departure, Professor Tai has taken half of my life with him." Seeing my astonishment, he added, as if making a note for one of his poems, "This is no exaggeration. In the past, when I had a problem, I could always call him. If he too could not remember what I wanted to know, he could usually give me a clue on how to find out. Now, there is no one to consult with and no one to turn to for consultation." The sorrow of losing a trusted friend who had shared with him the joy of Literature and Wine was undisguisedly carved on his face and echoed in his voice. I fumbled for words to comfort him, but ended up sitting there in sympathetic silence. When his legs had become even weaker, he had to depend on a wheelchair even at home, and a nurse was hired to take care of him all the time. In the gloomy twilight, he was sitting trapped in the wheelchair, looking lonely and helpless. I recalled the beginning lines of his poem "The Loneliness of Poets," "Through the ages, poets have been lonely. If there were no loneliness, they could not produce poetry." Professor Cheng was a poet. Losing his friends in his old age and conscious of the ebbing of his own life, what he was feeling could not be just loneliness! His conversation now mainly revolved around his declining physical condition, though he was working slowly and determinedly on putting in order his poetic and academic writings. Obviously, an inexpressible and unavoidable anxiety was troubling him.

Before going abroad at the beginning of this summer vacation, I had bought a box of Professor Cheng's favorite cakes and telephoned to see whether I could go and say goodbye to him. To my surprise, the one who talked to me on the phone was a nurse. She urged against my going, saying, "Your teacher suddenly lost his memory three days ago. Now he is in bed and cannot receive visitors." This unexpected development left me dumbfounded. "Is it dangerous? Will it last for some time? Is he in pain?" While I was asking this series of questions, the very feeble but clear-minded figure I had seen two weeks before appeared vividly in my mind. It made me think that it must have been a joke of Heaven to have made such a keen mind so suddenly lose its memory. "Such things are hard to say. Some people may survive for a long time, while others may go quite soon," she informed me from her professional experience.

On my trip, I had forebodings all the way. The one wish coming repeatedly to my mind was the hope to see my teacher when I returned to Taiwan. But I was not sure that the frail old man could stand the torture of disease too long! The sad memory of Professor Tai being tortured by cancer could not be put out of my mind.

Early in the morning of July 28, I had a long-distance call from Ko Ch'ing-ming, a colleague in the Chinese Department. He told me that Professor Cheng had passed away. Ch'ing-ming well knew how anxious and uneasy I had been before leaving Taiwan. He repeatedly said, "Professor Cheng passed away without too much pain. He died peacefully, composed." Late on a September evening I returned to Taiwan. The next evening I prepared a box of cakes to take to Lane

74, Wen-chou Street. Ping-shu and I embraced each other in tears. She recounted the details of his last days and the day he died. He had passed away very serenely. I looked around at the well-arranged bookshelves, the scrolls of calligraphy and the paintings on the walls. Everything was kept just the same as it was. Maybe it was because I was not in Taipei when he had died, and did not see his body, so even when I heard her tell me all the details, I could not be convinced that it was true. It was as if as I was seated on the sofa, my teacher would come out from his study, waddling and coughing, a Professor Cheng, though walking with difficulty, no longer confined to a wheelchair.

Walking out of Lane 74, Wen-chou Street without Professor Cheng, I slowly walked across Hsin-hai Road, and entered the other end of Wen-chou Street. Stars were twinkling in the Taipei sky, still awaiting the autumn, and the stifling air of summer was swirling about everywhere. Once more I missed so much that mid-spring morning of three years ago. Tears streamed down my cheeks. In the middle of the road, I stopped suddenly. I would never see Professor Tai again in Lane 18 of Wen-chou Street. I was told that his Japanese-style house had already disappeared. A high-rise of cement and steel was under construction in full swing there. Ever since the passing away of Professor Tai, I had not had the courage to go near that area. I hesitantly proceeded towards it, sometimes stepping back to give way for cars to pass.

I don't know how long I had walked when I finally came to the beginning of Lane 18, Wen-chou Street. In the dim night light, there stood a row of unfinished apartments. I stood at the spot that should have been the old Number 6. Looking intensely amidst the rough cement columns, I seemed to see a study in a modest wooden house. Looking again, I thought I saw two respected scholars sitting in the study talking. Then, I heard their warm, hearty conversation and felt the warmth of the spring sun.

Translated by Pang-yuan CHI 齊邦媛

PAI Hsien-yung 白先勇

Even the Tree Isn't the Same
— *In memory of my late friend,*
Wang Kuo-hsiang

樹猶如此 [*]
——紀念亡友王國祥君

In the western corner of the back garden of my house, right next to the fence, there was once a row of three Italian cypresses, trees that originate from the coastal region of southern Europe and are quite distinct from all other cypresses. The trunk soars up, straight as a pencil, to a height of sixty or seventy feet, and two people holding hands can just reach around its girth at the base. Above, the branches are compact and do not grow out in wild profusion, so the tree seems to rise out from the earth as if majestically holding up the sky, a richly verdant and powerful pillar, like a great stone obelisk. The seaside climate of southern California is warm, just like that of the Mediterranean, and Italian cypresses can be seen everywhere. In some of the huge mansions with their extensive gardens, people grow them closely together in a line, so that from a distance they form a single wall, a luxuriant green fence rising up into the clouds.

I moved into the house in Hidden Valley in 1973. It is called Hidden Valley because the area is surrounded by mountains on three sides and also is thickly wooded, making the place seem secluded.

---

[*] From Choong Yee Voon 鍾怡雯 and Chen Ta-wei 陳大為 eds. *Tianxia sanwenxuan* 《天下散文選》 [Commonwealth's selection of essays], Taipei: Commonwealth Publishing Co., 2001.

Although located in the city, hills shield its view, making it difficult to find. When I first went in search of the house using the address in the newspaper, I turned this way and that, only finding it after getting lost many times. Finally, behind a hill, nestled deeply in a valley, I suddenly came upon it. Dusk was falling as I drove along the hilly road into Hidden Valley and I was greeted by the contrasting shades of green from the mountains and the trees stretching out in front of me. I just felt it was a perfectly quiet and sheltered place. But I never imagined I would still be living in the valley today, more than twenty years later.

Number 940 Barcelona Drive is halfway up the slope, and it is a very ordinary one-story building. One might say that certain people and houses are made for each other, and I fell for this one as soon as I saw it, mainly because of the big trees both in front and behind. In front of the house, a massive and quite ancient, pagoda-like pine towered majestically, and behind it a pair of Chinese elms swayed gracefully and seductively like weeping willows. On both sides, there were dense thickets of shrubs shutting out the neighbors, and the whole building was secluded under the shade of the trees. I loved this kind of house hidden away among the woods, and the price was just right, so I paid the deposit right away.

The house itself was well maintained and needed no attention. The problem was the flowers and shrubs growing outside. The owner was particularly fond of ivy, and everywhere the garden was full of this creeper, wheedling its way into every corner. Ivy has an amazing persistence, and getting rid of it takes a huge amount of time and effort. Not only that, but there were daisies, poppies, and hibiscus, none of which are plants that I like. To pull them all out took a massive amount of work, and it was far more than I could achieve on my own. Fortunately, that summer my good friend from high school, Wang Kuo-hsiang, came over from the East Coast to Santa Barbara and helped me, and the two of us worked together to clear this Hidden Valley garden and plant the flowers and trees of my choice, providing the basis for the way the garden subsequently turned out.

Wang Kuo-hsiang was at that time doing his postdoctoral research at Pennsylvania State University. He only had one and a half months of vacation, but we spent all of thirty days on the gardening. Every day we started at nine in the morning and did not stop till the onset of evening at five or six called an end to our toil. We cleared the undergrowth, pulled out the unwanted plants, and piled up several truckloads of branches and shrubs till finally the garden was emptied down to its bare outline. Both Kuo-hsiang and I were novices at gardening, so by the end of the day our whole bodies ached, but fortunately the summer climate in Santa Barbara is not too hot, and so working shoulder to shoulder under the gentle breeze and mild sun did not seem too arduous.

Santa Barbara is a wine-producing region, and there is a company there that makes an apricot wine called "Aprivert" which is crisp and sweet, a top-quality wine. When chilled, it is exceptionally palatable. Our neighbor had a plum tree, and half of one branch extended into my garden. This plum tree was rather special, having a very large fruit called a sugar-plum, with plenty of blood-red juice, sweet as honey. In July of that year, the whole tree was laden with mouth-watering fruit, hanging there like little red globes. Initially, Kuo-hsiang and I were a little concerned that picking someone else's fruit in broad daylight was not quite right, but later we discovered that according to the law in California, if a tree extends into your property, then the fruit is yours, and so, with full legal backing, we fetched a ladder and Kuo-hsiang climbed up into the tree while I picked up the fruit down below, and in a moment we had collected a whole bucketful of dark red plums. After finishing work, when the sun sank beneath the horizon, we would sit on the lawn under the gentle breeze sipping Aprivert and eating sugar-plums, and we soon recovered from the weariness of the day.

Santa Barbara has been called the "Pacific Paradise." The scenery of the city really does make it captivating, but I am convinced that one of its main attractions is the richness of the seafood: stone crab, lobster, sea urchin and abalone are all local specialties, Stone crabs in particular, with their hard shell, soft and succulent flesh and giant claws, are a delicacy in Santa Barbara. At the time, Americans did not really know how to eat crabs in their shells, so at the fish market on the wharf, live crabs were just a dollar each for female crabs and one-fifty for males. Being from Zhejiang, it was natural for Wang Kuo-hsiang to love this kind of food, and whenever we went to the fish market, we brought back four or five huge crabs which we then ate steamed. The key to steaming a crab is timing, as half a minute too long and it is overdone, but half a minute too little and it is still raw. Wang Kuo-hsiang relied entirely on instinct, so he would be watching the shell slowly turning red and then, muttering "done," he would pluck the crab from the pot, confident that it would be steamed just right. Then with sliced ginger and rice vinegar on the side and a jar of warmed Shaohsing wine, that would be our dinner. Over the summer the two of us wolfed down at least several dozen stone crabs. That year I had just obtained tenure, and *Taipei People* had been published not long before. After Kuo-hsiang had graduated from the University of California at Berkeley, he had started his first job in postdoctoral research at Pennsylvania State University, and at the time he was still full of confidence and enthusiasm for theoretical physics. We had aspirations for the future, our prospects were golden, and we were completely oblivious to the cruel vicissitudes of fate.

The garden was all tidied up and ready, but selecting what to plant took considerable thought. Of all the possible flowers, I love camellias the most. Camellias are exquisite, the white ones crisply refined, the red ones luxuriantly beautiful, and the pink ones charmingly cute, and so each has its own special appeal. Even when not flowering, the plant is an attractive deep green. Camellias originate from China, where they grow abundantly on the Yunnan-

Guizhou Plateau, and they only reached America via Europe. They love humidity and are well suited to acid soil, so with the moderating influence of its sea mists, Santa Barbara happens to be in the camellia region of America, and the flowers grow exceptionally well there. We decided that camellias would form the core of our plants, and we searched through all the nurseries in town till finally selecting about thirty sprigs of all colors and varieties. Sometimes the names of camellias in America can be quite evocative, so white ones can be "Swan Lake," pink ones "Elegant Beauty," and there is a red one called "General Eisenhower"—this last is the American camellia par excellence, and the one planted in my back garden did indeed grow so exuberantly that it stood there with the proud demeanor of a grand general.

After the flowers were planted, the final question was what to do with the empty space remaining in the western corner of the back garden. The owner had originally erected a swing there, and after the frame was removed, all that remained was an empty corner. As it was not a large area, it could not accommodate any trees with too wide a spread. So Wang Kuo-hsiang suggested, "Why don't we plant Italian cypresses there?" This was a good idea, since an Italian cypress does not take up much space and grows straight up without spreading out too far, so we decided to buy three saplings and planted them in a row along the fence. Even though they were just three or four feet high at that time, Kuo-hsiang predicted, "When these three cypresses are fully grown, they'll certainly be taller than all the rest of your trees!" And indeed, the three Italian cypresses did grow to lord it over all the others, forming a prominent landmark in my garden.

Over the years, the trees and flowers flourished and the garden gradually took shape. During that time, Wang Kuo-hsiang changed jobs a number of times, moving to Canada and also to Texas. His postdoctoral research did not progress smoothly. Theoretical physics is a profound science with few career opportunities. Because

American students regard it as a difficult subjcet, not many people study it, and consequently there are only a limited number of teaching positions. During those years, American universities faced budgetary cutbacks, and jobs were hard to obtain. With only a handful of physics departments from the more prestigious colleges offering positions in theoretical physics, it was tough elbowing your way in. Arizona State University once offered Wang Kuo-hsiang a position, but he turned it down. When he had originally opted for theoretical physics at National Taiwan University, he was inspired by Li Cheng-tao and Yang Chen-ning winning the Nobel Prize, and later at Berkeley, he had been guided by some leading teachers (at the time the staff of the Berkeley Physics Department included six Nobel laureates). With top teachers at a prestigious college, Wang Kuo-hsiang naturally held high aspirations for his own future, but when he realised that his research in theoretical physics involved no important breakthrough and that he would never become a top physicist, he decided to give up physics completely and change his career to the high-tech field. Of course, this meant he could no longer achieve his lifetime's goals, and this forever remained a gnawing disappointment. Subsequently, he found a steady job at the Hughes Corporation in Los Angeles doing research on artificial satellites. During the Gulf War, the artificial satellites used by the American forces were built by Hughes.

In those years, whenever Wang Kuo-hsiang had a vacation, he generally came to stay in Santa Barbara, and as soon as he reached my house, he would go straight into the garden and check on the flowers and trees we had planted. If he had not been there for a while, the sight of the three Italian cypresses in the back garden would make him exclaim, "Wow, they've shot up yet again!" A cypress grows about ten feet a year and reaches its full height within a few years, a grand tree standing loftily at sixty or seventy feet. Of the three, the middle one was the most vigorous, and being much taller than the other two, together they formed a three-pronged outline like the Chinese character for "mountain" (山). The climate in the valley is quite humid, so the cypresses grew luxuriantly verdant, and when they caught the evening sun, they shone resplendently, a truly eye-catching sight. In March and April, all the camellias in the garden blossomed. The trees seemed to be covered with little white swans, and as the pink flowers were even more beautiful, my garden really captured the exuberance of spring.

1989 was the year of the horse, an inauspicious year, and that summer in Mainland China the June Fourth Incident in Tiananmen Square, with the lives of hundreds and thousands of young people suddenly extinguished. For a while I sat glued to the television watching the events unfurl and rarely went into the garden. Then, one day I suddenly noticed that the leaves on the middle of the three cypresses in the back garden had developed yellow spots. At first I thought it was because of the aridity of the summer, with the plants struggling to cope with the drought, and I never expected that within a few days a whole tree sixty or seventy feet tall could suddenly dry up and die, as if it had been struck by lightning. If you touched them, the pointed leaves fell to the ground, and in this way an evergreen tree that had been standing there so proudly, lording it over all the others, in just a few days completely died. The strange thing was that the cypresses on either side were both fine, the same deep green as before with no hint of disease, so it was totally shocking that just the middle tree stood out so prominently, withered and dead. I had no choice but to get someone to chop it down and cart it away. and from then on there was a big, empty space in my back garden. For a cypress to die like that for no apparent reason upset me deeply for many days, and in my heart I felt it was an unlucky omen, as if some disaster was about to strike. Not long after, Wang Kuo-hsiang fell ill.

That summer, Kuo-hsiang was constantly coughing, even though in the twenty years he had been in America he had always been healthy, never even catching a cold. When he went to see the doctor for a check up and the results of the blood test came back, it was found that his red blood count was only half that of a normal person, at a little over six grams per litre. When the doctor did a bone-marrow extraction and the results came out, Kuo-hsiang called me and said, "My old disease has returned, as the doctor says it's aplastic anemia." When Kuohsiang said this, his voice was steady, as always calm in the face of adversity, with a scientist's rationality and self-control, but when I heard that long, strange name for the disease, I felt a cold chill descend over me, as a whole host of terrifying memories surfaced once more.

Many years before, in the summer of 1960, one morning I had hurried alone to the Hematology Department of Taipei Central Clinic to await the result of a laboratory test, and the director of the department, Dr. Huang Tien-szu, came out and told me, "Your friend Wang Kuo-hsiang is suffering from aplastic anemia." That was the first time I had heard of this unfamiliar disease. Dr. Huang probably saw my complete bewilderment, so he went on and carefully explained the nature and causes of aplastic anemia. It is a very rare blood disease, where the bone marrow loses its ability to produce blood and no longer makes enough new blood cells, and as a result the levels of red blood cells, platelets, and hemoglobin all become low. The causes are complex, with a variety of chemical, physical, and viral possibilities. Finally, Dr. Huang solemnly told me, "This is a very serious kind of blood disease." In fact, even with the great advances of modern medicine, it is still the case that no specialised drugs have been developed to deal with this very tricky condition, and so most of the treatment just depends on steroids to stimulate the blood-creation function of the bone marrow. Another line of treatment is a bone-marrow transplant, but nobody had heard of this at that time in Taipei. As I left the Central Clinic that day, of course I was totally shattered, but as I was young and ignorant, I did not fully comprehend the seriousness of the disease, and I thought that just so long as it was not terminal, there was still hope of recovery. In fact, the recovery rate for sufferers of aplastic anemia is exceptionally low, and only about five per cent of patients can, for some unknown reason, get better on their own.

The first time Wang Kuo-hsiang suffered from aplastic anemia, he was about to become a third-year student in the Physics Depanment at National Taiwan University. He had little choice but to take a break, so he quit studying for two years. His condition became quite serious, and every month he had to go to the hospital for a blood transfusion of at least 500cc. Because his platelets were low and his blood-clotting ability was reduced, his gums often bled, his eyes became bloodshot, and his eyesight suffered. The most prominent feature of Kuo-hsiang's character was his drive to win at all costs, a staunch determination never to accept failure, and this stubborn willpower helped him for the time being to ward off the devastating ravages of the disease. All I could do was stand by his side and give him encouragement and spiritual support. As his family had moved to Taichung, he underwent treatment while staying on his own with relatives in Taipei so that he could easily get to see the doctors. After class, I often cycled over from National Taiwan University to Chaochou Street to visit him. At the time, I had just started working with my classmates on the publication of *Modern Literature*; it was at its most probing and exhilarating stage, so of course I talked with him about every little detail of the new journal. When he saw my excitement, he was pleased, and even in the midst of his illness he succeeded in getting two new subscriptions for the journal, and he also became a loyal reader. In fact, Wang Kuo-hsiang's contribution to *Modern Literature* was quite substantial, as that kind of publication with low circulation had regular financial crises. Subsequently, in my first few years as a lecturer at the University of California, my salary was limited, and we were constantly in severe financial straits in order to scrape together the funds to publish the journal. While Kuohsiang was studying for his doctorate at Berkeley, he had a full scholarship, as well as over four hundred dollars a month for living expenses. After he became aware of my difficulties, every month he would save one or two hundred US Dollars, which he donated to rescue *Modern Literature*, and this continued for quite some time. As he could certainly not be regarded as well off, this was a substantial sum of money, and if it had not been for his long-term financial support, I fear that *Modern Literature* would have folded long before.

I had known Wang Kuo-hsiang since the age of seventeen when we were both in the second year at Chien-Kuo High School, and right from the start we had a special kind of bond between us, like brothers sworn to stand together through thick and thin. On graduating from high school, I had the opportunity of direct entry into National Taiwan University, but because I wanted to study water engineering with the dream of going to build a dam in the Three Gorges of the Yangtze River, and also because I could not wait to leave home in my quest for freedoms, I applied for direct entry into National Cheng-Kung University in Tainan, which at the time was the only place with a Department of Hydraulic Engineering. Wang Kuo-hsiang also had a similar idea. As he was a top student in his class, there should have been no problem passing the entrance exam into National Taiwan University, but after discussing it with me, he took the exam for the Department of Electrical Engineering, also at Cheng-Kung University. We rented somewhere to live near the campus in a district originally set aside for military personnel, but after one year of an easy-going university lifestyle, I found my interests did not really tally with what I was studying, so I re-took the entrance exam to the Department of Foreign Languages at National Taiwan University and returned to Taipei. Kuo-hsiang persevered at Cheng-Kung University for one more year, although he also could stand it no more. Engineering was definitely not right for him, as he discovered that his true vocation was research into theoretical science. So he applied to take the examination to switch to National Taiwan University and also to change to the Department of Physics. At the time, switching not only university but also departments and even schools within the university was exceptionally difficult, especially as he was applying for National Taiwan University. However, he was successful, and in fact he was the only person who was successful that year. But just as we were numbed in out celebrations at overcoming all obstacles and finally attaining university places to pursue our true interests, Wang Kuo-hsiang perversely met with misfortune and became sick with that extremely rare form of blood disease.

After undergoing treatment with Western medicine for over a year, Wang Kuo-hsiang's condition was showing no signs of improvement, and the astronomical cost of the treatment was gradually causing financial problems for his family, but just as they were feeling completely trapped in this impossible situation, Kuo-hsiang found salvation. His family heard that a famous doctor from south China called Dr. Xi Fuyi had treated an overseas student from Korea who was similarly suffering from aplastic anemia, and though the condition of this student was so serious that the Western doctors had given up hope, he was cured by Dr. Xi. I had always relied on Western medicine and held a prejudice against traditional Chinese medicine. In the prescription that Dr. Xi prepared for Kuo-hsiang, there were many kinds of herbal remedies, and there was also rhinoceros horn. I did not then understand that, in Chinese medicine, rhinoceros horn is an ingredient for cleansing the blood, so I was surprised at its use, and also that such a small packet of rhinoceros horn powder could be so expensive, But after Kuo-hsiang started taking the medicine prescribed by Dr. Xi, he indeed did get better day by day, and within six months he no longer needed any more blood transfusions. Many years later when Kuohsiang and I were in America, we once went to look at the animals in the world-famous zoo in San Diego California, and there was a group of seven rhinoceroses, both young and old. That was the first time I had really studied this mysterious beast, and I had never before realised that if you look at it closely, the skin of this huge animal is as thick as a suit of armor, and with its horn protruding from the end of its nose like a sharp axe pointing at the sky, it has the aura of a noble warrior. Probably because rhinoceros horn had once cured Kuo-hsiang, I was indescribably well-disposed towards that herd of exceptionally fierce beasts, and I stood in front of the railings gazing at them for quite a while.

Wang Kuo-hsiang and I were too optimistic in our belief that aplastic anemia was a nightmare from the past and Kuo-hsiang was one of the five per cent of lucky ones. We never anticipated that this stubbornly persistent disease could lie dormant for over twenty years and then suddenly reappear like some terrible monster emerging from a deep sleep to strike back with bared teeth and rattling claws. Kuo-hsiang was now over fifty, so naturally his body's power of resistance was much weaker than when he was young, and when the sickness returned, the condition was even more serious. From then on, the two of us embarked on a terrible battle against the monstrous disease in a life-and-death struggle that lasted for three years.

Seeing that Wang Kuo-hsiang's disease had been cured the first time using a combination of Chinese and Western medicine, this time we naturally adopted the same policy. Kuo-hsiang found the prescription that Dr. Xi Fuyi had prepared over twenty years previously and we asked friends and relatives in Taipei to take it to Dr. Xi to look at. Dr. Xi adjusted some of the medicines in it and also added a few elements: *astragulus*, *sheng-shu-di*, *dang-shen*, *lingusticum*, and *shou-wu*, all of which are herbal medicines for supplementing the blood and boosting the energy, and amongst the ingredients there was of course rhinoceros horn. Fortunately we could obtain these medicines in the Chinese medicine shops in Monterey Park City, Los Angeles, where there was a well-established shop called "De Cheng Shop" run by someone from Hong Kong that had a wide range of stock at reasonable prices. Those few years, I often went to fetch medicines for Kuo-hsiang, and after so many visits, the boss and shop assistant of De Cheng Shop came to know me well. Because the rhinoceros is a protected rare species, it is illegal to sell rhinoceros horn in America, so initially the shop assistant in De Cheng Shop was unwilling to bring it out. However, after we pleaded with him for a long time, he did produce a piece of rhinoceros horn from a small locked metal box, shaved some off and sold it to us. But after twenty years, Kuo-hsiang's medical condition was not the same, and as he was not in Taiwan and so was unable to go to see Dr. Xi for a check-up, there was of course no way to adjust the medicines. This time, taking Chinese medicine had no effect. For three years, however, Kuo-hsiang never stopped taking herbal medicines, because Western medicine still had no special treatment for his condition and just as before simply relied on a wide range of steroids. We discussed with the doctors the possibility of a bone marrow transplant, but they maintained that a transplant was too dangerous for a fifty-year-old patient, and moreover locating a donor with an exact blood match was as difficult as finding a needle in a haystack.

For those three years, Wang Kuo-hsiang relied entirely on blood transfusions to stay alive, and sometimes he needed two a month. Our emotions went up and down with the unpredictable fluctuations in his red blood levels, and if his blood count stayed above nine, we felt a little reassured, but if it fell to six, then we had to prepare to go into the hospital for a transfusion that weekend. Kuo-hsiang had insurance with Kaiser Permanente, one of America's largest medical insurance organisations. The headquarters of Kaiser in the heart of Los Angeles is a row of massive buildings extending over several blocks, and the hospital is such a labyrinth that after you turn a few corners, you have no idea where you are. I must have gone into that hospital at least forty or fifty times, but I still regularly ended up somewhere strange, perhaps the Radiation Department or the Ear Nose and Throat Department. As every building looks exactly the same from the outside, the rows of glass doors and windows have a cold, impersonal glare. This style of modernist buildings is almost Kafkaesque, and when you go inside, it is as if you have blundered on to an alien planet.

As there was always the possibility of a reaction to the transfusions, I generally drove Wang Kuo-hsiang to and from the hospital. Fortunately the transfusions were arranged on the weekends, so when my classes were over on Friday, I went over to where Kuo-hsiang lived in Los Angeles and then we drove in together the following morning. Even though the transfusions began at eight on Saturday morning, it would be four or five in the afternoon before the complete 500cc transfusion was finished, so we left the house at six in the morning. Los Angeles is frighteningly large, so wherever you go, it is quite normal to take an hour by car to get there, and the traffic congestion on Route 10 is notorious especially during the morning rush hour. People who live in Los Angeles waste most of their lives on this octopus-like highway network. As a result of getting up so early, while I was with Wang Kuo-hsiang during the transfusion, I couldn't help dozing off, but no matter how long I slept, as soon as I opened my eyes, there would be that packet of blood hanging on the frame, the deep red liquid seeping drop by drop along the plastic tube into the vein on the inside of Kuo-hsiang's arm. Those drops of blood continued like the perpetual dribble in an hourglass. But lying on the bed, Wang Kuo-hsiang was able to keep totally calm as he received the eight-hour infusion of this elixir of life. The veins on the inside of both of his arms had been pierced with so many needles that they became bruised and swollen, but he never uttered a single word of complaint. He endured suffering with incredible fortitude, so when he did groan in pain, that meant the agony must be beyond what any ordinary person could tolerate. I have rarely seen patients who could bear suffering in silence the way Wang Kuo-hsiang did, and this kind of stoicism arose out of his indomitable self-control and determination not to allow anyone else to see his helplessness in the face of his affliction. But both of us understood that this was an incomparably arduous struggle, which needed the support we could get from all the confidence, rationality, and determination we could muster. We could never show any weakness or reveal any fear to the monstrous disease, so when we were together, it seemed like we were constantly reminding each other always to stay strong and never relax.

In fact, if Wang Kuo-hsiang's physical condition would permit it, we did our best to enjoy life even in the face of adversity, so whenever he completed a transfusion and there was a sudden recovery in his spirit and physical strength and also some color in his cheeks, although we knew that this good health was artificial and temporary, we took the opportunity to appreciate a moment of normality. Driving home through Monterey Park, we would go for a meal at a restaurant that we had always loved, and probably in an effort to make up for the whole day spent in the hospital, our appetites were especially good. We often went to the North Sea Seafood Restaurant because this Cantonese restaurant has authentic Hong Kong cuisine, and its Bi Feng Tang fried crab is just right. After our meal, we would rent some videos. We had never before watched quite so many series from China, Hong Kong and Taiwan, (such as *Dream of the Red Chambers*, *Thirteen Manchu Emperors*, and *Yan Feng-ying*) and as we followed the twists and turns of the plots, an evening would easily slip by. Of course, Wang Kuo-hsiang also maintained great interest in world events. It was the time when the communist regimes In Eastern Europe and the Soviet Union were crumbling, so every day we watched television avidly. Seeing the Germans drinking champagne in celebration as they climbed on top of the Berlin Wall, both of us clapped and cheered, and in that moment, aplastic anemia was completely forgotten. Wang Kuo-hsiang had just bought a small house in El Monte in 1988, and at the back there was a small garden, but within a year of moving in, he became ill before there was time to sort out the garden. Before he fell sick, he found in a supermarket a pair of dark brown urns originally intended for preserving duck eggs. On them a scene showing two dragons fighting over a ball was carved in relief, and the ancient simplicity of these duck-egg urns was really charming. When Kuo-hsiang brought them back home, he used an electric drill to make holes and prepare them for use as flowerpots. One Sunday when he was in especially good spirits, I drove him to a garden center to find some flowers. We discovered that osmanthus also grows in California, and this was like suddenly discovering a special treasure, so we bought two sprigs and planted them in the duck-egg urns. From then on, these two osmanthus plants became Kuo-hsiang's companion in sickness, and right up to the time that he became seriously ill, he never forgot to go into the garden and water them regularly.

As Wang Kuo-hsiang became very sick, though he was reluctant to let me see it, I could fully empathize with his feelings of depression and fear when he was on his own, as my own spirits would also sink when I was quietly by myself. I once privately asked, and the senior doctor in charge of his case told me that although Kuo-hsiang's aplastic anemia had been held in check for twenty years, it had now reached the final stage. This use of the term "final stage" was a real shock, and the doctor did not say anything further as I did not want to hear any more and was unwilling to let him continue. But an issue that brought me out in a cold sweat often churned about in my mind like the rising and falling of the tide: what would happen if this time it turned out that Wang Kuo-hsiang did not recover from his disease? In fact, his condition often became critical so we were subjected to constant worry. One evening when I came back from a party at a friend's house in Los Angeles, I found Kuohsiang lying prone on the sofa in a half-conscious state, and I quickly took him to the hospital. That evening I drove along the highway at over eighty miles per hour, and even though I am not a very skilled driver and also have a poor sense of direction, everyone can find what is needed in the face of adversity, and I covered a journey that would usually take forty minutes in half that time. When the doctor's tests came out, they showed that Kuo-hsiang's blood sugar levels had reached 800 MC/DL, and if we had been delayed by another quarter of an hour, he would probably have suffered brain damage. Basically his long-term use of steroids had caused his blood sugar levels to rise. The emergency room of a hospital is always a place of life and death, and the emergency room at Kaiser is many times larger than that of an average hospital, so of course the struggle between life and death in there is even more intense. You just watch the doctors and nurses rushing and jostling about while the patients are stuck in small cubicles separated by white sheets as if they have been completely forgotten, and just wait helplessly for a doctor to come and attend to you. When they do finally deign to look in, after a brief inspection they are gone again. I accompanied Wang Kuo-hsiang in and out of that emergency room many times, and every time we waited till dawn before he was finally admitted into a proper hospital ward.

As soon as Wang Kuo-hsiang became sick, I started scouring everywhere for news on treatment for aplastic anemia. My own doctor in Taiwan was Wu Te-lang, the Dean of Chang-Keng School of Medicine, and he introduced me to a senior doctor at the Hematology Department of Chang-Keng, Dr. Shih Li-yun. I wrote to Dr. Shih sending her Wang Kuo-hsiang's medical history and arranged to visit her at home when I next went to Taiwan. At the same time I searched all over Mainland China for books and articles about dealing with similar diseases using Chinese medicine, and I read in a medical journal about how the Director of Hematology at Shuguang Chinese Hospital in Shanghai, Dr. Wu Zhengxiang, treated this kind of condition, though in Mainland China they referred to it by a slightly different name from the one used in Taiwan. I also read in a Mainland newspaper that there was a Chinese doctor in Shijia Village, Hebei Province, who had a special program for handling the disease, and he had established a specialized clinic for his therapy. I discovered that instances of the disease in the Mainland were actually not that rare, and Chinese and Wesern medicine had been used together to treat it for many years, with quite a good success rate for some of the programs. So I decided to go for a trip to the Mainland myself, in the hope that I might find a doctor or medication that could cure Kuo-hsiang. When I discussed my plans with him, he said, "In that case, I'll trouble you to do it for me." Wang Kuo-hsiang was not very good with words, but everything he did say came right from the heart. His whole life, he was constantly terrified of causing trouble to others, so when he did ask for help, it really was as a last resort.

In 1990, before I went to the Mainland, I first went to Taiwan to visit Dr. Shih Li-yun in Chang-Keng Hospital in Linkou. Dr. Shih told me that she was in the process of treating a number of patients with aplastic anemia, and the method of treatment used was much the same as in America. When Dr. Shih looked at Wang Kuo-hsiang's medical record, she did not say very much, so I guessed that she was unwilling to tell me how difficult it was to treat his condition.

I took with me to Shanghai a box containing a thick pile of Wang Kuo-hsiang's medical records, and accompanied by my friend in Shanghai, Professor Lu Shiqing of Fudan University, I went to Shuguang Hospital to consult Dr. Wu Zhengxiang. Shuguang is the most famous Chinese hospital in Shanghai and is quite large. Dr. Wu explained to me in considerable detail about all kinds of possible causes and treatments for the condition from the perspective of Chinese medicine. Shuguang Hospital combines Chinese and Western medicine in its therapies for the disease, so on the one hand there are blood transfusions while on the other they also use Chinese medications that promote a long-term balance and concentrate on cleansing the blood and boosting the energy. Dr. Wu discussed Wang Kuohsiang's medical condition with me a number of times, and finally he wrote me a prescription and insisted I maintain regular telephone contact with him. I also heard that there was a famous doctor in Zhejiang Chinese Hospital, so I went on a trip to Hangzhou as well to visit this elderly Chinese doctor there. His diagnosis was quite mysterious, and the prescription he wrote even stranger. It is only when someone close to you is seriously ill that you can understand exactly why people clutch at straws in the face of acute sickness. At that time, if someone had told me that there was a miracle worker living at the top of a Himalayan mountain, I would also have climbed to the top to beg for a wonder cure from him. At that time, saving Wang Kuo-hsiang's life was more important than anything else for me.

The day after I flew to Beijing, I took a train to Shijia Village together with Professor Yuan Liangjun of the School of Social Science and we stayed the night at the Hebei Province government guesthouse. That evening in the guesthouse, I met an engineer from America who was also a graduate from Cheng-Kung University and had originally gone to America as an overseas student from Taiwan. He especially came to see me because he knew I was in Mainland China to find a doctor on behalf of a friend. I was perplexed how there could be another visitor from America in that kind of remote place, but as soon as we met, the engineer told me his story: his wife had been in a car crash the year before, and she had been in a coma ever since, remaining in a vegetative state. The engineer sought medical help everywhere without success until finally he heard that in Shijia Village there was a well-known *qigong* master who had opened a clinic to use *qigong* in the treatment of patients. So he quit his high-salary job, sold off all his assets, and moved his wife Shijia Village to receive *qigong* treatment. He told me that every day, four or five *qigong* masters would take turns infusing his wife with energy, and when he recounted that his wife already had some movement in her fingers and showed some signs of response, his face lit up with hope. I was deeply moved by the intensity of love and faith that could make him burn his bridges in giving up everything to transport his wife thousands of miles to find a doctor in this remote part of northern China. I have long forgotten the engineer's name, but over the years I have often thought about him and his wife, though I do not know whether she finally regained consciousness or not. A lew years later, I myself came to experience the wonders of Chinese *qigong* as I was successfully treated for dizziness by a *qigong* master, and I subsequently became a firm believer in *qigong*. Originally when the engineer told me about the marvels of *qigong*, it had certainly moved me, and I wanted to get Wang Kuo-hsiang to go to Mainland China to receive this treatment. But he needed regular blood transfusions, and he easily became acutely sick, so in reality it was not feasible for him to undergo such a long journey. This matter has always left me with nagging doubts, that if Kuo-hsiang could at that time have tried out *qigong*, maybe there was a possibility of him recovering.

The next morning, I went to visit the clinic that specialised in treating aplastic anemia, and I met the chief doctor there. It turned out that it was a very basic, small hospital with about ten patients, and from their appearance they were all quite sick. The doctor was young, but he spoke with plenty of confidence, and when I was leaving, he sold me two big packets of herbal medicine, which was ground to a fine powder in order to facilitate carrying it. I took these two bags of pungent medical powder back with me to Beijing. It was already the end of September, so it was the start of autumn, the best season in Beijing. That was the first time I had been in the city, so naturally I had to visit the Forbidden City and the Ming Tombs, but I could muster little enthusiasm as my heart was not there. My hotel was near to Wangfujing, not far from Tiananmen. In the evening, I strolled down for a look at Tiananmen Square, only to find the largest plaza in the world quite empty. Apart from the soldiers from the People's Liberation Army on guard, there were only a few scattered pedestrians. Compared with the time of the June the Fourth Incident one year before when it was seething with people bubbling with excitement, Tiananmen Square had the deserted, ominously desolate air of the aftermath of a disaster. That night, the wretchedness in my heart matched the cold breeze of the Beijing autumn evening. I had searched everywhere in Mainland China, but my conclusion was that there was no special treatment for aplastic anemia in China. Wang Kuo-hsiang had of course harbored considerable hope in my trip to China, and I dreaded disappointing him.

When I got back to America, I discussed it with Wang Kuo-hsiang and he eventually decided to use the prescription prepared by Dr. Wu Zhengxiang of Shuguang Hospital, seeing as the ingredients were relatively mild. On the other hand, the two big packets of medical powder that I had hauled all the way back were not used. But Kuo-hsiang's sickness was getting more serious every day. In the first year, he had managed to go to work, but the journey there was an hour each way by car, and in the end his strength was not up to it, so he quit his job at the Hughes Corporation. Fortunately he had bought disability insurance, so he did not face financial ruin as a consequence of the sickness. The second year, as a result of the use of so many steroids, he ended up with diabetes. Furthermore, his long-term anemia affected his heart, so he developed an irregular heartbeat, and gradually even moving around became difficult for him.

In January 1992, on Wang Kuo-hsiang's fifty-fifth birthday, I saw that he was in good spirits and suggested we go and celebrate his birthday at the North Sea Seafood Restaurant. On the way there, we chatted about what dishes we would order, and this talk of food really whetted our appetites. There is a flight of about twenty steps between the car park for the North Sea Seafood Restaurant and the building itself, and Kuo-hsiang held on to the railing while he climbed up, but he was gasping for breath by the time he had reached halfway. His heart probably could not take it, and it looked like he was really suffering, so I quickly went forward and supported him, telling him to sit on the steps and rest for a while. He wheezed for a moment, and then he stood up in an effort to climb on up. I knew that he was unwilling to ruin the atmosphere by admitting defeat, so I myself suggested, "Let's not eat here. Let's go home and have some long-life noodles." I never imagined his body could be so weak that even a few steps were a problem. We went home and cooked two bowls of plain noodles, and that was how we spent his final birthday. On Sunday evening, I had to go back to Santa Barbara, and as Kuo-hsiang saw me off, in the rear-view mirror of the car I caught a glimpse of him standing alone in front of the door. Over the past two years with so much sickness, his hair that was already prematurely white had become really sparse, and it presented quite a shocking sight in the fading evening light. After I drove onto the highway, I was suddenly overwhelmed by a burst of desperate sadness. I stopped the car by the side of the road and laid my head on the steering wheel, sobbing uncontrollably. I was bitterly despondent that Wang Kuo-hsiang could bravely endure so much, persevering with such effort in the battle against the monstrous disease, but in the end he had still been ground down to this emaciated state. Moreover, I had devoted every possible ounce of energy to looking after his sick body, but in the end I could only watch helplessly as his life ebbed away drop by drop. I had always believed that man could triumph over the forces of nature, but if you are constantly fighting against the odds, ultimately human strength cannot overcome fate. Everybody must die at some time, and there is nothing we can do about it.

During the summer vacation, I moved into Wang Kuo-hsiang's El Monte home, as an emergency could occur at any time, On the evening of August 13, after buying groceries at the supermarket, I came home to find him having difficulty breathing, so I quickly dialed 911 to summon an ambulance. They used an oxygen mask to revive him and then immediately carried him into the ambulance and drove to the hospital with the siren wailing. On Friday, after two days in hospital, Kuo-hsiang's spirits seemed better. He had been in and out of hospital many times, so this kind of situation had already become routine and I thought that he would probably be able to leave the following day. I spent the afternoon with him, chatting about this and that, and at eight in the evening he told me, "You go back and get something to eat." I left the *World Journal* for him to read and said, "I'll come and collect you tomorrow morning." Those were the last things we said to each other. Early on Saturday morning, the hospital called to inform me that Wang Kuo-hsiang had slipped into a coma and had been admitted into an intensive care ward. I hurried over and found him lying there with his body stuffed full of tubes. His supervising doctor told me that they were not planning to use a cardio-defibrillator if his heart failed, and I nodded in agreement, as this use of electrical resuscitation causes too much suffering for the patient. Kuo-hsiang was in a coma for two days, and then on Monday August 17, I had a frightening premonition that he would not make it through the day. At midday, I went to the hospital cafeteria for a hurried meal and then rushed back to the intensive care ward to watch over him. On the monitor, his heart was getting weaker and weaker. At five o'clock, the doctor on duty came in. I gazed steadily at Kuo-hsiang's heartbeat on the monitor, and at twenty past five, his heart finally stopped. I held his hand and so was with him as he took his final journey from this world. In that moment, a chasm opened between the living and the dead, and in the world of the living, I took my leave of Wang Kuo-hsiang.

In 1954, during the summer vacation forty-four years ago, Wang Kuo-hsiang and I had both been rushing to a supplementary class at Chien-Kuo High School in preparation for the university entrance examination. Though in the same year, we were in different classes so we did not know each other, but on that day it happened that we were both late, and as we jostled and barged into one another while both scrambling up the stairs, that was how we first met, and we remained friends for thirty-eight years. Wang Kuo-hsiang was a kind-hearted person: he treated people well, looked after his parents, and was loyal to his friends. He totally abhorred hypocrisy, so he always directly spoke the truth, and I once teased him that if he ever told a lie, his tongue would end up tied in a knot. Being dedicated to research, he would fight fiercely for his principles, and inevitably he sometimes offended people, so in his career he encountered obstacles. He was a gifted scientist, and he should have been successful in the realm of physics, but it was just unfortunate that in the second year of university he became seriously sick and this affected his brain. At Hughes, his research on artificial satellites did result in substantial achievements, but he would have progressed much further if the fates had not intervened, interrupting his career prematurely. At the age of fifty-five, he died too young. For all the years that Wang Kuo-hsiang and I knew one another, we always helped each other, providing mutual support through difficult times. With the two of us working together to cope with the trials and tribulations of daily life, we could always persevere, but when the final blow fell from that monstrous disease and the god of death, despite expending every ounce of energy, it was all completely in vain.

After organising the funeral arrangements for Wang Kuo-hsiang, I returned to Santa Barbara, where the summer was already over. That year, there was a serious drought in the area, and the city authorities had restricted the use of water, forbidding the watering of plants. After several months away from home, I found that the lawn in my front garden had dried out and become a plot of parched yellow. Because I had been rushing so often to Los Angeles, I had neglected the care of my garden, so all the shrubs were drab and listless, and one camellia after another had turned sickly and was barely clinging to life. My home become a wasteland. After taking Kuo-hsiang's ashes back to Taiwan and laying them to rest in Shantao Temple, I returned to America and started work on rebuilding my garden. Just like people, plants that are hurt need a long period of care. I expended two years of my blood and sweat before each of those camellias recovered. After retirement, one has plenty of time, so I began travelling all over the place in search of prize blooms, and these proliferated till I now have a wide range in my garden. I also brought back the two osmanthus plants from Wang Kuo-hsiang's house. As they had already matured, the duck-egg urns were too small, so I transplanted both of them to a corner of my garden, allowing them to find a home in the soil. Each year as winter recedes and spring arrives, the sixty or seventy camellias in my garden blossom in a tumultuous profusion of resplendent reds and delicate whites. The original camellias that I planted together with Wang Kuo-hsiang are now twenty years old and have grown as tall as the eaves of the building, and when they are all in flower, there are over one hundred blooms for each camellia. In the mild spring weather, I can sit in a deckchair in the garden, sipping tea and reading the newspaper, and with a multitude of flowers as company, for a while I can soak in the the glorious moment. The only thing missing from this idyllic scene is that, if I raise my eyes, I can forever see in the western corner of the garden, between the two remaining Italian cypresses, a starkly empty space, and this deep void is just filled with white clouds drifting by. In the creation of the world, when there was a tear in the fabric of the sky, even the Goddess Nuwa was unable to repair the damage.

Translated by David and Ellen DETERDING 戴德巍、陳艷玲

Pang-yuan CHI 齊邦媛

A Day in the Life
一生中的一天[*]

It was a morning in June when I walked, focused and calm, into classroom number 24, first picked up a piece of chalk as was my wont, and then proceeded to open the textbook, *The Norton Anthology of English Literature*. I began to teach the very last lesson of my life. Together, the students and I had previously made the difficult journey across T. S. Eliot's *Waste Land* (1922) and covered the territory of two world wars. We had treaded almost another half century, until our travels through shock and despair to renewal had all of a sudden taken us right up to the year 1983 and the poem "River" by the then soon-to-be Poet Laureate Ted Hughes (1930-1998). For half his life, Hughes wrote nature poems reveling in the raw ferocity of the all-encompassing life force, which he pinned down in the minute observation of birds, beasts and reptiles. He relates his grand vision when he writes about the river that "fallen from heaven, lies across the lap of his mother, broken by world:

> But water will go on
> Issuing from heaven
> . . .
> And will wash itself of all deaths."

---

[*] From Pang-yuan Chi's 齊邦媛 collection of essays *Yisheng zhong de yitien*《一生中的一天》 [A day in the life], Taipei: Elite Publishing Co., 2004.

With that eternal hope, I closed the textbook. I concluded with a summary of the development of English literature from the 10th century to the present day, echoing the opening remarks of my first lesson nearly a year ago. When the bell began to ring, I looked at the upturned faces of my several dozen students and said goodbye, wishing them that their studies would make their lives happier. I made it short and stepped down from the dais quietly. It has always been my style of teaching to eschew idle talk about non-curriculum-related topics, and to avoid in particular any display of my personal moods and emotions. In conformance with this approach, I now parted without tears.

Stepping into the corridor outside the classroom, I was carrying a large bouquet of pale purple, pink and white peacock flowers in my hands. Every single blossom was a silent farewell that needed no words. Farewell, teacher! On many a fine morning we sat tied to our seats by that literary history of yours, awe-inspiring and sometimes profound beyond ready understanding. We would listen to your voice floating from one epoch into the next as we watched the trees and sky outside the window. Adieu, teacher. In the long years ahead, I may remember a few verses you recited, or a few things you said—about literature, and about life.

Still holding the flowers, I walked down the old corridor that was mottled and stained with age. Suddenly, a picture flashed across my mind: me entering this same corridor for the first time, a youth with long hair. A myriad of emotions welled up in my chest. Early retirement, what did that really mean? Retired from what? What would my life look like from now on?

The graduate school end-of-term exams were scheduled for later the same day. I was standing by the window of classroom number 16, observing how afternoon tranquility was slowly settling on the university campus. A few bicycles were flitting past under the azure sky, a few students walking towards the library with books under their arms . . . . After a while, a car pulled up in front of the

Fu Memorial Bell. A bride stepped out in a flowing white gown and began to pose for wedding pictures. Probably a last look back on her old life before taking the plunge into a more serious future. Many years ago, I also could be said to have "married" myself off from this selfsame old building, only to come back again. The journey through the choppy seas of life had proved to be quite eventful, and I found it hard to recall the feelings of the young bride.

After answering questions from the students, I returned to my place next to the window to find that the originally sunny skies were now almost completely covered by low-hanging dark rain clouds. The bride hurriedly gathered her long dress and rushed back into the ribbon-festooned car. Thick drops started falling very suddenly, quickly turning into dense sheets of rain. In the distance one could hear dull thuds of thunder that were gradually moving closer, until it seemed that they were all assembled right above the campus, the continuous pounding leaving hardly any breathing space. Now and then, a flash of lightning appeared to be darting in through one window and out through another, exploding in the little square yard on the other side of the classroom. The students would raise their heads from their exam papers to look at me, and then, as if reassured by my unruffled posture, bow their heads again and continue to write furiously. The incessant thunderclaps reverberating through my entire body, I saw the rain pouring onto the broad leaves of the Indian almond tree outside the window. The leaves were undergoing their seasonal change of color and slanting downwards under the heavy downpour. Behind the thick rain curtain, the red brick administrative building on the other side had become all but invisible. The more than twenty students and I were as a lonely isle amidst the sound of the torrential rain that surrounded us on all sides like a cascading waterfall, somehow bringing us closer together. This feeling made me even less certain of what would be the proper way to bid farewell to my students. It was not just this class of students I was leaving behind, it were entire decades in which I had experienced many exciting twists and turns, and had grown and changed together with countless students.

As abruptly as it had begun, the thunder shower ended. After I had collected the exam papers, I stood at the corridor window waiting for the water to subside a bit. I knew that at this moment there would hardly be any space where a pedestrian could tread on Hsinsheng South Road just outside the university gate. While I stood there in hesitation, several students walked up to keep me company, and we decided to brave the water for a short distance to go to another building and sit for a while in the coffee shop there. We were laughing and joking as we gingerly avoided the big and small puddles on our way. It was almost as if you could hear the sound of the thirsty soil greedily sucking up the rainwater. Through cracks in the clouds, sunshine was flitting over the broad leaves of the trees, and the patches of reemerging blue sky, slowly widening, were reflected in the water puddles with white clouds fleeting across. Amidst this display of nature's forces, I ventured a new start.

Was it not possible that this magnificent spectacle was a heaven-sent inspiration, a generous gift to enlighten me? The maker of all things was telling me in the most poignant and profuse manner that in the larger scheme of a transient world, youth and old age, black hair and hoary head, are but subtle shifts occurring in the wink of an eye. Since you do not have the power to change that, just keep on going with a happy song on your lips! Thunder and lightning, rain and snow will accompany you on your road, as will the bright rays of the sun.

Translated by David VAN DER PEET 范德培

LIAO Yu-hui 廖玉蕙

If Memories Were Like the Wind
如果記憶像風*

As a student in junior high school, my daughter's academic performance was mediocre, but she had a sweet personality—cheerful, charming, tender and considerate. We were perfectly happy with her, though once in a while, our thoughts might have been overshadowed by the prospect of her struggling in the relentless exam-oriented educational system where only the fittest survive. When our friends talked about how their daughters threw tantrums or were forever at odds with them, we were thankful that our daughter was different.

Last year, during the summer vacation, my son, who was hoping to enter high school, came back home one day with his entrance exam results, forwarded to him through his old school. While we were nervously matching his scores against the basic requirements of individual high schools, my daughter came back from her summer school.

"All hell has broken loose!" she shouted in our direction.

This was what my daughter was like back then, day in and day out. The moment she got back from school and put down her school bag, she would follow me around the house, enumerating the day's happenings, things big and small, relevant and irrelevant. But that day, the adults were not in the mood for such small talk.

* From Liao Yu-hui's 廖玉蕙 *Xinshiji sanwenjia: Liao Yu-hui jingxuanji*《新世紀散文家：廖玉蕙精選集》(*Selected Essays of Liao Yu-hui*), Taipei: Chiuko Publishing, 2002.

"Quiet, please! Go and eat on your own. I'm helping your brother to look for a school," I said.

We finally finished with our calculations a little bit later. Tension had been gripping the whole family for quite some time because of the all-important high school entrance exam, but at that moment, I was thankful the stress was finally relieved. However, just as my son and I started talking about the school he might be qualified for, my daughter came barging in again.

"All hell has broken loose! My teacher wants you to go see the Dean of Student Affairs," she said with an air of mystery.

An invitation to the Dean's office generally means trouble. My poor heart, which had scarcely begun to enjoy a little peace, was agitated again.

"What happened? Why the Dean's office? What for?" I almost jumped up from my chair in alarm.

Taken aback by my strong reaction, my daughter tried to play down the event.

"I was beaten up by a classmate. She's also beaten up other classmates. Their parents reported it to the school . . . . Anyway, our teacher is asking you to go to the Dean's office. Go and you'll find out."

Now, such news shocked me even more! How could my daughter, who had always been courteous and docile, get involved in a fight? When did this happen? Why did she never mention it? Why hadn't we detected anything?

"It happened quite a while ago, when you went to Nanjing for a conference. One day, when I was reading on the floor of our Japanese-style study, Dad noticed bruises on my leg and asked me about them. I lied, saying I got them in a fall. But what really happened was that I was beaten up by a classmate. I didn't tell the truth because I didn't want to worry him," she explained.

"Why did your classmate beat you up? What had you done to her?"

"I have no idea."

How come my daughter was beaten up and didn't even know why? Things might not be as simple as they appeared! That evening, I was in for an even greater shock when I called her teacher. My daughter was beaten up not just once, but four times! According to the teacher, the fight was initiated by three girls, all from problem families. The leader, called R, lived with her maternal grandmother. When called to the office, the grandma banged on the desk, angrily rebuking the staff for wronging her granddaughter. Quite a few girls suffered intimidation or beating of some kind, but my daughter's case was the most serious: she was beaten up four times in ten days. The teacher suggested that I formally report the case to the Dean's Office, which would facilitate an investigation.

When I put down the phone, my hands were trembling. How could my daughter, who had always been talkative and never kept anything from me, have managed to withhold from me things of such enormity, not betraying a clue of her agony all this time since I came back from Mainland China? She must have been tormented by the stress pent up inside of her. Just as I guessed, after a lot of prodding and coaxing by her father and me, she finally broke down.

"K threatened me, saying that if I should dare to say anything to our teacher or my parents, she would push me from the top of the building, and see that I die an ugly death," she said between sobs.

I felt a chill running down my spine.

"Besides, I didn't want to worry you and Dad," she added.

I felt a stab of pain in my heart. Our daughter was a gentle and reasonable girl, who did not usually get into trouble. That's why we'd never seen the need to warn her about bullying on campus, thinking that she would never experience it. Yet, it seemed that it was her docile nature that made her an easy target for bullies and had landed her in such a plight. Even more saddening was the realization that we, as parents, had failed terribly to secure her trust in us.

After talking it over with my husband, we decided to postpone filing a formal complaint with the Dean. We believed that a formal complaint would do nothing other than worsen the situation. We decided to take the matter into our own hands. Of course, one important factor that contributed to this decision was that we did not believe that children 13 or 14 years of age were incorrigible. They were at worst misled and had temporarily gone astray. Later when I found out that all these children were from problem families, and were deprived of love and care, my heart was further softened. Consequently, I managed to find the telephone numbers of two of the three girls, T and R. The third girl K was not in my daughter's class. She reportedly had no permanent residence and had regularly been in and out of police stations and juvenile detention halls.

When I explained politely on the phone that I was a parent of a student, the grandmother of R, who answered the phone, began to berate the Dean's staff members, accusing them of groundless slander. The verbal barrage went on for quite a few minutes. I listened silently for as long as I could; then I assured her that I didn't call to condemn her granddaughter, but to get a better understanding of the situation. The old woman hesitated for a while; then she barked out to her granddaughter:

"Hey, her mom has come for you!"

Vague noises could be heard from the other end of the receiver, noises of resistance.

"What are you afraid of? Her mom sounded pretty polite!" the old lady blustered.

Over the phone, the young girl adamantly denied ever hitting anybody. I had no intention of forcing a confession out of her, though. My only purpose was to let her know that parents were paying attention to this matter. I reminded her that even if she didn't participate in the fighting, just egging them on was also wrong.

The second girl, T, sounded as if she had every reason for bullying my daughter.

"She deserved it! At school, I don't do well, and neither does she.

But I don't understand why the teacher always greets her with a smile, and me with a long face. I can't take it !"

What ridiculous reasoning! But I needed to remain calm and patient to let her see reason.

"If you don't like my daughter you don't have to be friends with her. If she does anything wrong, you can be direct and tell her; or you can tell your teacher or even tell me. No matter what, hitting people is wrong! When I heard that my daughter had been beaten up, I felt terrible! Imagine, if you were the one beaten up, wouldn't your parents feel upset?"

"No way! My dad wouldn't feel a thing! My dad says if you do wrong, you deserve a good thrashing," she answered stubbornly.

Later I found out that at home T got hit for the slightest offence. Whenever her father hit her, he spared no mercy.

Throughout the conversation, my daughter was listening nervously by my side, holding her breath. She kept passing small notes to me, reminding me: "Please, don't irritate them, or I'll have a rough time!"

I hung up the phone. I was speechless.

Both girls finally promised to do what I implored of them—that they would not only stop harassing my daughter, but would take it upon themselves to protect her. I believed that these "big kids" would keep their promise, in the same way men of the streets hold to their own ethical standards and sense of honor. Besides, no really big grudge existed between the kids, anyway.

However, during noon break one day, my daughter ran all the way home in a panic. She said that K, who was very elusive, suddenly showed up at the school gate after having skipped school for some time. She was not dressed in her uniform that day. She made it known that she would "fix" my daughter one more time. Fortunately, T alerted my daughter and escorted her to the backdoor, rescuing her from disaster.

I looked at my daughter's face, drawn with fear, and I was filled with rage. What kind of world was this? If the school could not even ensure the safety of the students, what was the use of all those high-sounding slogans of "education," "edification," and "enlightenment"?

I phoned the Dean. He sounded very concerned and supportive.

"I did have a glimpse of K at the school gate a short while ago. I'll go and find her. As soon as I get hold of her, I'll get back to you," he promised.

In less than ten minutes, the phone rang. I requested to talk to K. I had to stifle my anger before talking to her. But as soon as her timid greeting "Mama Tsai" came through the phone, my heart began to soften. This time, I did not ask her why she wanted to fight my daughter. It dawned on me that these rebellious kids needed little provocation for a fight. Things as small as a wrong look or a careless brush against them might just trigger off a fight.

I tried to initiate a friendly chat with her.

"I've heard that you haven't been to school. Everybody goes to school, but you just wander about by yourself. Don't you feel bad?"

"Sometimes I do," she answered quietly.

"Why don't you go to school to be with your classmates?
You can have fun and study together."

"But I don't like going to class," she said.

"Then what do you like? Do you like reading novels?"

"I guess so."

I wanted her to feel my sincerity for her. "There're a lot of books in my house . . . novels, stories. When you're free, come to our house with my daughter. Don't wander the streets. You may run into bad people."

The girl politely said thank you. Meanwhile I was struggling inside whether to mention the fights, but finally decided against it. I hung up the phone with a sigh, and my face was covered with tears. What kind of environment had made this child "homeless," I wondered. What kind of parents would let their child wander the streets?

As for my daughter, I followed the Dean's suggestions and told her:

"Next time when something like this happens again, go and get help from the Dean's office. Do you understand?" I said emphatically.

"Do you think I didn't want to do that? When they surrounded me I simply couldn't go anywhere," my daughter sounded as if she had been terribly wronged.

A few days later, my son came back from playing basketball at his old school, and told us what had happened that day.

"While I was playing ball today, somebody shouted out K's name. I turned my head and I saw her. What a pipsqueak! Sister is a real wimp to be afraid of her! I'd have fought it out with her," he said, wiping away his sweat.

My daughter raised her objections immediately.

"You don't know her like I do! She's thin and small alright, but sometimes her mad dog eyes send shivers down your spine. You feel as if she is going to pounce upon you and tear you to pieces! It's scary!"

But in the ensuing days, there seemed to be peace. According to my daughter, nobody had given her any more trouble. We were relieved and thankful that the whole thing seemed to have blown over.

Early this year I attended a cross-straits conference on Chinese fiction sponsored by the *China Times*. For two full days I participated in that literary gathering at Eslite Art Gallery. Then, when I came back home that evening, my husband confided to me something that had obviously upset him.

"Something strange is going on! For the whole weekend, our daughter just buried herself in writing. She drew lines on the paper and filled them up with her small handwriting. I have no clue what she was writing about. She wouldn't let me have a look."

That night, as the children were finally ready for bed, I went into my daughter's room to be alone with her. I asked her whether she had something to tell me. She said no, but I wouldn't settle for that.

"Haven't we made a deal? We've promised each other that there would be no secrets between us," I reminded her.

She took out pages of writing from her school bag. There were about five or six of them, written on both sides. They were vivid descriptions of her nightmares and details about her being beaten up, very much like the transcription of a police interrogation. As I read them, tears came pouring out like rain. I almost broke down. At first I thought it was just a child's way of venting her anger, but it turned out to be a true story of grim and gory campus violence.

In her small handwriting, she gave the following account:

The first time: It was a Friday. K of Class 15 came and told me to see her at the school gate after school. When school was over, there she was, dressed attractively, even wearing perfume. She lured me to the apartment building next door. We went to the second floor. I had only just put down my school bag and turned round when she barked out a question totally incomprehensible to me, her countenance a total turnaround from a moment ago. Before I had time to answer, she slapped my face a few times. I was in a daze. She slapped me! I couldn't believe it! I'd never done anything to her, and there had never been any reason for a grudge. Why would she hit me? I hit back. Then the two of us got into a fight, with her pulling my hair and me tugging at her clothes. She grabbed me by the hair, trying to fling me down but ended up bringing me to my knees, so that I was "totally defeated," so to speak. But that's not all. The next moment, she grabbed me from the floor, growling a threat: "If you dare to tell anyone about this, I'll push you off from here!"

I was scared to death. The whole thing got my asthma going, and as I was gasping for breath, a twenty-something-year-old woman suddenly came out of the small crowd of bystanders, yelling at me: "Wheeze till you drop, sweetheart!" To that, she added another slap on my face. I was brought down to my knees again. I was so scared that I had to obey everything she said.

When I left that apartment building, I burst out crying. I cried because I hated myself for being such a wimp. Besides, I couldn't swallow such humiliation! I couldn't accept the fact that I had been roughed up like this, without the slightest knowledge of why. She said I talked in a "cocky" way, what does "cocky" mean? I have never been so humiliated! I've never been hit by anybody, not even by my parents! What right did she have to hit me? I hate her! I've never hated anybody in my life, but now I've decided that we're sworn enemies!"

The second time: At noon one day during summer school, K, who didn't attend summer school, suddenly appeared. She asked me to have a talk on the twelfth floor of the apartment building where she had fought me last time. Since I didn't have the guts to say no, I followed her obediently. As soon as we arrived, she said: "Last time, you pulled my clothes, almost stripping me naked. Today, you have a choice: run home naked, or get slugged." She looked scary. After a moment's thinking, I chose the latter. She had a peculiar way of hitting people. She hit not only my face but also the back of my head. My face felt burning hot, and my head seemed to have swollen to the size of a basketball. The pain was so excruciating that I begged her to stop. I touched my teeth and there was blood on my hand. "I'm letting you off today and you're damn lucky I am!" While I was leaving, she threatened me again: "one word of this and you will die . . . ."

The third time: This time, they had planned to "fix" another classmate, but she escaped, and I became the substitute. Again they asked a few off-the-wall questions; each question was accompanied by a punch. It was pretty rough. With T and K hitting and kicking me together, I was hurt all over. There was a dark bruise on my knee, which took a long time to heal. Like last time, my mouth bled badly. Oh, I'm such a coward . . . !"

"The fourth time: While the class was visiting the Technology

and Information Center, T pushed me into the rest room, hit and kicked me . . . .

"K, have I done anything so wrong that I'm such a nuisance to you? Why do you have to beat up people? What good does it do you? It only makes you . . . .

One day I dreamed that I'd become a police officer. Our section chief wanted me to go to some apartment building to catch two criminals who were on the run—and they were K and T. When I got there, I could see that they were beating up people. I went up immediately to stop them. Then I grabbed K's arms, handcuffed her from behind and handed her over to my colleague to be taken back to the police station. Then I turned to talk to T, rather coldly.

"This time, I'm letting you off. I'm giving you a chance to change your ways. Don't let me catch you again. Don't let me down."

"Who the heck are you?" asked T.

I showed her my ID. She was so scared that she immediately knelt down in front of me . . . ."

The other day, I dreamed of K again. Her eyes had completely lost their hard look. She looked forlorn.

"Go home! If you don't go home, your mother will be worried sick," I tried to persuade her.

K asked me who I was. I told her I was the person she'd beaten up three times. I persuaded her to change her ways and be good. I even helped her to find her mother. She was so happy that she shed tears of joy . . . .

. . . .

As I was reading, I couldn't fight back my tears. Only then did I realize that we had shown sentimental kindness to evil only at the expense of our daughter. Such acts of cruelty as she had suffered had done far greater damage to her than we had imagined. Such behavior was really detestable, abominable! I had to admit with shame that if I had known what atrocities those kids were capable of inflicting upon my daughter, I'd not have been so merciful when I dealt with those two little brutes. I earnestly believe that no mother in the world would ever tolerate such cruelty to her children. How shameful that I have failed in my responsibility to protect my daughter!

But all these things had happened about half a year ago. I wondered why they had come back to haunt her again.

"Didn't you promise Mom that you would forget the whole thing and let bygones be bygones?" I asked my daughter.

"Recently, because of the exam, the teacher rearranged the seats. T and R, who used to bully me, are now seated to my left and to my front. I'm scared! Though they no longer bully me, I can't help trembling whenever I think of what happened in the past . . . ."

I hugged my daughter. My heart was greatly troubled.

"Let me talk to the teacher. Let me ask her to rearrange the seating. How about that?" I tried to comfort her.

At that, my daughter's whole body tensed up. She was all nerves.

"No, if they find out about it, I'll be in for it! I promise I'll stand up to them!" she pleaded.

My husband and I could not sleep all night. We were at the end of our rope. Our daughter was meek, totally defenseless. We had to deal with the situation carefully, or she would be traumatized even more. For the first time, we mulled over the possibility of transferring her to another school. For the next few days, we called a few private Christian schools, but their answer was the same—transfer students had to take a series of stringent screening tests. When I thought of my daughter's lackluster academic performance, I sadly abandoned this idea. Inside I was even grumbling that God seemed to favor intelligent people more than weak ones. Driving home from school, staring at the bleak highway in front of me, I felt that our future was equally bleak. At that moment, I was overcome with grief. And in the loneliness of my car, I cried.

Just when we were physically and emotionally almost completely drained, our daughter came back one day with some good news.

"The teacher said that she would rearrange our seats next week. Nothing to worry about any more! . . . Mama, I'm really sorry."

This had finally come as a result of my conversation with her teacher. One night I finally decided to talk to the teacher without my daughter's knowledge. I suggested that my daughter should be seated away from those two girls when the time came to rearrange the seats. When the teacher knew what my daughter had been through, she apologized profusely and promised to remedy the situation as soon as possible. Before hanging up the phone, she shared with me her favorable impressions of my daughter.

"That daughter of yours is really adorable! Despite everything, she bears no grudge against any of the girls. During the last tug-of-war competition between the classes, she cheered T on. I noticed that she almost shouted herself hoarse, and her chubby face was very pink. For me, sometimes a whole day's teaching can be draining, but during class, when I catch her eye, she will always give me a smile. Mrs. Tsai, you're also a teacher. You should understand the kind of feeling that makes a teacher's hard work worthwhile. Your daughter is really a lovely child!"

Toward evening the next day when my daughter came back from school, I followed the teacher's advice and went with her to the roof on the seventh floor. We set all her writings on fire. We hoped that the devastating memories could be consigned to the past.

The pages were finally reduced to ashes. When I turned round for a broom to clean them up, a gust of wind had already blown them away. My daughter stared into the sky, as if in a trance. "If only memories were like the wind," she said quietly to herself.

Will our memories really be like the wind?

Translated by May Li-ming TANG 湯麗明

LUNG Yingtai 龍應台

Best of Both Worlds:
Wisteria Tea House and Starbucks
在紫藤廬與Starbucks之間[*]

Taiwan's Insularity

In 1968, an electronics industry leader and his U.S. corporate president visited Taipei to see whether this was the right location for their company's first Asian factory. In the end, however, they opted for Singapore. Why not Taipei? The entrepreneur explained to me that Taipei seemed somehow closed off, that people just did not know what was happening around the world, and that the general level of English proficiency was quite low. In other words, Taipei was not international enough.

In 2002, Lonely Planet brought out an updated edition of its Taiwan guidebook. The author had clearly put little effort into the revision, as there was almost nothing about new developments in Taipei in it. But the author did provide an overall impression of Taiwan's capital, which he described as one of the most unapproachable cities in Asia. In other words, Taipei seems isolated, barely connected with the outside world, and with a lower than average English fluency: not the kind of city where international travelers are going to feel at ease, let alone at home.

---

[*] From Yen Kun-yang 顏崑陽 et al eds. *Jiushiher nien san-wen xuan*《九十二年散文選》 (The Best Taiwanese Essays, 2004). Taipei: Elite Publishing Co., 2004.

Can it be? Thirty-five years have passed since 1968 and Taiwan is still closed off, still out of touch with the rest of the world?

Yes, it's true. Anyone who has traveled much can see immediately that Taiwan is comparatively insular. There are few foreign travelers at Chiang Kai-shek International Airport. The English on the street signs in the capital is an utter mess. Pick up a newspaper and you are finished with the international section in five minutes flat. The content of cable television news is a collective indictment of our self-centeredness: ten times as much coverage for a child who swallowed nails while playing than for Ethiopia's starving millions; footage of a dog chewing betel nuts in Nantou dwarfs the Argentinean presidential election in importance; nude demonstrators at a G-8 summit fill up the television screen, without as much as a single commentary on their cause. 24 hours a day, the people of Taiwan are force-fed detailed images of loud-mouthed politicians, whose antics often escalate into scuffles and even brawls. Issues of international concern—war, the environment, poverty, famine, intellectual advances, sudden changes in the old order, latent crises—seem not to exist in Taiwan.

"That's absurd," you may argue, "Taiwan *is* international: just look at the concentration of Starbucks in Taipei, the highest in the world. And what about the all-night convenience stores, on almost every street corner." There are indeed ways in which our capital city seems cosmopolitan. Want to hear the hippest hip hop music and see the latest fashions? Taipei's the place to be. Release dates for Hollywood movies are among the earliest in the world. Moreover, the yearly rhythm we beat out is international: we celebrate Valentine's Day on February 14, hold a costume parade for Halloween in late October, and cook Thanksgiving turkey dinner in November. Come Christmas in December and the whole town turns out to sing and dance in City Hall Square. Even the Presidential Office gets in on the act on New Year's Eve, setting off fireworks, popping champagne corks, and counting down the seconds to midnight, when you grab the nearest person for a celebratory kiss.

Finally, the newly elected national government is now asking for English versions of all official documents. Civil servants must now undergo English testing. The entire population is studying the language! The final goal of all these efforts is to make English an official language. So who says Taiwan is closed off?

Who to Emulate?

But what on earth is "internationalization"?

If "modernization" means the introduction of new farming techniques used on the existing soil of traditional culture—such as democratic institutions, the scientific spirit, and industrial technology—for the benefit of a new philosophy of accommodation and a new lifestyle, and if "globalization" signals an unprecedented perforation of traditional ethnic and national borders as deep-rooted cultural institutions are now self-adjusting to the rhythm of modern technology and economy, then a nation's cultural and social heritages—its laws, beliefs, morals, values—will all have to be redefined.

Modernization is the holy grail of a great many developing nations, and globalization is rapidly becoming a reality. In the new order, developed nations are trying to capitalize on established advantages, while developing countries are faced with the danger of "becoming invisible" even as they ride the tide of opportunity.

Where does the concept of "internationalization" fit in? It would seem to indicate becoming international, but what does that mean? Who is international and what are they like? In making English one of our official languages, are we trying to emulate England and the United States? Or India and the Philippines? Or Hong Kong and Singapore? When the government announces the adoption of a foreign language as a lingua franca, have they thought seriously about the country's destiny and its place in the world? Are they willing and able to ensure its survival?

Like a Shepherd through the Pasture

It was 1978, my first trip to Europe, the continent of the Enlightenment and the Industrial Revolution, where many of the world's advanced nations were to be found. My head was stuffed with bright-eyed imaginings about what "modernized" countries were like. But fresh out of the airport, motoring along the Franco-German frontier, I was surprised at the absence of the surreal high-tech cityscapes I had been expecting. Framed by my window was a medieval landscape illuminated by the slanting rays of the setting sun. Villages were nestled at the verge of forest groves and fields of wheat. The orderly pattern of redroofed, white-walled houses set off the serene balance of church steeples amid a symphony of dogs and chickens.

The car had to stop when nearly a hundred fluffy sheep trundled across the road like children going home from school, shoving and jostling and shouting. Looking off into the pasture, I saw a shepherd walking slowly over, his flock milling around him. He wore a beard and a raincoat and held a staff in his hand. The dusk dyed the sheep a pastel shade, and the sharp extraneous smell of grass wafted through the air.

I was shocked! Where were the proud monuments of "modernization"? All there was to see was "tradition," tradition that was serene and peaceful, and close to the soil. As the man and his sheep drew nigh from the rich green pasture, I felt like a thirsty traveler in the presence of an Old Testament shepherd.

A subsequent period of lengthy residence in Europe confirmed my first impressions time and time again: tradition is still a vital part of the European way of life. People carry on the traditional ceremonies for the different stages of life, knowing on every occasion what songs to sing, what colors to wear, what flowers to send, and what words to speak. As with birth, age, sickness and death, so with spring, summer, autumn and winter: the seasons are cadenced, with the Carnival parade at winter's end to ward off evil, egg painting at Easter to celebrate life, street dancing at midsummer to break from work, and solemn reflection at Christmas to pray for blessings. Age-old practices have not warped or disappeared because of modernization. In Rome, Paris, and Berlin, the works of the past— a fallen city wall, a ruined church, or a cobblestone street—are protected and restored, no matter what the expense. Thus, modern technology is used to preserve the feeling and essence of tradition.

This is no shallow poetic nostalgia. As we soar up into the vast unknown like a helium balloon, tradition is a tether tying us safely to the ground. Tradition helps us maintain our composure through the trials of life and live in harmony with the seasons—spring flowers, autumn moon, winter snow. It is like the firm ground beneath our feet, or like a solid tree that we can lean on. Tradition is the old poem that makes us weep, and the writer—long dead and gone— with whom our spirits communicate.

Tradition is not a nostalgic mood. It is a necessity, essential for our survival. I discovered in Europe that my original understanding of "modernization" was incomplete. For advanced countries, modernization is the means; protecting tradition is the end. The massive sums that are invested in the environment, the efforts that go into related research and development, are only to recover the perfect simplicity of tradition: "narrow bridge, flowing brook, human abode." The final goal of modernization is not to propel ourselves aimlessly into the unknown, but rather to return to our own language and culture, to our own history and belief, and to our own soil.

A Crisis of Culture

Thereupon I saw that the more advanced a country, the greater its capacity to protect culture, and the more culture is protected, the more self-assurance the people have. By contrast, the more backward a nation, the worse the loss or even disintegration of culture becomes. A country in such dire straits can neither keep its bearings nor plot a course into the future.

Taiwanese people celebrate the day of lovers but know nothing of Saint Valentine; they hold costume parades but are unclear about the meaning of the Carnival; they eat turkey dinner but cannot say to whom they are thankful; they join in the Christmas revelry but do not settle down for any religious reflection. Every seasonal celebration must be linked back to its religious or cultural roots. Adopting other people's celebrations is analogous to picking up somebody's ancestral tablets without having any idea about how or who to worship!

It is easy to import the hustle and bustle of festive celebrations, but not the cultural meaning. Uprooted, celebrations are reduced to empty consumerism. Neglected are one's own cultural observances, which have since time immemorial punctuated the seasons with occasions for gratitude, cleansing, soul searching, and prayer. If our cultural roots wither and die, how can we invest our communal life with meaning? A few speak words of wisdom in times of trouble, but most have no clue what to do.

Taiwan's leaders want to make English an official language, but they know not what they do. They treat language as a tool that people can "pick up" just as easily as you can grab some dead piece of wood to use as a club.

Language is not a club. It is a great and sturdy tree, whose roots are inextricable from the ground of culture and history. Transplanting language is transplanting culture and history, values and beliefs, for these things are intertwined. Consider colonialism. Consolidating colonial rule involves changing the identity and outlook of the colonized people. The first step in the process is to get the colonized people to take the language of the colonizer as their own language. This is how English came to be widely used in Hong Kong and Singapore, where people not only speak English but also understand how the Anglophone world operates. History has made it easier for Singapore and Hong Kong to engage directly with the international community, but perhaps there has been a price, paid not in currency but in culture. The ascendancy of English has weakened Chinese and Malay, but has also failed to seed an Anglophone culture rich enough to rival that of New York or London. If culture is a soil, then in Singapore and Hong Kong there is no soil deep or rich enough to support the growth of a towering tree.

Knowledge is the Key

Taiwan is not an English-speaking country, never having been colonized by an English-speaking power. So why list English as an official language? What might the consequences of this decision be? Clearly, the politicians in Taipei do not have reasonable answers to these questions. They have only this foolhardy plan that will surely oust us from our niche.

If internationalization is not adopting other people's festivals or languages, then what exactly is it?

It is knowledge of self and other. In knowing ourselves, we gain a sense of our place in the world and of our foundational values. In knowing others, we are able to explain our language, institutions and customs—our unique perspective—in terms that others will understand. Internationalization does not mean being the same as others but rather being able to tell others how we are different. As such, "internationalization" means finding a reasonable way to make ourselves understood. It is not an end but a means.

Finding "a way to make oneself understood" requires knowledge. Not knowing the colonial history of Africa, you will think that the sorrows of the Taiwanese people are the greatest that the world has ever known. Not knowing how the world reacts to the Chinese market, you will only view "the China problem" through the lens of politics. Not knowing international commerce, you will continue seeing Taiwanese entrepreneurs in China as traitors and not as an economic vanguard. To be international, we must understand the rivalry between the United States and Europe in the wake of the Persian Gulf War, the compromise politics of the United Nations, the post-glasnost transformation of Russia, the position of the new China in the international order, and the enormous challenges that globalization presents to sovereignty and culture. If we lack such understanding, how can we possibly find the right words to let the international community understand Taiwan? Without international knowledge, our explanations are wasted breath.

The more advanced the nation, the more its people know about the world. A mastery of such knowledge makes a nation powerful, for knowledge *is* power, after all, and competence increases with knowledge. If television is an index of culture, consider television in Taiwan and the nature of the knowledge it imparts: local news is broadcast unremittingly, blowing our own importance out of all proportion. This navel gazing is a sign not only of the backwardness of our nation but also of a sickness in our culture. We complacently allow television stations to deprive us of our right to know. We remain apathetic and ignorant about the rest of the world, and yet we still complain that nobody understands our plight, we still lament that we are the orphans of the whole world. Are we not being just a little contradictory?

Starbucks or Wisteria Tea House?

I like drinking coffee at Starbucks, not necessarily because they sell the best coffee, but because no matter where I am I know what it will be like before I go in. Cold rain starts falling in Jerusalem, London, Beijing, or Hong Kong; and then you see that familiar sign glowing at the next street corner. You are a stranger to the city, but you know that a tasty bagel and a nice warm Grande Latte are waiting for you just a few steps away.

"Globalization" is what makes you feel at home away from home, and vice versa.

I also like drinking tea and meeting friends at Wisteria Tea House. Amid the aroma of tea, someone reminisces about the great personages who once gathered within these walls and about the history they helped to make. Others, impassioned souls, plan out the next program of social reform. The wisteria blooms leisurely all the while, for there is no sense of hurry here. It knows the history of Taipei City too well.

There are fifty-eight Starbucks in Taipei and only one Wisteria Tea House. There are six thousand six hundred Starbucks worldwide and still only one Wisteria Tea House.

Internationalization does not mean renovating Wisteria Tea House into one more Starbucks. It means instead opening our gate and showing Starbucks in, while at the same time ensuring that Wisteria Tea House's soft and lovely light continues to shine. It also means knowing how to show this light to others, knowing how to familiarize people with how Wisteria Tea House is—how "I" am—different.

The more Starbucks there are, the more important Wisteria Tea House is.

Translated by Darryl STERK 石岱崙

Yin Dih 隱地

God-of-the-Day
一日神*

A happy day, an angry day . . . a day of sweetness, and a day of bitterness . . . . The god of creation, the god of destruction, the god of protection . . . . Can anyone escape these gods? They have cast their omnipresent nets between heaven and earth.

It appears as if the three gods have divided the world up into three parts. But this is a vast world, how can there be only three gods? The three gods each have their minions, and in truth these are the big and small gods of the universe, controlling the fates of the countless creatures inhabiting this world. As human beings, we yearn to create our own destinies and to carve out our own paths. When the gods hear our plans, they laugh and jeer behind our backs.

It has been said that there is a god-of-the-day that few have heard of. This god is with us for only one out of the 365 days of the year. He stays with us for a day and then departs. As such, his presence is hardly felt, and he often escapes our attention.

The god-of-the-day is light-footed. He arrives at daybreak and leaves at night, bidding us farewell after a day's company. When will we meet again? None of us knows.

We don't know where he is. But we know that he was here, and we know that he has departed.

When do the gods-of-the-day change guard? The changes are

* From Yin Dih 隱地, *Yireshen*《一日神》(God-of-the-Day). Taipei: Élite Publishing Co., 2011, 9-23.

imperceptible. It takes only a day to turn good news into bad news. Why such big difference?

A person can be perfectly fine one day, and wake up to find that the world has changed overnight.

It is not right, something is not right. You look into the mirror one morning and see an abominable, scruffy old man. Only yesterday you were still a handsome chap. What happened to your looks? You do not like what you see. You comb your hair again and again, but your hair refuses to stay put and, worse, it continues to lack luster. Continued attempts to tame your unruly hair remain futile, resulting in a spillage of problems.

Bygones. Has life withered away just like that? Sixty years. Six decades have gone by. What happened to a life that is supposed to go on forever? The best of my days are over. Spring blossoms and autumn moon have become things of the past. I have yet to bask in summer glory, but that too, seems to have become a dream that is out of my reach?

He passes each day with trepidation. The best time of the day is in the morning, and he worries that his day will start with a bad omen—and behold, a bad hair in the morning ruins the entire day. Happiness is always fleeting, while the sense of ennui drags on and on like sleepless nights, making his stomach churn, banishing his appetite and wrecking his day. Today's god-of-the-day is not a malicious demon, but he must be a god of lassitude, dragging my day down into the dumps. Quick, let's fend him off with a tenderness of heart and try to avoid friction. To talk sense, one must talk to someone who is rational. The same rule applies to gods and spirits. If the god-of-the-day is irrational, you must try to get out of his way. If you survive the day, all will be well. If you fail to do so, it could cost you your life, and you could end up lifeless, like a ghost.

"I failed to dodge the bullet!" Indeed, there are more ghosts than people in this world. So you have to be more careful day to day. Fortunately, the god of protection is always there, and the mischievous god-of-the-day can only bother you for a day. Tomorrow, a god with a smiling face will come your way.

How good it is to be alive. If you can sail through the dark night and wake up at dawn to trees, flowers, clouds floating in the bright blue sky, and the slowly rising sun . . . . How wonderful life is, with birdsong and coffee and Bach's unaccompanied cello suites, forming ripples of joy that surround you.

When he was in his twenties, he was like an ascending airplane. The world flew by before him, up, up and away, even his tiny pecker soared upwards. When he was in his forties, he read *How to Succeed before You Turn Forty*. The book stated, "If you are not healthy at forty, you will never become healthy; if you are not successful at forty, you will never be successful; if you are not rich at forty, you will never be rich . . . ." When he was in his sixties, he was transformed from an atheist into a polytheist, and he was able to sense the presence of god everywhere. He was even convinced that there is a god-of-the-day each and every day. The god of creation created him, and everyone should be thankful to the gods who created them. Who is my god of creation? One day, he suddenly asked himself this question. He wanted to pay homage to his gods with kindness and appreciation. "You don't need to pay homage to me, just be careful not to enrage your god of destruction!" came words of advice as if from the blue sky. He couldn't see his god of protection's face, but could clearly perceive genuine concern in his voice. His god of creation created him, and wanted his "creation" to live a long life on earth. Gods of destruction are everywhere, but they are preoccupied with their affairs and prefer to leave you alone as long as you don't provoke them. "Indeed," says your god of protection, "as long as you stay out of trouble, I can enjoy a carefree and easy life as well."

Ever since detecting the presence of gods, he started to exercise caution in his day-to-day dealings, but there were quite a few mischievous gods-of-the-day who enjoyed playing pranks on him, giving him a sense of illusion.

He had two bunches of keys, one for his office, and one for his home. He was always looking for his keys or his glasses or his wallet. The gods-of-the-day who played pranks on him liked to play hide-and-go-seek with him, hiding these objects from him—the objects had no feet, but somehow they were able to run here and there. He remembered placing something on the table, but somehow that something was nowhere to be found. "God-of-the-day, oh god-of-the-day, I am getting older, and I can't recall where I put my stuff. Please stop giving me a hard time. You must have moved my things around, making me hunt high and low for them."

One day there was a meeting of all the residents of the community. The thirty-two households bickered viciously, blaming each other. They all had fenced-in gardens, and they all planted flowers and trees in their gardens. When the trees grew tall, their branches and leaves would intrude into neighboring gardens, giving rise to tension between the neighbors. One would exercise one's rights by trimming the intruding branches and leaves with shears, and the other would retaliate by doing the same. This went back and forth, and before long, the neighbors became enemies.

Which god is responsible for this? Creating hostility between neighbors? If this god were only a god-of-the-day, then a good quarrel followed by some reflections and apologies from both sides would have resolved the conflict. But this isn't something that could be resolved by the god-of-the-day. There is a god-of-the-month who, in turn, has to answer to the god-of-the-year. Some people become lifelong enemies because of conflicts over a tree, and their quarrels escalate into armed conflict, resulting in casualties. Instead of living a good life, they all end up ghosts.

"I am going to stay out of the way of the god of destruction, and live my days in peace!" He prayed in his heart to the god-of-the-day. Yes, just one day of peace and quiet will suffice, because having had that, even if tomorrow ushers in trouble, I will be able to bear it and stomach it, because suffering is the common fate of human beings.

"Is that so?" the god of anger hiding behind the door is incredulous. He can make you seethe with anger from dawn to dusk. Once he gets on your case, you'll end up with a poker face and boil with rage for no particular reason, and the more you think about it, the more you feel as if the whole world is against you. Thinking about the past will only make you angrier. You are angered by your own anger and wonder why other people can smile but not you. You toss and turn in bed, unable to fall asleep, and that of course makes you angry about your insomnia. Your rage keeps you up all night. People prone to anger are often infuriated by their own fury.

Tomorrow and tomorrow, there are so many tomorrows. Oh, god-of-the-day, I have been upset all day today, and I don't like my angry self. Please grant me a day of serenity and peace tomorrow. As for the tomorrow of the tomorrow of my tomorrow, my god-of-the-day, I am your subject, I have seen all there is to see and tasted all there is to taste, the sweet and sour, as well as the bitter and pungent. So, before I bid farewell to this world, all I want is to breathe easy, to live an ordinary life among ordinary people.

Extreme emotions do harm to the body. Peace and tranquility is what I want. God-of-the-day, please send old-fashioned and gentle gods to protect me. As for the whimsical and naughty gods-of-the-day, please send them to hot-blooded teenagers who crave excitement. Let them mingle and have a blast!

Translated by Michelle Min-chia WU 吳敏嘉

Wen-hsing WANG 王文興

Flaw
欠缺[*]

I must have been eleven that year, because I had just enrolled in junior high. At that time we were still living on Tung-An Street, our earliest home in Taipei, and had not yet moved to Tung-Hua Street, after which we moved again to Lien-Yun Street. But it has always been my impression that the earlier the home, the more superior it seemed; every time we moved, it was to a less attractive place. Perhaps it was the nostalgia for early childhood, strongest for the earliest years, that gave rise to such an illusion.

Tung-An Street was a quiet little alley, with less than a hundred families along its entire length. Slightly curved around its middle, the street stretched all the way to the great gray river at the end. Actually, viewed from the vantage point of the river bank, there were very few pedestrians on the street, which, with its palish body and meandering path, was in reality a small river itself. Such was the tranquil picture when I was eleven; later, as small cars were allowed to pass through the street, the atmosphere of quiet seclusion was lost altogether. My present reminiscences hark back to the era before the arrival of the cars.

In any event, on Tung-An Street then, cats could be seen strolling lazily along the top of the low walls, from one house to the next. The whole landscape was filled with glistening green foliage and

---

[*] From Wang Wen-Hsing 王文興, *Shiwu pein xiaoshuo* 《十五篇小說》 (*Fifteen Short Stories*), Taipei: Hong Fan Publishing Co., 1979, 163-176.

delicately fragrant odors from the profusion of flowers and plants growing in the front yards. Flowers especially took to the Tung-An Street inhabitants; they bloomed in the spring and they blossomed in the fall. Most unforgettable however, were the evenings of that tiny street, when silent street lamps illumined the darkness of the road. Night seemed even quieter than day. The little grocery stores, unlike their counterparts in the crowded city, closed up at half-past nine. Midnight began at half-past nine. Night enjoyed its deepest and longest sleep on this street. Light breezes rustled among the leaves while remote stars twinkled in the skies, and after a few hours, night passed, day broke. In the early morning mist, the owners of the small grocery stores, still unlike their counterparts in the city, began taking down the wooden panels to the shops.

In spring that year, a young seamstress opened shop at the end of the street near the river. It was at a time when Taipei, still untouched by the glamours of affluence, was just beginning to prosper, and a number of three-storied buildings could be seen cropping up here and there. Ever since the previous winter, we children had been watching with interest the construction of such a building on the vacant lot in front of our houses. Our feelings were excitement mingled with sadness; we were excited because, as children, we felt an immense satisfaction with all novel experiences; new sights, new sounds, new objects, new undertakings; and sad because we were losing our favorite playground for after-school ball games. The building was completed in spring, and the young woman moved in. The house consisted of three compartments, and was three stories tall. The young woman and her family occupied the entire compartment on the right, while the second and third floors served as family rooms. It was said that she owned the entire building and we children had naturally assumed that she would occupy all the space herself, but it turned out she reserved only one compartment for her own use and offered the others for rent. A week after they had been taken she changed her mind and sold them off. And we felt a slight tinge of regret for her that she had been able to occupy only a part of the building.

I was a precocious child then, although I looked at least two years younger than my eleven years. Like all underdeveloped children however, my mental growth compensated for my physical weakness by being two years beyond my age. One day, I discovered that I was in love with the young woman. The realization dawned upon me during the spring vacation, right after the soft spring showers, in the blossom-filled month of April.

Being a sensitive and ingrown child, I had an instinctive fear of glamourous and sophisticated women, and took only to those with kind faces (I still do now). The woman at the dressmaking shop was exactly the type I liked.

She was about thirty-five or so, and did not wear much make-up (this was very important). She wore neither rouge nor powder on her face and only a tiny trace of lipstick on her lips, which were often parted in a white warm smile. Her eyes were not only beautiful, but, even more important, glowed with gentle kindness. My love for her stemmed not only from approval of her looks, but was rooted in sincere admiration for the goodness of her character as well.

Love in a precocious child, like a heavy blossom atop a frail stem, was a burden too heavy to bear. Only then did I realize the consuming nature of love; if the blazing flames were the joys of love it was the burning of the fuel itself which made these flames possible. I found it impossible that true happiness could consist in achieving joy from the masochistic burning of one's own self. Although I had been in the world for a mere eleven short years then, I had undergone enough minor suffering to be able to devise a means of avoiding pain; that was: if you happened to form an emotional attachment to a certain thing or a certain person, the best thing to do was to immediately look for a fault therein, upon which you would then be able to withhold your affection and thus lighten the burden. During the next few days, I often concealed myself directly opposite her shop and scrutinized her with cold detachment, in an effort to discover some ugliness in her. But the longer I watched, the more beautiful she seemed. I realized then that love had so deeply embedded itself that there was no way of uprooting it. I would have to live with it.

It was already the last day of the spring vacation. I made up my mind to enjoy it to the full by playing outdoors for the whole day. Early in the morning, I went over to our new playground (which had been relocated at the vacant lot in front of the garbage heap beside the grocery store) to wait for the other children to gather. We started our ball game much earlier that morning than usual—it must have been before eight o'clock, for our shrill cries woke an office worker living in one of the wooden buildings. Still clad in his pyjamas, he opened the window and leaned out to scold loudly. Our ball often hit the ragged old woman who kept a cigarette stand next to the garbage heap and she tried to chase us away with a broom, but as she lacked the strength and energy, could only stand brandishing her broom like a sentinel in front of her stand, hitting out at whoever ran near her, but we were all careful to stay away. On top of it all, Ah Chiu's pet mongrel kept dashing among us madly. For some reason or other he seemed to have pick me for his target, jumping on me repeatedly and causing me to fall several times. It was only when Ah Chiu's mother appeared and summoned him and his four brothers back to breakfast that we finally broke up the game and dispersed. The sun had splashed the entire street golden by then. Thick greenery clustered over the tops of the plaster walls. Market-bound housewives were already holding summer parasoles to ward off the sunlight, whose beams had become so strong lately that some buds were bursting into flower before their time. I left thirsty and wormed my way into Liu Shiao-tung's yard in order to drink from their faucet. Water flowed over my face and neck, where I left it for the sun to dry. As I passed the dressmaking shop, I saw the young woman standing in the doorway talking with another lady, teasing now and then the baby the latter held in her arms. I climbed up the incline at the end of Tung-An Street, walked down the steps on the other side and headed for the river.

The river under the sunlight was alive with undulating glitter, like a million thumb-tacks rising and falling in rhythm. On the opposite bank, two ox-carts were crawling along the sandy beach. Standing under a newly-budding tree, I could smell the fragrance of the baked earth along the river bank and feel the coolness of the river breeze on my skin. As I walked away from the tree, I raised my voice and started singing "Crossing the Sea in Summer." Keeping time with my hands, I went singing all the way up the river. I walked into a bamboo grove, found a relatively flat patch of land and lay myself down.

In front of me stretched the river, glimmering through the bamboo leaves; at my back was a piece of farmland colorful as a Persian rug. The huge patches of green were rice paddies; big blocks of rich dark brown were earth freshly plowed but yet unsowed; slender strips of light green, like the thin glass squares used under microscopes, were can tendrils, while the golden patches were vegetable blossoms, swaying in the spring breeze. The short dark figures of the farmers could be glimpsed working in the distance, and occasionally the faint odor of manure drifted in from the fields.

I lay quietly, thinking of all kinds of whimsical things, but they were all happy thoughts; I allowed my fancies to roam like the breeze-driven clouds in the sky. I turned over, and, resting my chin upon my arms, gazed at the river through the bamboo leaves. I thought of the young seamstress. I had no one in whom I could confide my love, only the river. Later this river also became the witness to my pains in learning to swim. I would often steal away from home, make my way alone to the river under the summer sun, and, bracing myself against fears of drowning, would try to teach myself the art of floating above water. But I never did succeed. I gave up my efforts finally, because I no longer had the courage to struggle.

The river could not respond to my confidences either. I returned to my former position on my back and covered my face with a handkerchief.

I lay until the sun had travelled directly overhead, then removed the handkerchief and sat up. Thinking that my mother would be waiting for me to go home for lunch, I stood up and headed for home. The farmers had all disappeared from the fields. Probably they too had gone home to eat.

At home I saw our Taiwanese amah. She had not gone home yet and was still doing the ironing. As soon as she saw me, she asked:

"Young Master, have you seen my Tsun-hsiung?" I replied that I had not.

"Weren't you playing with him outdoors?"

I said I was not.

"I can't think where he could've gone. I told him to come and help me mop the floors, but there hasn't been a trace of him all morning. My Tsun-hsiung just can't compare with Young Master, Ma'am. Young Master is smart, and works hard; so young and already in junior high; he'll be in senior high next, and after that, a top official." She said, shaking out one of my father's shirts.

Our amah often praised me thus, remarking that 1 would proceed to senior high school after finishing junior high. She could not imagine a college education beyond that of senior high, so, after that, I was to become a high official.

Mother answered her in broken Taiwanese:

"It'll be the same with you. Tsun-hsiung will also go to school, also earn money and support you."

"Thank you, Ma'am, thank you. But I was born to suffer, Ma'am. Tsun-hsiung's father died early, leaving me alone to raise him. I have no other hopes, only that Tsun-hsiung will be like Young Master, work hard in school—study in junior high and afterwards in senior high—no matter how hard I have to work, wash clothes all my life even, I want him to be educated."

"He won't disappoint you," my mother replied.

Amah only sighed.

That kind old woman. I still remember her broad tan face, like a piece of dark bread, warm and glowing, the perfect blending of simple goodness and unpretentious love. Where she had gone, no one knew. As I grew older, gentle people like her were harder and harder to come by. They are not the kind to adapt easily within an increasingly complex society, I suppose. I also recall another minor detail about her, the result of the peculiar powers of childhood observation: I often noticed her bare feet, with ten stout toes fanning out, pattering along on the shining floors of our house. The reason I found this extraordinary perhaps was that we all wore slippers in the house and there were many pairs of spare slippers in the hallway reserved for guests. Amah probably had never become used to this alien custom and thus never wore any. I often mused to myself then that even if she consented to wear slippers like the rest of us, where would we find such a large pair to fit her?

That was the last day of the spring vacation. Another detail I remember was that I went out and bought a diary that afternoon. A certain fascination for the surrounding phenomena, interest for the musings within my mind (for my newly-sprung love), and for spring itself urged me to imitate Liu Shiao-tung's elder brother and keep a diary. All my reminiscences for the day were faithfully recorded that evening in the first entry of my diary.

After the spring vacation, love continued to plague me, as if urging me to some action, to do something which would bring me closer to her, albeit only in my feeling. I thought of taking something to her shop and asking her to mend it for me (a sorry means of courtship, I admit). But that shop of hers took only women's clothing. I could not think of anything else, so one day (when no other solution offers itself, the only solution becomes the workable solution) I finally brought along a Boy Scouts jacket with a missing button to her shop.

Her shop was tastefully furnished. Pictures cut from Japanese fashion magazines adorned the walls, and a vase of bright red roses stood on a small table in one corner. Four girls were sitting in the room, talking and laughing among themselves as they pedalled on machines spread with pieces of brightly colored material.

"What do you want, little one?" A round-faced girl wearing a string of imitation pearls lifted her head and asked.

"I want a button sewn," I said, turning to the seamstress, who stood at the table measuring a dress, "can you do it?"

The woman took my jacket and said: "Ah Hsieu, sew the button on for him." She handed the jacket over to the round-faced girl, then turned and went on with her measuring.

I felt the sorrow of rejection.

"Which button is it?" The girl asked me.

I told her, with my eyes on the woman.

"How much?" I asked the woman.

"A dollar." Replied the girl.

The woman seemed not to have heard my question, for she did not even lift her head. My grief sank its roots into the depths of my heart. But after a while I saw the woman put on a pair of glasses, and curiosity gradually took the place of sorrow. I found it strange that she should wear glasses, as if it were the least probable thing in the world. I did not like the way she looked with glasses; she no longer looked like herself. Moreover, she was wearing them too low, they made her look old, and gave her an owl-like expression.

Suddenly aware that I had stood gazing in the shop much longer than necessary, I asked the round-faced girl:

"Can I come back and get it later?"

"No, stay. It'll be ready in a minute."

I waited nervously in the shop for her to finish. I glanced again at the pictures of the Japanese women on the walls. They were all very pretty, with dazzling smiles, but strangely, their eyelids all had only single creases. I looked again at the roses in the corner. They were still flaming red. Feeling that they seemed to be redder than roses usually were, I took a more careful look and discovered that they were plastic flowers.

After a while, a boy came down the stairs, munching a piece of fruit. He was taller than I, also in a Boy Scouts uniform, and was wearing a pair of glasses. With sudden intuition, I realized this was her son. I had seen two smaller children with her, but had never seen this one; like all new-comers to the neighborhood, he never came out to join our games. Amidst surprised confusion I, who was secretly in love with his mother, watched him as he went upstairs again with a water bottle.

After the button had been replaced, I hurried out the door with the jacket. In the doorway I met our amah coming in. Afraid that she would report me to my mother, for I had come to the shop without her knowledge, I slipped away as unobtrusively as I could.

Despite the fact that I had been received with cold indifference at her shop, that I had seen a son of hers who was much older than I, my love did not change; the love of a child does not change easily. I still gave her all the passion of my eleven years.

Thus I loyally allowed my love to continue, without hope, without fullfillment, and without anyone's awareness. This hopelessness however colored my love with a nuance of melancholy beauty. Actually, I could not tell whether this sense of futility gave me sorrow or happiness. But I was sure of one thing, that, with such love, I was happier than adults in one respect. I was spared from any unnecessary anxiety; I did not have to worry over the fact that one day my love would suddenly come to an end. As long as my admiration existed, my love existed. Looking back now, I should say I was quite happy then.

The trip I made to her shop, I recall, was the only time I undertook such a venture. I never found another opportunity; besides, for some reason I suddenly lost all courage, and found myself deeply ashamed over the incident. Whenever I thought of myself going into her shop on the mere pretext of replacing a button, my shame would grow until the experience became a positive terror, causing me to sweat in anguish. For three days afterward I did not have the heart to pass in front of her shop. Courage is a strange thing: the first plunge should never be merited as true courage until tested by subsequent tries.

Although I was never in her shop again, I was often in front of it. Opposite her shop was a dry goods store which sold all kinds of tidbits for children and from whence I frequently stood vigil. Munching on a cracker, I watched as she moved around in her shop. Sometimes I would see her husband, a man of thirty-some, riding a motorcycle and said to be working in a commercial bank. Strangely enough, I never felt a trace of jealousy for this man. This showed, I suppose, that I was still a long way from maturity. I did not seem to realize the full significance of the word "husband." I thought of him as merely another member of her household, like her brother, her uncle, or her brother-in-law. But should she be talking with another man, for instance if she chatted momentarily with the barber next door, my jealous rage would lead me to visualize the barber lying on the ground, with a dagger in his heart.

Thus the days slipped by, one after another, like the turning pages of my diary. Soon it was summer and the end of the school term approached. I began to worry about my grades; I was very weak in algebra, and was afraid I would not be able to pass in the finals. My algebra teacher had already warned half-jokingly that he expected to see me again next semester. I shook with fear; I had never in my life had to repeat a grade, and now the threat loomed large. Yet mingled with the anxiety was a sense of unbound expectation, expectation for the freedom, the happiness, and the unlimited possibilities of the summer vacation. Under the dark shadow of the finals, I sat for hours on end with the algebra text in front of me, but, instead of studying, I often simply gazed at it anxiously. I grew thin and pale.

Finally, the heavy, burdensome finals were over. Al! the students hurled themselves into the free skies of the summer vacation like birds escaping from captivity. I was merely one ecstatic soul among thousands. Countless youngsters, burdened by the exams, eagerly awaited the arrival of the summer vacation, and, in waiting, imagined that it would never become a reality, or else suffered their joys of expectation to be almost cancelled by the pains of suffering.

That first morning of the vacation, I opened my eleven-year-old eyes to the riotous singing of birds and a world brilliant with sunshine. Exams were a thing of the past. No matter how badly I did on them, they were no longer on my mind. All children, perhaps, are unable to worry over the past. Sitting up in bed, a shiver of excitement told me beyond a shadow of doubt that the summer vacation had finally arrived. That certainty did not come from any indication on the calendar, but from a certain sound, a certain odor, a patch of sunlight, all distinctively characteristic. I heard the shrill buzz of the cicadas, saw the reflection of a basin of water shimmering on the ceiling, smelled the cool fragrance of mothballs as my mother took out our winter clothing from the trunks and laid them out in the sun— and I knew that this was it. Happiness was that child as he jumped out of bed.

Each year with the awareness of summer came the re-minder to sort out our fishing gear. We would rummage among the coal bins in the kitchen and come out with a slender bamboo pole which our mothers had discarded (and which we had painstakingly whittled ourselves), take it to the bathroom and, with great effort, try to clean it, thinking of the great catches in store this year, although for the most part we were able to bait only frogs.

I found my fishing pole that day as usual, and cleaned it up as before. But holding it in my hands I all of a sudden felt that it was much too homely. It was my own handiwork, of which I had once been so proud, but now I saw its crudeness. I felt that I needed a brand new fishing pole, a *bona fide* one, not a plain home-made one like this. I wanted one with a reel, a tinkler, and one that was gracefully pliant like a whip. I made up my mind to ask my father to buy me one. I had high hopes of getting it, because I had an indisputable reason: I was *eleven*.

I threw my fishing pole back into the coal bin.

I headed for the garbage heap to look for my friends. It had been two whole weeks since we played our last ball game, all because of the final exams. Our mothers would not let us play.

I passed by the dressmaking shop, hoping to catch a glimpse of the young woman, but today her shop was closed. She must be out with her family. I felt a little disheartened. I saw her every day, but one day in which I did not was enough to give me that feeling of void.

My friends were already in the middle of a game. I hurriedly joined in and immediately became involved in the ferocious battle. We played happily until noon. The side I was on lost and they blamed me, while I blamed myself for joining the wrong side. But we all determined valiantly to fight again tomorrow and win. As I walked home, the dressmaking shop was still closed. Again I experienced a loss.

At home my mother was complaining over the fact that Amah had failed to show up that morning to do the laundry, and that if she was too busy to come she should have sent Tsun-hsiung over with a message. Then she turned upon me and said that I had disappeared all morning like a pigeon let out of the cage; she wanted me to go and look for Amah, but she could not even find me. I was headed for sure trouble if I played like that every day, and I should not spend all my time in ball games even though it was the summer vacation. Naturally, these words were ones I liked least to hear.

After lunch I felt drowsy. The white hot sunshine outside made it hard to keep my eyes open; in the room a few flies were buzzing intermittently upon the dining-room table. Unconsciously I dozed off for about ten minutes. Awaking, I gazed at the bright sunlight outside the window and the flies on the table in the room and a familiar sensation dawned upon me. How could I have forgotten?

Summer vacations were always boring after all.

Just then Mrs. Liu, who lived next door, came over for her daily chat with my mother. With hair curlers bobbing she stepped in the doorway and asked:

"Is your mother at home, little one?"

"I'm in the kitchen, Mrs. Liu," my mother called, "find a seat and I'll be out in a minute." But Mrs. Liu had already traced the voice into the kitchen.

Then they both emerged. My mother's hands were covered with soap suds. She found a piece of cloth and started wiping them.

"How come you're doing the wash yourself?" Mrs. Liu asked as she sat down.

"Amah didn't show up today, I thought I might as well."

"That's what I came to tell you," Mrs. Liu said, setting her curlers bobbing again. "You know what's happened to Amah? She's lost all her money. Twenty thousand dollars of savings, and she lost them all last night. No wonder she's sick."

"Oh? Is that so? I didn't know she had so much saved up." My mother remarked in surprise.

"All the money she earned by working day and night as a washerwoman, saved up bit by bit. She says she's saving the money for her son's education. Worse luck that she should lose it all. But this time lots of other people on our street were hard hit too. Mrs. Yeh lost ten thousand, seems like she just put the money in a couple of days ago, and it being the money for the fuel coupons of her husband's office at that. Mrs. Wu lost three thousand. It's all that witch's fault, and now the whole family's skipped."

"Who're you talking about?"

"That woman in the dressmaking shop. You can't imagine how unscrupulous she is. One hundred fifty thousand, gone just like that. Who'd believe she was capable of doing such a thing? Everyone saw that her business was good and trusted her, saw that she offered higher interest, of course, and never dreamed she would suddenly skip out like that. Sheer betrayal, that's what it is."

"Unbelievable," my mother mused, "she seemed to be such an honest person. Oh, poor Amah, what is she going to do . . . . "

I did not stay to hear my mother finish. I ran out of the house and headed straight for the dressmaking shop.

The shop was still closed. A few women were standing near the doorway chatting. I stood gazing at the shop as pieces of the conversation nearby drifted into my ears.

"They left in the middle of the night. No one knows where they are now."

"They could report her to the police, have her arrested."

"No use. All she'll have to do is declare herself bankrupt, and she wouldn't have a care in the world. Besides, now that she's got the money, the law can't touch her."

"It was all planned," another said, "you notice she was in a hurry to sell most of this building as soon as she moved in."

"They say she sold this shop of hers last week too."

A few maids were peering in from the windows on the right. I went over and looked in through a small pane of glass: the room was empty, all the sewing machines and the furniture were gone.

"Just imagine, she didn't even pay the girls their wages. How mean can one get?"

Hearing this I suddenly felt my ears burn with anger. Mrs. Liu had already left when I got home. Seeing me, my mother murmured:

"Unbelievable, just unbelievable. People are getting worse and worse. More people get rich and more cheating goes on. People are getting prosperous, but if morals go bad, what's the use of all this prosperity? Luckily we aren't rich; otherwise, who knows? We might also have been duped."

Our family was not rich. My father was teaching in a high school then, and, in Taiwan, a teacher was by no means well off. But was Amah well off? I thought. Why cheat her out of all her money? And those girls who had worked for nothing, why deprive them of their wages?

I went with a book up to the rooftop that evening; I had decided to heed my mother and do a little studying. The sky above was a soft quiet blue. I sat on the reddish tiles and leaned my head against the railing.

I could see the dressmaking shop down across the street. The door was still closed, but the chatting women had gone.

Thinking of the young woman, of her comely yet gentle face, I found it hard to believe that she was a fraud. But she *was* a *fraud.* Every time I told myself the truth, my heart contracted in pain.

I still cherished my love for her. I wanted to keep that love. I closed my eyes and thought of her lily-like face yet I was always reminded of her blemish. I saw the ugliness of that face; and the flower hung down and withered.

Dusk slowly enveloped Tung-An Street; wisps of pale smoke began to curl from the chimneys nearby. I found the scene in front of me misting, and discovered that my eyes were filled with tears.

Oh, youth, perhaps my sadness then was due not only to a woman's having disappointed me, but to the discovery that some element in life had been deluding me, and had been deluding me for a long time. The sorrow and the anguish of the discovery disturbed me deeply.

From that day on, I understood a bit more; I learned that disillusions were an integral part of life, and that more disillusions were to come. From that day on, I had forgotten the beauty of that woman, although I never could forget the details of this incident. No wonder; that was my first love.

Translated by Chu-yun CHEN 陳竺筠

LIN Hwai-min 林懷民

The Boy in the Red Shirt
穿紅襯衫的男孩[*]

I did not really like Hsiao Heh the first time I saw him.

Perhaps it was due to his long and messy hair, with sideburns extending to both sides of his jaws. Perhaps it was due to his clothes, too red and too dirty—I never cared for men in loud colors, particularly in that brilliant and aggressive red.

Perhaps it was due to none of these, but rather to his attitude that he did not give a damn.

Even if the sky fell he would not bat an eye. He seemed to have come from another race unknown to my life.

As we left the Fengs' house, Chia-ke lit a cigarette and started grumbling. Mrs. Feng must have lost her mind in her longing for her son, he said. Otherwise, she would not have welcomed into her home such a gypsy-like juvenile delinquent.

Juvenile delinquent? Hsiao Heh probably was not that bad, yet his appearance was indeed most incongruous with Professor Feng's elegant living room.

This was merely our impression, he himself was quite at home. He would leaf through a book or touch a vase. Then, slumping into a sofa, he would pick up a cigarette, cross his legs, and settle back to puff in great leisure.

---

* From National Institute for Compilation and Translation 國立編譯館 ed., *Qingshaonien taiwan wenku xiaoshuo duben 1: chuan hong chenshan de nanhai* 《青少年台灣文庫──小說讀本 1：穿紅襯衫的男孩》(*Taiwanese Literature Reader for Teenagers—Short Stories 1: The Boy in The Red Shirt*), Taipei: Wu-Nan Book Inc., 2006, 164-189.

That day, Hsiao Heh was at the Fengs' to repair their record player. Mrs. Feng had nothing but praise for his versatility and talent. It seemed he could fix anything in a matter of minutes, from stopped-up toilets to leaking water pipes. He even built the latticework for the grape vine in the front yard. He was not at all like us college students, who knew nothing besides studying and having a good time. When we had been there visiting one evening, the fuse had blown. The room was plunged into darkness, but none of us could do the repair work.

Hsiao Heh grinned in response to Mrs. Feng's compliments, exposing two rows of uneven white teeth. From his right foot dangled an old worn out slipper. He acted as if he were really superior to us because of his versatility.

With his famed pipe in hand, Professor Feng regarded Hsiao Heh with an indulgent smile. The lines on his face softened, making him seem like a different person from the stern man in the classroom.

Chia-ke could never stand being on the sideline. Mrs. Feng's incessant praises of Hsiao Heh finally drove him to leave. Without mentioning the recommendation letter which he had intended to ask Professor Feng to write, Chia-ke dragged Ping-mei and me along and we said our goodbyes.

Ping-mei was very much displeased. As soon as Chia-ke started to grumble, she retorted:

"You're only jealous. In what way has he offended you? College boys like you are all self-important and pretentious. After one has seen your kind for too long, one feels that Hsiao Heh is rather loveable. He laughs when he wants to, in a natural and spontaneous way."

Chia-ke was taken aback. He adjusted his glasses, but before he could answer, Ping-mei added:

"Sometimes I feel that only people like him are really alive. Unlike us . . . ."

"F . . . ! " Chia-ke resorted to swearing whenever he became angered. "You can go after him. Nobody is stopping you."

I felt most uncomfortable seeing them quarrel. Being caught in the middle, I never knew which side to help. I hurriedly told them I had to go back to finish a reading report.

I might have come across Hsiao Heh before, but as I did not know him I never noticed him.

Since that night, it was as if he had suddenly leaped out from some obscure corner, I would encounter him at least two or three times a week. He would be either roaming aimlessly in the neighborhood of the school, or slurping down a large bowl of noodles with lots of red peppers at a Shantung-style food stand. Most of the time he wore that flamboyant red shirt and a pair of faded blue jeans.

One night, I came out of the library and found him again by the noodle stand. After we finished eating, we walked off together.

Mrs. Feng had told me that he was a high school graduate. I had nothing else to say, so I asked him why he had not gone to college, and why he wasted his time fooling around.

Hsiao Heh raised his eye-brows and asked me instead: "What's the use of going to college? What good is it—if one does not like studying, but studies just because others are doing it?"

He told me that since childhood days he had never been interested in books. All his father's beatings were but for "shit!" After he finally got through a technical high school and finished his military service, his father said that, as he was the eldest son, he should stay on the farm and help out. He ran away from home instead, and had lived on his own ever since.

"What did you do?"

"Oh, a lot. In the beginning I worked as a surveyor in the mountains. Minerology was my major. If nothing else, at least I learned the techniques of simple surveying. After that, I returned to Tainan and painted billboards for movies. Then I worked for a plumbing and electrical service shop. After four months I had a fight with the boss' son . . ."

"What happened?"

"F—, that son of a bitch, he made a sales-girl pregnant, then coaxed her into becoming a waitress in a fruit shop in Kaohsiung. There he forced her to have an abortion, then abandoned her."

"Why? What for? Did you like the girl?"

"Not at all," Hsiao Heh waved his hand. "That girl had no looks. It was later when he kept harassing the young apprentice. I couldn't stand it and quarreled with him. He thought being the boss' son, he could beat up the people in the shop. He slapped me, F—him. I beat him up."

"Oh."

"Just at that time, a former classmate of mine asked me to work on a fishing boat, so I went out to sea. But I didn't work too long either. I get bored very easily and can't stick to one thing for long." He shrugged. "So, I came to Taipei to do odd jobs."

"Why didn't you go back home?"

"It's not to say there's anything bad with farming, I just can't take it. Day in and day out, you watch over that same piece of land. How boring! I like odd jobs. You pick up as much work as you like, or nothing at all if you don't. You don't have to wait on the pleasure of anybody. I like Taipei, it makes you feel that if you work hard, someday you can also have a lot of things, a lot of money."

He talked with such enthusiasm that I had to admit that Ping-mei was right. She had said that Hsiao Heh had in him something that attracted people—a kind of spirit. That was something I lacked most. Unexpectedly, Hsiao Heh asked me:

"What are you going to do in the future? You graduate this summer."

"Military service."

"I mean after you finish your military obligation."

Of course I knew what he had meant. I just did not know what I would do.

"Do you also want to go to the United States and study there?"

I guessed I sort of wanted to go abroad, everyone went. People who knew me all said it would be a waste of my excellent academic record if I did not go abroad. Chia-ke and Ping-mei would go at all cost; they were already applying for admission into graduate schools. But, Yun-kang already had a showdown with me: "If you go, go by yourself."

She kept saying that, judging from the stories she read, the life for a foreign student abroad was really tough. I said most stories were fiction. She retorted that a distant cousin of hers had spent one out of three years in the United States in a mental asylum. Her family had thought the girl was having a great time until a classmate of hers wrote and told them the truth.

"You can succeed all the same if you stay in this country," she said with great eloquence. "If you want to go abroad that much, wait till you are rich, then travel and have something like a trip around the world. It will be just as nice. We can work hard to make money; when we have made enough, we can travel and spend all we have. Then we return and start all over again."

As for herself, she could not care less about going abroad. Her greatest wish was to someday get away from everything and play golf under the sun. The grass on the golf course looked so tempting; walking on it would be so relaxing.

Well then, I would not go abroad. Not that I had to stay and accompany Yun-kang in playing golf. To tell the truth, I did not exactly understand why I should go abroad. Yet, on the other hand, what would I do if I did not go? Teach? It seemed an ideal job for an idle man like me.

So I said to Hsiao Heh:

"I'll probably teach."

"What's so good about teaching? You work so hard and earn no more than two to three thousand dollars a month. With a bit of luck, I can earn that much right now."

"But don't you think your kind of life is very unstable, very insecure?"

"Who cares? I like this kind of freedom and independence. I'll survive."

He shrugged and continued:

"You sound like Mrs. Feng. She takes every opportunity to urge me to get married and have a career. Ha, get married and have a career!—I just came from the professor's home. You know why I was over there? I went there to build a chicken coop for them. Mrs. Feng said that she's going to raise chickens. What a fuss! They're not short of money. They brought up their children, each one left and remained abroad. And now she wants to raise chickens!"

I understood well why Mrs. Feng wanted to raise chickens. Every time I went to her home, I saw her busy knitting, one piece after another. Professor Feng told her that she did not have to bother, that there were plenty of such things in the United States. Mrs. Feng would not listen, but continued to knit those hats, scarves, or socks. The only difference was that formerly she knitted for her children, now she did it for her three grandchildren. Professor Feng had his own interest to occupy himself with. He would lie in a reclining chair, pipe in mouth, and read those Kung Fu novels in which two combating factions contended for supremacy. When he got tired of reading, he would stand up and, with his hands behind his back, pace the living room floor.

Naturally I would not tell Hsiao Heh all this; he probably knew more than I did. At that moment we reached where I lived. Quite casually I told him I lived on the second floor and to drop by anytime.

About ten days later, Hsiao Heh did indeed arrive, but not to see me. My landlord had hired him to paint the newly renovated rooms.

For two days, the whole house was permeated with the pungent odor of new paint, as well as the melodious whistling of one hit tune after another. Even Chia-ke he had not thought a fellow like that could whistle so well.

The last weekend in September, I went to climb Mount Kuan-Yin with several of my schoolmates. When I got back, I ran upstairs, eager for a bath.

The door was ajar, but Chia-ke was not in. Hsiao-Heh was sound asleep with his head on my beloved *War and Peace*. His long legs were bent, his mouth half open. That same red shirt, unchanged for many days, was soiled and brownish looking. His beard grew wild around his chin, and he was covered with paint.

When I returned to the room after my bath, he was sitting there thumbing through a magazine. He greeted me with a broad smile, as if it was the most natural thing to do in letting himself into my room. He scratched his tangled mass of hair and said:

"I worked my ass of for three days and two nights. F—, I nearly collapsed." He searched his pockets and found a squashed pack of cigarettes. He then looked for matches.

"What kind of work?" I found Chia-ke's matches on the desk and passed them over to him.

"Painting the arches for the National Day celebrations. I did it all myself. Made two thousand five hundred dollars. But I won't get the money till two days later."

"Oh," I could not help but admire him. I only earned four hundred and fifty dollars a month working as a tutor, taking grief from my pupil.

He lit a cigarette and inhaled deeply. Letting out the smoke, he stretched himself. He said he came over because my place was closer to the bus stop. He was too tired and lazy to make it back to that "pigsty" of his.

I had been to his "pigsty" once. I was sent by Mrs. Feng to ask him to paint her chicken coop. Professor Feng thought it was unnecessary to have a chicken coop painted. But she insisted on it and wanted it painted green. What freakish imagination!

Hsiao Heh had been out, and I found only his "friends". His place was at the end of a deep alley. It was so dirty and dark, a light had to be left on in the daytime. He did not mind, saying that "it is but a place to lie down." Within this space of about thirty square feet, four and sometimes as many as six or seven people were accommodated. His "friends" were all young fellows working at odd jobs. They traded information about working opportunities, shared the work among themselves, and looked after one another.

"When you came in a while ago, was Chia-ke in?"

Hsiao Heh shook his head. He said the apartment had not been locked. Even if it had been, he claimed, he could have gotten in anyway.

"You can open locks?"

"No," he gestured with the hand which held the cigarette. He said he could climb in from the top window near the hallway, which he knew was never locked. "Oh!"

"I'm really good at climbing. Do you know why people call me Hsiao Heh? Back in high school, we did not have money to pay for movies, so we sneaked into the movie houses by climbing over the surrounding walls. I was always the first one to get to the top of the wall, from where I would pull up those who could not climb. Once we saw a film about hunting in Africa. There was this nimble little black monkey who was always climbing all over the place. So they called me Hsiao Heh the Monkey. Later, they just dropped the monkey and called me Hsiao Heh."

"You could probably star in a Kung Fu movie." Hsiao Heh's eyes flickered as he recalled with a broad smile:

"One summer I painted signboards in Tainan. A restaurant by the canal hired me to paint its sign. They wanted the sign painted outside the third floor wall so that people could see it from afar. I built a scaffold. It took me several days to finish the job. By then I had run out of money, but the restaurant refused to pay till their manager checked my work. I was starved. I looked up a friend who worked on a boat. He was also broke and hungry. He deserved it though, he had lost his money gambling. We pooled what change there was left in our pockets. It wasn't even enough for a soft drink. We sat in the boat, staring at the patches of green and red lights reflecting in the canal, and listening to the roars of laughter coming from that restaurant. Our mouth watered.

"I told my friend that sitting idly would not solve our problem, that it would be better to try and get something to eat from the restaurant. They should have paid me, anyway. After business hours were over, I went to the kitchen on the third floor under the pretence that I had left a paint brush there. When the cook went out to get a drink of water, I got hold of three roast ducks and threw them out the window to my friend who was in the back alley. But he was so clumsy he did not catch any of them. The ducks fell and rolled in the sand and mud. We could not get them cleaned, no matter how many times we washed the ducks. It was better than nothing though. We pretended the roast ducks were flavored with pepper-salt and chewed every bone clean. Afterwards, we lay down on the gangplank and chatted, till somehow we both fell asleep."

I was stunned; what kind of life was that! Yet he made a joke of it amidst swirls of cigarette smoke. "Do you often steal?"

"No," he frowned, somewhat surprised that I should ask such a question. "That was the only time. Really, I never stole afterwards. I was very upset that they delayed my pay."

Although some people could lie without showing it on their face, I believed Hsiao Heh was telling the truth. We were sitting so close that I could tell by his eyes that he was not lying.

"Let's change the subject!" Hsiao Heh threw the cigarette butt on the floor, stubbed it out with his shoe, then turned to me:

"Hey," he never seemed to learn to call me by my name: "Can I have this?"

He thrust a magazine at me. On the opened page was an advertisement of motorcycles.

"You meet the nicest people on Hondas." The illustration showed a group of people on Hondas, including a fat woman with her curly haired dog, a young man with his girl friend, and a housewife with flowers.

I told him to take it if he wanted it.

He tore the page off, folded it and put it into his shirt pocket:

"I am collecting motorcycle ads. I'm going to buy one."

"A Honda, like the one in that ad?"

"Oh," he wrinkled his nose and said with a sneer: "That kind of motorcycle is for kids. I'm going to buy a 120 c.c. one. I have not decided on the make, but it must be red."

"Why must it be red?"

Hsiao Heh lowered his head. Looking at his two hands, he slowly said: "No particular reason. A person should have something that belongs to himself, some color that represents him."

I noticed for the first time that though he was not sturdy in appearance, he had a pair of large, solid hands. They were covered with specks of paint and marked with scars and thick calluses of various sizes, hands that had lived.

"Since high-school days, I have liked red clothes," he laughed gently. "My old man was disgusted to see me in this color, grumbling that the family was unfortunate in having such a rascal. Yet, the more he resented and opposed, the more I wanted to be in red."

He jerked his head up:

"Why must I dress myself like others just to please them? Names were given by parents; there you have no choice. Names are for others to call you by, but clothes you put on to make yourself happy. I like red. Red clothes make me aware of my own existence, make me know myself in a crowd of people. Fresh red reminds you that you are alive, that you must go on, that you cannot lie down.

"Sometimes when I feel dispirited, I want to become a little ill, or even to be wounded, to bleed, or to have a little pain here, a slight ache there. These feelings can tell you that you are still living. This is the most important thing: to let yourself know that you are alive. Otherwise, you won't be able to achieve anything."

I sat dumbfounded in my shorts, clutching the towel I had brought in from the bathroom.

I had never known that so much principle was involved in dressing, and that one must have a color of his own. Suddenly I was full of self-pity. I did not have a particular color of my own; no color meant much to me.

If I had to choose one from a myriad of colors for myself, I would feel lost — may be I would even choose the color that Hsiao Heh liked. How could I say for certain that I disliked red clothes? I had never given this much thought before. And that night at the Fengs' house when Hsiao Heh's red shirt irritated me, perhaps it was because deep inside I had also wanted to wear red clothes but had not dared to.

If everyone in the world was as "brave" as Hsiao Heh, and appeared in the color that he liked, the world would probably be more festive and more beautiful.

I stood up and hung up the towel, determined not to be influenced by Hsiao Heh in my thinking. By then I already had rather absurd associations: For according to Hsiao Heh's assertions, people like me not only did not have individuality, they seemed no better than the women who sell themselves to anyone.

Hsiao Heh took out the ad and was studying it again.

I poured two glasses of water and handed one to him.

"Then, why do you want to buy a motorcycle?"

"To ride!" his expression once more indicated that such a question was "superfluous."

"Pu-ppp"

"Pu-po, po, po, pu—"

Hsiao Heh clasped the imaginary handles with great energy, his eyes squinting and his mouth twisted to one side. He cocked one eyebrow, and hunching his back, he leaned slightly with his left shoulder.

"Whoosh! Turn! Give it gas! Whoosh! You are breathless, there is only speed. Whoosh! What a thrill!" A series of indistinct roars from his throat. They sounded less like the noise of a motorcycle than of a car or a jet.

The noise came to a stop. Hsiao Heh opened his eyes.

"Can you ride a motorcycle?"

I shook my head, not wanting to tell him that I had not the slightest wish to attempt it. Newspaper reports about those motorcyclists who died in traffic accidents were enough to scare me.

"Did you see *The Great Escape*?"

I quickly nodded.

"Remember? Steve McQueen rode a motorcycle and pu, there he went over the barbed wire fence. That was something! Just to have one experience like that, I would die content." He gulped down the glass of water.

Hsiao Heh slammed his hand down on the edge of the bed. His lips pressed tightly, he turned his chin up.

"I will buy one, even if I have to give my life. The latest next year. When I get pay of two thousand five hundred dollars, I'll add five hundred more to round it out to three thousand. With that sum I can get into a cooperative group and pay for three shares. By New Year, it will have grown to four thousand five hundred. Meanwhile, I will try to make a little extra. Then . . . ."

Suddenly I could no longer stand his aggressive seriousness nor that confident "If I want to do it, I can" attitude. I interrupted:

"Then you will buy the motorcycle, take a girl for a ride and show off. Right?"

The faint smile at the corner of his lips vanished. His eyelids suddenly lowered as he said with a raised voice:

"Never, F— those girls!"

Hsiao Heh cocked his head and gave me a searching look:

"Girls are not as obedient as machines. They are like eels, too slippery to hold on to." He ended with a roar of laughter. Then with a wave of his hand:

"It does not matter what you say. All the same, I will have a motorcycle someday.

That is my only dream."

As he spoke, he slid back down on the bed, using his arm for a pillow. Eyes closed, a smile surfaced on his dirt streaked face; peaceful, content.

I felt a surge of admiration. Though over twenty years old, Hsiao Heh looked very young and was one of those luckiest kind of people in the world. He was like an innocent child who held the world in his palm.

He must have told Mrs. Feng about his intention to buy a motorcycle, for several days later when she saw me, she shook her head and said she was increasingly puzzled by the motivations of the younger generation.

Why would one spend his hard-earned money on such a good-for-nothing motorcycle? One should rather save the money, marry and start a career.

"That boy!" She sighed and shook her head vigorously: "Times have really changed."

I did not see Hsiao Heh again for a long time. Sometimes I came across him on the streets, but we exchanged nothing more than a hurried greeting. I noticed that his hair had grown longer, his chin seemed more pointed, his forehead looked more prominent and his eyes were sunken. He rode a bicycle, parts of which made a clanking noise that could be heard from far away.

The weather had become very cold, and he changed into a jacket which was red on some days and blue on others. I said he finally changed his color. Ping-mei said his was still the old color, red. Later, when the matter became clarified, Chia-ke was proven right in having maintained that the fellow was wearing a reversible jacket.

I got up rather late on a Sunday. When I went for my breakfast at nearly ten o'clock, I met Hsiao Heh unexpectedly in the soybean milk shop. His red jacket was coated with dust and his eyes were bloodshot. He appeared exhausted and dejected. I asked him what was wrong.

He said, "making money."

"Now I'll do anything, as along as I get paid."

"You do not know, some swindler got away with my three thousand dollars. That f . . . ing bastard, it was said he ran away to the East Coast with a woman, someone else's mistress. I have no doubt I will get my money back. After all, Taiwan is only that big. Yet, I will have to start all over again. As you know, the most basic motorcycle costs over ten thousand dollars."

"What for, Hsiao Heh?" I put down my sesame roll and cruller. "Why in such a hurry? Take your time. If you wreck your health, even if you get a motorcycle, you won't be able to ride it. By the way, why don't you get one on installment?"

"I don't want it that way," he gulped down his soy-bean milk, wiped his mouth with the back of his hand, stood up and was ready to go:

"Installments! That means you have not paid in full and the thing is not really yours. I want something to be completely mine!" I felt I had swallowed a fly with my soybean milk. I wished I had been a millionaire so that I could have bought a motorcycle for him, though I knew he would never accept.

In May, Chia-ke and Ping-mei received news of their applications. Ping-mei was given a tuition scholarship by the University of California. The University of Wisconsin promised Chia-ke a scholarship of eight hundred dollars a semester. They were both happy. Ping-mei decided to go first, while Chia-ke would follow after military service.

Since he had been guaranteed a scholarship, Chia-ke did not work as hard for the graduation examination as he did for other examinations in the past. While he took everything with a carefree air, I prepared my lessons with great pain and tension. Even though there were two more examinations to pass the next day, he took the devil-may-care attitude and went to the movies.

After staying up for several nights, I was dead tired. I fell asleep before eleven, fully clothed, with the book still in my hand. I was awakened by Chia-ke when he opened the door.

"That guy Hsiao Heh is really mad," he said while taking off his coat and tie. He had just seen Hsiao Heh riding a motorcycle back and forth at great speed in the narrow streets. The motorcycle looked very odd; a red heart and a naked girl were painted on the windshield.

"Perhaps he bought it second hand," I said.

A few days later, I saw the motorcycle myself.

By the judicious decision of the head of our Department, our class gave up the tradition of holding a dinner for the professors as a token of gratitude. Instead, we wrote letters to thank our professors for their instruction in the past years. This new practice received favorable comments in the newspapers, and other schools followed suit.

Yet, without the formal dinner party, we felt something was missing in our graduation. Several members of the class decided to have a farewell dinner on the eve of the commencement exercises. After all, this would be the last time together; overseas students would soon return to their homes, and a few others like Ping-mei would go to the United States. Who could know if we would ever see each other again.

It was a buffet held in a Western-style restaurant. That day, Ping-mei wore a new chi-pao and carefully put on her make-up. Chia-ke and I waited for her a long time. When we arrived at Chungshan North Road by taxi, we were already twenty minutes late.

As we got out of the taxi, we saw a crowd of people across the street, all with heads raised and necks strained backward. Up there, outside the fourth floor of the building, a man was performing "the flying trapeze."

A fan of westerns and detective movies, Chia-ke naturally would not want to miss such an exciting scene. We joined the crowd to watch.

That man was painting characters on the wall. There was no scaffold. A thick rope was tied around his waist, one end of which was pulled to the fifth floor balcony, the other end reached the ground where a man of slight build held it tightly.

The daredevil fellow grasped the rope with his left hand, his feet pressed against the wall. His right hand held a brush and he painted the characters stroke by stroke. Three of the four characters (International Gallery of Art) had already been finished and he was working on the last one.

Perhaps the paint was used up for the man stuck the brush in his waist band, held the rope tight with both hands, and started to "walk" across the wall of smooth porcelain tiles. Waiting for him at a window on the fourth floor was another man with hands extended, holding a small bucket of paint.

It was near evening and there was a breeze which made the rope snap, ruffled the man's hair and caused his trousers to balloon out. The people below were agape and breathless, their hearts pounding and their necks sore.

"What if the rope breaks?" Ping-mei asked with her hand to her heart.

What worried me was not the rope, but that man's legs. His legs were so long and thin that he did not seem to have any hips. I was afraid they might bend and fail him. Watching a man dangling in mid-air was worse than seeing him actually fall.

Chia-ke took off his glasses and cleaned them repeatedly in his neurotic way. When he finally put them back on and looked around, he exclaimed: "Isn't that Hsiao Heh's motorcycle?" Upon hearing Hsiao Hehs' name, the boy holding the rope jerked his head around to look at us. His forehead beaded with sweat, he stared steadily at me and grinned. I recognized him, Ah-tu, a roommate of Hsiao Heh's. The last time I went to their "pigsty", I had found him instead of Hsiao Heh and had exchanged a few words with him.

I raised my head again and looked at the man leaning against the window mixing his paint. Was he not wearing the red shirt that seembed to engulf the whole building in flames?

Strange, as soon as I knew that it was Hsiao Heh, I stopped worrying. I remembered the pair of powerful, big hands he had. And I remembered why he was called Hsiao Heh.

"Ah-tu, what is this all about?"

"Don't talk to me!" he yelled without turning his head.

He was right. I kept quiet.

Yet, before one minute elapsed, Ah-tu could not restrain himself: "With this fellow, you can't do anything. You know the new regulation. That English letters on signboards can not be larger than Chinese characters? The owner wanted to change the English letters to Chinese characters. Hsiao Heh wanted the job, saying that it was a heaven-sent good fortune to make five hundred dollars just by covering some English words and painting in four Chinese characters. He did not want to be bothered with building a scaffold, saying it was ridiculous to build one for four characters. I could not talk him out of it. He always must have his way. No one can stop him . . ."

"Stop talking," Ping-mei called out. "Hold your rope tight! What if the man should fall to his death, what will you do then?"

Ah-tu threw her a dirty look.

Ping-mei clasped her mouth as she realized that the mention of death at such a moment was ill-timed. She then said she had had enough and wanted to leave. After all, we were already more than thirty minutes late for the buffet.

As we turned the corner, Chia-ke took out a handkerchief and wiped away his perspiration.

"That guy must be tired of living, prizing money more than his life."

Ping-mei opened her mouth, ready for a retort. I stopped her with a glare.

After dinner on our way back, Ping-mei thought of Hsiao Heh and wondered what had happened to him.

Naturally, Hsiao Heh did not fall and kill himself. At least, there was no such report in the newspaper the next day. Furthermore, he came to see me.

That was on the eve of my departure from Taipei, and Chia-ke had already gone home to Taichung. I went to a movie with Yun-kang, had a snack, and then took her home. It was past midnight when I groped my way back to the apartment.

I took off my clothes, washed my face, and was just about to turn off the light when there came a knock on the door. I opened the door, and there was Hsiao Heh. For once he wore a white T-shirt. It made his face seem even darker.

He said several of his friends came up from the South and the "pigsty" could not accommodate them al. He hoped to stay in my apartment for the night.

"No problem. Come in. You can sleep in Chia-ke's bed."

Unlike me who needed to be fully tucked up even in hot weather, Hsiao Heh did not want any cover. I handed him a blanket which he folded up for a pillow.

"Hey, I saw your exciting performance the other day."

"What performance?"

"Flying trapeze. I also saw your motorcycle with that picture of the beautiful girl."

"Oh," Hsiao Heh smiled, his eyes sparkling. Elated, he said: "That was nothing. When someone wants to give you five hundred dollars, you can hardly refuse. The motorcycle wasn't mine, I have already returned it."

He lit a cigarette:

"Were you out on a date? I stopped by at eleven and your landlord said you are leaving tomorrow."

I told him that I would be enlisted next Monday, that I had just accompanied Yun-kang to see a movie, and that we had decided to be engaged by the end of the year.

"Oh," he let out a long whistle.

"Really, what about you, Hsiao Heh?" Suddenly I was like an old lady, full of good intentions. "Have you not thought about this? A family, after all, is very important. If you want to have one, you had better hurry. We will be old in no time." I really did not know what I was talking about.

Hsiao Heh was still laughing.

"How does that saying go? Girls are like eels?" Puffing on a cigarette, he knitted his brows. His gaze penetrated through the smoke on to the darkness beyond the window.

It was not a new story. But when Hsiao Heh told it, even I who had never experienced emotional setbacks could feel how heavy the blow was.

He was painting signboards for a furniture shop in Tainan. Frequent contacts brought him together with the shop owner's daughter and they fell in love. Her family opposed him because he did not have money nor a steady job. To show that he could settle down, and really work hard, Hsiao Heh went to work for an electrical repair shop.

His mother sent someone to propose the match, but the girl's family turned it down.

"F—, at the time, I really wanted to get a knife and cut down her father," he said. "Then when I thought about it, that was not necessary. If she had wanted to be with me, we could have eloped. But all she would say was that she did not want to hurt her parents."

Hsiao Heh left her and went on his own way. Not much later, he lost his job at the electrical repair shop.

"On my first trip back from the sea, they told me she got married and went to Chia-yi. And only two months ago she had told me that she would only marry me. Girls!"

"Did you ever see each other again?"

"Last year, during the Tomb Sweeping Festival. I was going home and came across her on the train. She boarded the train in Chia-yi with a child in her arms. There was no seat. I stood up and gave her my seat. She tried to talk to me, but I ignored her and went to another carriage. What was there to talk about? F . . . "

"Therefore, girls are like eels?"

Hsiao Heh threw the cigarette butt out the window. A spark of redness vanished in the darkness. He shrugged.

"Maybe I should not blame her. Human beings are all the same, they are like fishes, impossible to hold on to. I can't even be certain of myself. How can I know what I will be like tomorrow? It is even true with dogs, not to mention men. A dog may follow you around faithfully. But the day a bitch wags her tail at him, he will be gone. You can call till you're hoarse, and you won't get him to come back. In this world, you cannot trust anything, except your own hands."

He spread his hands slightly. On his left thumb was a fresh scar. It was probably a cut from the rope the other day.

"You forget, there is one other thing."

"What?"

"Motorcycle."

He smiled faintly, and with a wave of his hand ended our conversation.

"Get some sleep. Tomorrow you have a half-day ride on the train."

It was no sooner said than done. He kicked off his slippers, climbed into bed, turned and faced the wall. In a short while, there came an even snoring. I was left alone. With my eyes fixed on the ceiling, I thought over many things.

"Whatever you say, someday I will have a motorcycle. This is my only dream."

That was probably a very practical dream, even though Mrs. Feng would disagree. To make life bearable, a person must have something that he could hold on to. Chia-ke and Ping-mei had their mind set on going abroad. Yun-kang had her hope of "some day,

when I can get away from everything and play golf under the sun."
As for Professor Feng, he had his Kung Fu novels and his pipe. While
his wife passed her time knitting, raising chickens, and waiting for
those pale blue aerograms from her children.

Whether Hsiao Heh would find things as he had imagined them
to be with the purchase of a motorcycle, that was a different matter.
What was important was that he had a dream that could be realized,
that he knew what he wanted, and that he was willing to pay a price
for the fulfillment of his dream.

Compared to him, I did not know whether I was lucky or not.
My life had not been as sensational and as eventful a life as his.
Worse still, I just drifted through life, feeling content with whatever
environment that I found myself in, without even a clear idea as to
why I was alive. I sighed, sincerely hoping that military life would
change me and make me stronger.

Within two months, I was transferred with my unit to Quemoy.
The new environment, new people, and the new life made me
gradually forget Hsiao Heh and his motorcycle.

At the end of the year, I had a week's leave and returned to Taipei
for my engagement to Yun-kang. Taking the opportunity, I also
picked up my diploma from the university and called on Professor
Feng.

The old couple was pleased to hear the news of my engagement.
Mrs. Feng even showed me the wedding picture of their second son,
who was married over Easter in New York City. While showing me
the picture, she told me, now, only her youngest daughter was left.
She said she was not worried in the least, as there were numerous
outstanding Chinese students in the United States.

Somehow I felt quite uncomfortable at her words, so I asked,
rather impertinently, whether she was still raising chickens.

"Not any more," Mrs. Feng said. "all my effort was wasted. Around
the Moon Festival, a chicken plague killed more than twenty of my
thirty chickens. I had the remaining ones killed and eaten. Besides, I

will not have so much free time anymore . . . ."

Professor Feng explained that his eldest daughter had given birth to a girl two months ago. Life in the United States was so hectic, his daughter could not take care of all three children. She had asked her parents to look after the baby and would bring the baby over after Christmas.

"Our whole life was burdened with children. Now just as we got rid of them all, this little trouble-maker descends upon us in our old age. I am afraid we will not have any more quiet days!"

Mrs. Feng gave him a cold stare, reproaching him for calling their granddaughter a little trouble-maker.

The wrinkled smiles on their faces made it known just how anxiously they were awaiting the little trouble-maker's arrival.

Mrs. Feng suddenly asked me:

"Remember Hsiao Heh? He went back to Tainan not long after your graduation. His father was said to be very sick. Once he had wanted to buy a motorcycle." She remarked dryly.

Chia-ke heard that Ping-mei had a new boy friend at the University of California. Once he completed his military service, he quickly got his papers in order and left Taiwan by the end of August. I started to teach as I had planned, while Yun-kang began working in a trading company.

One weekend, Yun-kang and I went to the movies. At the corner of Chung-hua Road a voice called out to me. I looked back and saw Hsiao Heh. I had not seen him for more than a year. Perhaps because of the grease smeared all over him, he looked older. His hair was still a mess, though the ends were quite neatly trimmed.

I introduced Yun-kang to him, but he said he had met her once.

"I am now working in this car repair shop, no more odd jobs."

"And the motorcycle?"

"Oh," he grinned, revealing the same rows of uneven white teeth, the same Hsiao Heh of the old days.

"Pretty soon. It's not easy. My father passed away last summer.

My family depended on me for everything. I persuaded my mother to rent out the land until my younger brother grows up and can work it. My younger sister has entered Chungshin University, has her mind set on learning. As her eldest brother, I was only too happy . . ."

We were in a great hurry, so did not talk too long. I left my address and asked him to come visit.

He did not come.

More than half a year went by. Yun-kang and I got married and my life seemed to have settled into a pattern. I had never been too active, and I became less so after my marriage. Often after I returned home from the office, I would sit before the television set and spend the evening there. Yun-kang said that I had grown old. I also felt that I was becoming more and more like Professor Feng, all except the pipe. Yun-kang still thought of her golf, though she never learned to play. I kept saying that one day we would.

One early morning in June, when I was still half asleep. I heard the distant sound of a motorcycle approaching. The motor came to a sudden stop. A moment later, the door bell shrilled.

"Damn it. Who would come at such an early hour?" Yun-kang pushed me.

I rubbed my eyes and went over to draw back the curtain.

There downstairs in the middle of the road stood Hsiao Heh in his red shirt. A brilliant red motorcycle stood beside him like a small stallion. It glistened in the morning sun, along with the dewdrops on the lawn.

I flew downstairs and opened the door.

"Hsiao Heh, you finally bought it!" I laid my hand excitedly on his shoulder.

He did not speak but smiled like a fool. The only time I had ever seen such a smile was when my colleague Mr. Huang became a father last month.

His radiant smile was infectious. I was at a loss for words.

"Fantastic, isn't it?"

That sounded stupid. I knew I need not say another word and Hsiao Heh would understand I was genuinely happy for him.

We had breakfast together and chatted at random. I told him that Ping-mei had written to say she was going to be married, but the bridegroom would not be Chia-ke. I also told him that the Fengs were too busy with their granddaughter to raise chickens.

After breakfast, Hsiao Heh offered to give me a ride to school. We drove all the way at lightning speed. While the world flew past us and swirled, I said uneasily:

"Ai, slow down, Hsiao Heh, slow down."

He stepped on the gas to its maximum capacity, he steered the motorcycle like a stallion, and laughed wildly. Gusts of strong wind blew his hair against my face.

I thought of when I was a child, I used to ride a bamboo pole as a horse and run through the street yelling, "the horse is coming, the horse is coming. Faster, horse, faster." Gradually, under the influence of high speed, I became intoxicated in that kind of suffocating sensuous gratification.

When we arrived at school, I let out a deep breath of relief and invited him to come see me as often as he could. Though the topic of our conversation had been limited to his passion for motorcycles and, though his cherished dream had already been realized, I was certain we could find other things to talk about.

Hsiao Heh promised readily, but he never did come.

Yun-kang went window shopping one Sunday and saw a purse she liked at the First Department Store. Feeling it was too expensive, she did not buy it. But she kept talking about it. On Thursday, she could not stand the temptation any longer and dragged me to see the purse and help her make a decision.

When we came out of the department store, it was drizzling. Happy with her new purchase, Yun-kang suggested that we stroll back in the rain.

As we passed the car repair shop, I went in to look for Hsiao Heh.

"Hsiao Heh?" a fat, middle-age man regarded me with knitted brows.

"Don't you know? Dead, for almost a month. That guy! I predicted long ago that anyone as crazy about racing motorcycles as he was would end up in an accident sooner or later. After work, he would always ride alone in the middle of the night on MacArthur Thruway. So, who knows what actually happened? He landed up down in the valley, and lay there overnight before he was discovered . . . ."

There was a man, a man whose shirt was as red as fire.

Translated by Yao-heng HU 胡耀恆

CHENG Ching-wen 鄭清文

The Three-Legged Horse
三腳馬*

0.

I took a three-hour bus ride from Taipei to the village where Lai Kuo-lin lives. He was a classmate at the technical college. We have recently seen each other, the first time in more than twenty years, during our class reunion. Everybody was asked to introduce himself during the occasion and that was how I came to learn that he had returned to his village where he now operates a wood-carving factory.

His factory was quite large, easily occupying an area of some 200 pings or more. The front serves as his display shop. The main purpose of my visit was to look for wood carvings of horses to add to my collection. I began this hobby many, many years ago and I now have in my possession more than 2,000 pieces, some made of wood, others carved from stones. It was the Year of the Horse and I wanted to take the opportunity to add a few more pieces to my collection.

He had already shown me quite a number of carvings. But perhaps because they were mass-produced, the articles appeared too regular and standard. As we were moving about looking at his goods, a quaint-looking horse at the corner suddenly caught my attention. The horse's eyes were downcast. The animal appeared as though it was grazing yet at another angle, it appeared not. A dark, gloomy expression was cast on its face that made the animal appear to be

---

* From *Juwairen*《局外人》 *The Outsider*, a collection of short stories by Cheng Ching-wen, Taichung: Hsueh-ying Publishing Co. (學英出版社), 1984.

suffering from pain, or was it a sense of remorse? I couldn't tell. I have never, in my long years of pursuing this hobby, seen such an expression in a horse carving. No, I don't think I have ever seen that even on a painting.

I picked it up for a closer look and then saw that it had one crippled leg. A feeling of surprise and pity suddenly engulfed me. The lines on the horse's body made it look more vivid and powerful than the other carvings. The facial expression, more especially, was something the other works could not match. This horse was not painted. Its rough surface texture suggested that it was not even sandpapered. Cuts and incisions were still clearly visible here and there. From the fact that it was placed in a least visible spot, I inferred that it was not given any importance at all. Lai Kuo-lin, after seeing how I had been handling the artwork and how I dallied to put it down, then told me:

"That horse was done by a strange man. He likes to carve disabled horses. Whenever we go to his place to pick up his works, he usually gives us the disabled ones just to complete the number. But he forbids us from selling them. He says that he'll replace them with good ones next time. So they serve the functions of loose change in our transactions."

"Do you have more of his works here? I mean ordinary horses," I asked.

"Yes, here's one," Lai Kuo-lin replied as he fished out one and handed it to me. "How do you find it?"

"This is strange. It's not much different from the rest. Perhaps it's because you use a mold. But its eyes are quite special. Other horses' eyes look toward the sides. His horse looks ahead. Besides, its mane, tail and leg hair are not identical. Still, it cannot compare with the crippled one. See, this one is a living horse and it has feelings too. It is no easy job to make animal carvings show emotional expressions," I said at length.

"We retouched those horses that he had carved. We think he's too lazy. He does not even sandpaper them. We have even deducted from his labor fees for this reason," Lai Kuo-lin explained.

"Does he carve a lot?" I asked with curiosity.

"I couldn't tell. He puts all his things in one pile. We could not tell which are completed works and which aren't. I have noticed though that he's doing less and less of what we like. We used to pick up his works once a week. Now, it takes two or three weeks, or even a month, before we make another visit. He puts off work on normal carvings and instead spends time chiseling on strange looking objects," Lai Kuo-lin replied.

"Won't he really sell? I mean those crippled horses?" I asked.

"I don't know. Who knows what's in his mind?"

"Would you bring me to see him?"

"What for?"

"I want to see what special things he has."

"Special things?"

"I mean crippled horses and such stuff."

Lai Kuo-lin brought me there on his motorcycle. After half an hour drive through a circuitous mountain road, we reached the sloping summit of a hill. Looking down, we saw a clearing between two hills. It was a village with some 20 houses or less.

Some of the houses were huddled together while some were sitting some distance away.

"That's the village of Shenp'u," Lai Kuo-lin said succinctly before starting the motorcycle again to go down the slope.

It was a simple structure made of mud bricks. The bricks were so eroded by the elements that the straws inside were clearly visible and had in fact loosened, jutting out like inchworms. The house was situated in a corner of the courtyard. The central hall was made of the same material, but it had an extra layer of white lime mortar, which gave the impression of relative tidiness.

The door was ajar so Lai Kuo-lin decided to give it a little push. Once inside, I immediately noticed the sweet smell of fresh wood.

Having stayed outdoor under bright sunshine for a long time, my eyes could not see a thing in the dark. We stood there for some moments before we gradually got accustomed and saw an old man sitting below a small bamboo-latticed window. The man was about sixty years old. His short hair was more gray than black and his beard and mustache were five or six centimeters long.

The old man opened his mouth, "Is that you, Kuo-lin?"

"Yes, Uncle Chi-hsiang. I brought you a visitor," Kuo-lin answered.

"A visitor? From where?" the old man briefly threw a glance at me.

"Taipei."

"Taipei City?"

"Yes," Kuo-lin responded.

By this time, my eyes had fully gotten used to the darkness of the room. Right below the small window was a working table, probably a foot high, on which a wooden mallet and all sorts of carving tools were laid. The old man was seated on a flat stool, his legs slightly bent and stretched forward. Between his legs was a block of wood, its shape still too rough to be identifiable. The floor was littered with wood bits. Some finished works were piled high in one corner.

"Is your friend from Taipei?" the old man asked again before I had enough time to clearly see the wood carvings.

"Yes. He was my classmate when I was studying in Taipei," Kuo-lin answered.

"Do you know that there is a place called Old Town in the suburbs of Taipei?"

"I am from Old Town. I had lived there for thirty years until I moved to Taipei City some ten years ago."

"In which part of the town did you live?"

"Right across the Police Station."

"Police Station? Was that the former site of the County Penitentiary?"

"Yes, it was."

"Telling from your age and where you've lived, you must've known me," the old man said as he slowly turned towards me.

"I . . . know you?"

"Can't you still remember?" he said while pointing his index finger towards his own nose bridge. A band of white skin stretched from the middle of his forehead down to his nose bridge. It appeared like some form of skin disease.

"Are you . . . ?"

"You've finally recognized me! I am 'White-nosed Raccoon'! Who's your father?"

I told him my father's name. I also told him that my father used to operate a shop selling woodcraft.

"I remember him. I once beat him."

"I know. My father once told me so."

"Is he still around?"

"No, he already passed away."

"Did he ever tell you anything about me?"

" . . . "

"Go on, I won't mind."

"My father said that the three-legged's are more detestable than the four-legged's."

He went silent for a moment then he picked up a four or five-inch picture frame from his working table. "Do you know her?"

"No."

"She's my woman."

"If I'm not wrong, her older sister and younger sister were teachers."

"Yes. Exactly."

"How about this person?" I asked while pointing to a two-inch picture at the frame's lower left-hand corner. The picture had yellowed with years.

"That was my first-ever photograph, taken the first time I went to

Taipei. I sent a copy to my mother."

He was bald in the picture. I looked at his nose bridge. There was no sign of the white band.

As if having guessed what was going on in my mind, he offered an explanation, "That was retouched by the photographer. He charged an extra five cents for that."

"Do you mean it was there from a very young age?"

"Yeah. When I was still small . . ."

I.

"Black-footed Elk, White-nosed Raccoon . . ."

Five boys headed by Ah Kou, all gripping to their wooden tops, half walked and half ran as they made their way towards the village burial grounds. Ah Hsiang, a head shorter than Ah Ho, the smallest of the five, was following closely behind.

"Black-footed Elk and White-nosed Raccoon, go back! Don't come with us!" Ah Chin, who was the last of the pack, said in a loud voice as he violently let go of his wooden top.

"I also have . . ." Ah Hsiang said. It was a cold day. Steam came out of his mouth as he spoke.

"What do you have? A penis?" Ah Cheng said.

"I also have a top."

"What top? Did you make it yourself? It's smaller than your balls!" Ah Chin quipped.

"My uncle promised to buy me one this big," Ah Hsiang said, gesturing with his fingers to make a hole the size of a rice bowl.

"It's too early to brag about it," Ah Chin replied.

"My uncle lives in Taipei."

"So what?"

"Go back or I'll take your pants off!"

Ah Hsiang was holding his top in one hand while the other hand tightly grasped his fly. A rope made of clothing material was wound around his waist. Ah Hsiang had a small built, making it impossible for him to fold and tighten the fly of his pants the way grown-up men do.

"Go back!" Ah Chin turned around and gave Ali Hsiang a push. Ah Hsiang made one step back. Ah Chin was the youngest son of Uncle Ah Fu. He was the very first person to call him "White-nosed Raccoon."

Uncle Ah Fu once caught a raccoon in one of his mountain trips. He put the animal inside a cage, thinking of selling it. The animal's fur was yellow with a tinge of black. A thin stripe of white hair covered the bridge of its nose and led down to a round and reddish nose tip. With one of its legs mangled by the trap, the raccoon limped heavily inside the cage.

"You're also a white-nosed raccoon," Ah Chin suddenly said as he pointed his finger at him.

From that day on, the name stuck. Nobody seemed to remember what his real name was.

He looked on with fear as the five turned a bend towards the other side of the bamboo fence.

He raised his hand and unleashed the top on the ground. The top skidded sideways.

"Shit! What a lousy top," Ah Hsiang gave out a curse.

He picked up the top and wound the rope around it. He then retraced his steps. Seeing a kettle of tea by the roadside, he squatted on the ground and helped himself with two bowls.

Then, he returned to the vegetable farm of Uncle Ah Fu. This small patch of farm land surrounded by mountains and hills used to be planted with sweet potatoes, cassava and peanuts due to its infertile soil. Uncle Ah Fu, who had frequented the outlying villages and towns, listened to suggestions and instead planted some leafy vegetables on a small plot.

Ah Hsiang felt a certain heaviness in his bladder but it wasn't really full. He stood beside the vegetable plot and waited. The curly white cabbage must have been growing for a month now, he thought. He noticed that the inner leaves had begun to curl inside. Along the plot's edge, there were three cabbages whose leaves had started to turn yellow. If not for Ah Chin, nobody would call him raccoon, he told himself.

A draft of cold air came blowing towards him. It made a hissing sound upon hitting the bamboo fence. He made a slight move to shrink his body, which made him become more aware of the pressure in his bladder. Looking around, he realized that nobody was around. He then quickly pulled up his pants and squeezed his bladder. A shower of urine, steaming in the cold air, spattered on the fourth cabbage. It moistened the leaves and dripped into the vegetable's core. He again put more pressure, aiming the projectile at another ball of cabbage. The liquid created bubbles on the surrounding soil but soon seeped into the lower layer. He felt very relieved. If anyone sees him, he would say he was applying fertilizer, he thought.

Suddenly, he heard a loud cry. Somebody rushed out from behind the bamboo fence.

Ah Hsiang shuddered in surprise. Before even realizing who it was, he felt his urine flowing back from where it just came from.

It was Ah Kou, Ah Chin and the rest. He couldn't believe his eyes. How could it be possible for them to have made a long turn and hid themselves behind the bamboo fence?

"I knew it was you, you White-nosed Raccoon!"

"What have I done?"

"You pissed on the vegetables!"

"I was fertilizing them for you. What's wrong with that?"

"Didn't you know that using warm urine can choke the vegetables? Look at those three cabbages."

"I have nothing to do with that."

"Who else would it be?"

"Really, it wasn't me. I tell you."

"Would the white-nosed raccoon admit having eaten a fruit if he really were the culprit? Let's catch the raccoon and skin it alive. Pull down his pants!" Ah Chin quickly got hold of Ah Hsiang as he said this.

"Stop it! Stop it!" Ah Hsiang struggled to break loose of Ah Chin's grip, his hands swaying violently and his feet kicking aimlessly.

Ah Jin grasped one of his hands which was holding the wooden top while Ah Ho and Ah Cheng held his legs. Only Ah Kou remained standing at one side, laughing all throughout the proceeding.

Ah Chin pulled down Ah Hsiang's pants. Immediately, the rope broke loose like bamboo shoot shedding an outer skin. The fly flapped open and the pants slid down Ah Hsiang's legs.

"Ha, ha, ha!" Ah Chin laughed with relish as he pulled off Ah Hsiang's pants and threw them into the air. They fluttered in the wind and fell on the ground.

"Ha, ha, ha!" everybody roared in laughter.

Ah Hsiang continued to wriggle violently. The air was getting cold and he felt it blowing on his bare buttocks and legs. Unmindful of the consequences, he picked up the top and forcefully stabbed the back of Ah Chin with it.

"Ouch!" Ah Chin shouted in pain. He instinctively felt his back with his hand. His fingers were drenched in blood.

"Son of a bitch!" Ah Chin turned around and swung his fist, aiming directly at Ah Hsiang's face.

Ah Hsiang felt his upper teeth colliding with the lower ones. He bit his own tongue. He sensed a salty taste inside the mouth and immediately knew he was bleeding inside.

II.

It was a bright sunny day. Against a backdrop of azure sky, the rolling mountains were lost in the distance. A pomegranate tree stood motionless in the windless expanse, its foliage thick and green in the bright sun.

Ah Hsiang had been walking for two hours now. The unpaved mountain path not wider than one or two meters meandered down the mountain towards the edge of a brook. This was the only way leading to the outside world. On a rainy day, this path becomes muddied and usually shows hoof prints of a passing ox. The next day, baked by heat under the sun, the mud becomes craggy and uncomfortable to walk on.

Ah Hsiang walked and ran on his barefeet. A bundle holding, his books and lunch box was strapped across his right shoulder and tied at the left side of his waist.

He continued walking a section of the mountain path then went down the brook and stepped on stones lying below the surface of the water. When the water level was low, the stones, laid at intervals of half a step, usually appeared above the running water. Passers-by step on these stones to cross to the other side. After a downpour, the water level rises, sometimes waist deep in some spots. It is said that during the storm season, the water level rises suddenly. One time, someone tried to brave the current and was swept away.

Someone was coming towards Ah Hsiang. It was Uncle Ah Fu. In the rural area, people who lived in a place some three hours away were still considered neighbors.

"Uncle Ah Fu," he greeted the man, unable to hide his embarrassment. He was afraid of meeting someone he knew along the way. But he was right in the middle of the brook and it was physically impossible to hide.

"Are you going to town, Ah Hsiang?"

Uncle Ah Fu did not ask why he's not in school today. Rural folks did not pay attention which day of the week it was: neither did they care if students missed their classes. Ah Hsiang immersed one foot into the water to give way to Uncle Ah Fu. The water felt cold and relaxing. Instinctively, he immersed the other foot. He sensed that the stone where he stood was slippery. It must be the moss, he said to himself. He steadied his footing and dipped both his hands in the water, enjoying its exhilarating effect.

What if Uncle Ah Fu meets his father and tells him about the encounter? How would he explain to his father? Ah Hsiang moved back to the stepping stones and looked towards Uncle Ah Fu. Deep inside, he felt a greater sense of fear for the new Japanese teacher. Mr. Inoue was a fair-skinned chubby man who appeared starkly different from the dark and emaciated residents of the village. On the second day of his arrival, Mr. Inoue told his students to move all desks and chairs to the back of the classroom. He then told everyone to kneel down on the floor. With a bamboo stick, he hit each one on the head. When it came to Ah Hsiang, Mr. Inoue hit him twice after noticing the bridge of his nose.

"Uneducated beasts and savages! Bakaro!" he cursed as he swung his stick. Nobody knew the reason for the show of violence. The following day, a tenth of the students did not come to class.

"What's the use of going to school?" somebody said.

"I will never go back and kneel before him. I only do that to my ancestors."

More than his classmates, Ah Hsiang received more rations of the beatings. He was hit at least once every one or two weeks. Each time, his head swelled and appeared to have developed boils. He could not think of any possible reason for the beatings except perhaps that white band on his nose bridge.

He didn't feel like attending school anymore but each time, he remembers his maternal uncle. It was this uncle who convinced his father to allow him to attend school in Neip'u, a village some one hour's walk from his own village.

"Be diligent in your studies and then come to Taipei when you finish," he used to encourage Ah Hsiang.

Ah Hsiang knew he would receive a beating again today. He wasn't supposed to be late but on his way to school he saw a strange-looking bird perched on a tree. The bird looked like a waterfowl but it had a caruncle above its beak. The caruncle appeared more like that of a duck, only much smaller. Ah Hsiang didn't know the name of this bird. He chased the bird for sometime before deciding to rush to school. Yet, he still arrived late.

The image of Mr. Inoue brandishing his bamboo stick filled his mind. He almost heard the sharp sound of the stick as it hit his head in the past. He knelt down on the floor hoping that the unavoidable can come instantly. Deep inside, he was really afraid of it. When it came, the impact hurt so much that he grimaced in pain, tears squeezed out between his closed eyelids.

Ah Hsiang lingered for sometime near the school, or more accurately, the indoctrination grounds. He remembered his uncle in Taipei and wished he could take the train to the city. At that time, he hadn't even been to the train station. He had learned from others that trains travel on rail tracks. All these could only be seen in the village of Waichuang.

He had walked passed the village of Chungp'u. By this time, the sun was high above the sky and its rays felt piercingly hot on his exposed skin. Ah Hsiang walked towards the shade under a tree and loosened his bundle to get his lunch box. The rice was enough but the viand consisted of merely three slices of salted radish and a small lump of fermented beans. Occasionally, his parents would buy salted fish in the market. In an instant, he swallowed everything into his stomach. He noticed that the sun was almost directly above where he stood. The distance from his house to the school in Neip'u was more than an hour's walk. From Neip'u to Chungp'u, he had walked for almost the same length of time. It would take him another hour or so to reach Waichuang, he mentally calculated.

His heartbeat started to grow faster again the way it did whenever he remembered Mr. Inoue's stick. At this moment, however, he had forgotten everything about his Japanese teacher.

He didn't have any idea of how a train looked like; neither did he know what's the shape of rail tracks. Although his uncle made a sketch on the rice paddy for him once, he now had only a very vague impression of it.

Once he asked his parents to bring him there but they said he was still too small to go.

Ah Hsiang climbed over a hillock. He then realized that it was a canyon. He was standing at the crest of the hill when he saw the rail track winding between the walls of the canyon. Was it really the rail track? He'd always thought it could only be seen in Waichuang. Ah Hsiang knew that where he stood now was not far from Waichuang.

The rail track stretched towards opposite directions. He couldn't tell which one was leading towards Taipei. He stood there motionless. Only his eyes switched alternately towards both directions. On one side, he saw the mouth of a cave some distance away.

He decided to climb down the slope. He found out that the rail tracks were laid on trunks of wood. Coal powder and rust littered the wooden surface. He then stooped down and took a closer look of the rail track. It was silvery smooth and shining. In fact, it glistened under the bright sunshine. He held his hand to touch the metal gingerly, the way he did when he had once secretly stroke the face of the image of the God of the Earth in the village temple.

"Choo . . . choo . . . choo," came the sound of the locomotive from the direction of the cave.

Awakened by the sound, he stood up and withdrew to the mountainside. The train brushed past his face in an instant. He didn't see a thing. When it had passed, he realized that people inside the car were watching and smiling at him.

Ah Hsiang took to his heels in chase. The train was proceeding in front of him. He continued running.

III.

As soon as he had finished elementary school, Ah Hsiang traveled to Taipei where he worked in an eatery that belonged to his uncle. He started with the meanest of tasks: sweeping the floor, washing dishes, clearing tables. . . Then he learned how to wait at tables and entertain patrons. Later, he also learned how to ride the bicycle and deliver orders. Ah Hsiang was a fast learner. He was especially good at finding his way around. Although he was new in the city, Ah Hsiang was more useful than older boys who came to the city earlier than him.

Satisfied with Ah Hsiang's performance, his uncle sometimes sent him to do the marketing or run an errand at the bank. It didn't take long before he became his uncle's most efficient assistant.

One day, around 11 o'clock late into the night, he delivered noodles to a cloth merchant in Jungting. There were four or five sales clerks playing cards.

"The noodle is here. Is it still hot?" One of them asked.

"Hey, Raccoon, how come there's very little soup. Did you drink it on the sly?" Someone else asked.

Ah Hsiang had delivered the noodle soup on his bike. It was unavoidable that some of the soup got spilled on the road. Besides, noodles absorb water if left to soak for too long.

"Yeah. He really looks like a white-nosed raccoon. Young man, I heard that you came from the mountains. I'm sure there are many raccoons there," a third commented jeeringly.

"Don't mind him. Shuffle the cards."

"Was it your father or your mother who's a raccoon?"

"Don't joke about that," the other said.

Ah Hsiang set the bowls of noodles on the table in silence. He did so with all his strength and his hands were shaking, fearful of further spilling out the soup. Then he replaced the lid of the serving box. By the time he sat on the bicycle saddle, tears were already rolling down his cheeks. With one foot resting on the ground, he wiped away the tears using the back of his palm. Why does everyone call me Raccoon? He left his village because everyone called him that. Once in the city, he came to know very few people. But as soon as they became familiar, they called him that name too.

These guys weren't familiar with him, but they still called him so. They had even insulted his parents. Ah Hsiang did not immediately return to the eatery. He went to the police station beside the park to report gambling.

Ah Hsiang had delivered noodles to the policemen before and was quite familiar with them. They wanted him to lead the way for the arrest. In the end, the gamblers were detained. Although Ah Hsiang only pointed the location to the police and did not show up during the actual arrest, the gamblers knew it was him who had reported them. When he delivered their orders inside the prison cell, Ah Hsiang was blamed and scolded repeatedly.

Ah Hsiang again reported to the police who then warned them that they would not be released if they behaved that way.

The experience made Ah Hsiang more convinced of his belief that there were only two kinds of people in this world: the bully and the bullied. Mr. Inoue belonged to the first. He belonged to the second type. But now, he saw how the sales clerks switched roles from the first to the second type. Similarly, Ah Hsiang felt that he had now turned into the bully.

After their release, the sales clerks came to see Ah Hsiang and his uncle at the eatery, vowing for a reprisal. But he was not intimidated. The police praised Ah Hsiang as a good citizen, a good Japanese citizen in fact. They encouraged him to continue his contacts with the police.

One night, during one of his deliveries, Ah Hsiang was attacked by several men in an alley. They pushed him down together with his bicycle and punched him severely. By the time he got up, noodles bowls and serving box were already damaged. Even the bicycle tires were not spared. He reported to the police but his attackers had long scampered away.

His uncle was extremely displeased when he returned to the

eatery.

"I have repeatedly told you that we must seriously engage in business and avoid meddling in other things but you do not listen. Now, it's best for you to return to your home town. I'll tell you to come after some time."

Ah Hsiang did not take the trip back. Instead, he ran to the police and told them about his predicament. Realizing that Ah Hsiang was an intelligent boy, the policemen asked him to work as a janitor. Ah Hsiang's knowledge of the Taiwanese dialect would be helpful. Besides, his experience in delivering noodles made him quite familiar with the locality and its residents. Sometimes, he joined the policemen in carrying out their duties. At times, he was assigned to gather information. Although Ah Hsiang was nominally a janitor, he was to some extent acting as a police informer.

At this point in time, what left a deep impression in the mind of Ah Hsiang was the prison cell built with wooden bars. He noticed that whoever are placed in that cell usually lose their cockiness. They become very yielding. Even intellectuals and rich traders come to beg him just for a bowl of water.

Sometimes, the policemen would bring the inmates to the bathroom located at the back of the precinct. Using water hoses, these inmates were doused with water, just like rats caught in a trap. They were watered dripping wet, their knees wobbling with cold. At times, policemen would insert a water hose into the mouth of an inmate and pump water down his throat while someone pinched his nose. This treatment made the inmates scream and swallow water until their bellies become bloated. Afterwards, they lay down on the floor while a policeman stepped on their stomach to make them vomit out the water.

Ah Hsiang was only a janitor and a boy. But because he was standing on the other side of the prison bars, inmates looked at him with appealing eyes. Nobody inside the prison cells had ever called him "White-nosed Raccoon."

Ah Hsiang would naturally always want to stand in this side of the prison bars but he wouldn't be a janitor all his life, not even an informer. He wanted to extend this prison cell into the whole of society. He would one day become a policeman, he often told himself. Only then can he command respect and fear from everyone.

He had shared his ambitions with the policemen who later told him tips on which books to read, how to read them and how to take the tests. He failed the first tests. The second time, not only did he pass the tests; he was one of the topnotchers.

IV.

Tseng Chi-hsiang and Wu Yu-lan were sitting side-by-side on the stone-paved staircase. The staircase had more than twenty steps, each step about 2 feet wide and 8 inches high. Its top level connects with a wide pathway leading to the Tz'uyou Temple while downward, it reaches the banks of Tashui River. The staircase actually formed part of the river dike and doubled as a quay.

A few stars were clearly visible in the pitch dark sky. Search lights that flashed from all directions lighted and faded. A few of the light beams crossed momentarily in the sky.

These precautions had lately become necessary. Japan had earlier declared war against the United States.

"No, my father insists that we cannot adopt Japanese wedding rites," Wu Yu-Ian said with her head facing down, her eyes looking intently at the flowing water of Tashui River. Reflections from the search lights gleamed and disappeared on the surface of the river.

"Your father is such a stubborn man."

"You can't call him that. He said that we have our own wedding rites."

"You're an educated person. You cannot behave like an uneducated person like him."

"My father also went to school, but he read books that were

different from ours. He used to say that sending my sister and myself to school was the most useless thing he ever did. He complained that we talk strange things and that he does not understand any of our sentences."

"My superior advised me to do so. Actually, it was more like a command."

"My brother-in-law also agreed that we get married according to our own rites. He'd been to the mainland to study."

"Don't ever mention him again. He's a dubious character. He needs my protection and he'll need me to save him one day. To have somebody like him for a relative is something disadvantageous to me. They'll lose their trust in me because of him, at least diminish their confidence in me. I have decided to adopt Japanese rites also because you have relatives like him."

"But father won't give us his permission if we don't use Chinese rites."

"If he doesn't give his permission, then . . ." Tseng Chi-hsiang suddenly stood up before he had finished the sentence. Wu Yu-lan also stood up.

"What do you think?"

". . ."

"Your decision is crucial. It has never been done in Taiwan and it will be special because it would be the first time. Are you not yet aware that the government is about to launch a campaign towards Japanization? In the future, not only weddings have to be done the Japanese way. Everyone will be asked to worship their gods and adopt Japanese names. In my case, for example, my surname Tseng can be changed into Katsute. Your surname, Wu, is also a Japanese surname, although quite rare and pronounced in a different way. Adopting Japanese names is necessary for thorough Japanization. Japan has already occupied many places in Southeast Asia. We'll go there some day, in that big place, and become leaders ourselves."

"My brother-in-law said that Japan will . . ."

"Don't say it. I know what you want to say. It will be a crime to say that. I'll have to make arrests. I cannot arrest you but in the case of your relatives, I cannot do anything. It is my duty to protect my country. Anybody who engages in rumor-mongering will be endangering the country. I'm sure Japan will win the war. My chief said it right. We must become models and start new trends. We'll live to see many people following us."

"What do you think?"

". . ."

"I'll fulfill any promise I have made to you."

Two months ago, the two of them played tennis at the back of the dormitory. The tennis court was a public facility, but owing to the nature of the game, only Japanese citizens, policemen, teachers and high school students, both boys and girls, could use the tennis courts.

After the game, the two went to his dormitory for a rest and to see his new tennis racket. It was not her first time there: she'd been there before but each time she had been accompanied by his friends.

Ah Hsiang learned how to play the game while he attended the training center. He also learned judo and fencing. Both judo and fencing are for self-protection. They were also means to get promoted. He's now a blackbelter. Playing tennis was an important part of his social activities. He'd eyed on this sport when he was still working as a janitor in Taipei.

Her tennis skills were nothing extraordinary. What he liked was her physical appearance in the tennis court. From the first time they played tennis, he had constantly thought of her. He remembered her wearing a short white blouse with matching shorts, socks and canvas shoes. Her hair was tied with a white kerchief. With tennis racket in one hand, she was slightly bending, he vividly recalled. He could still remember her sweet and melodious voice. He knew from the way she moved about that she came from a good family and had received good education.

She was much more educated than he was. Although she didn't go to some famous girls' high school, she was educated in a private exclusive school for girls. His elementary education was absolutely no comparison to hers.

Today, she was also all white from head to foot. The only difference was her somewhat disheveled hair. She removed her white hair band and, with her hand, fixed her hair towards the back. She was sitting quite close to him. Yet there was such a wide distance between the two of them. There was only one way of closing this distance—to conquer her. Now was an opportunity that rarely came.

He suddenly lunged at her.

"Talk it over with me if you want me. If you touch me again, I'll die right here before you," she said gloomily.

"Forgive me," he said kneeling down and with his hands stretched forward and his forehead almost touching the tatami mat, "I love you. Please promise me."

"..."

"Yu-lan . . ."

"Do your parents also favor Japanese rites?"

"My parents are rural folks. They won't have any opinion at all. Even if they disagree, I could convince them. If they still aren't convinced, I'll go on with my plan." His voice was firm and confident.

Slowly, he moved his gaze away from Wu Yu-lan and looked straight towards the other side of the river. Then he looked up to the sky. Search light beams were still criss-crossing the night sky. Tashui River flows towards the city of Taipei. From where he sat, he could vaguely figure out the shape of the building housing the Governor-General's Office.

"Splash!" The sound came from the farther end of the river. Somebody was throwing stones into the river.

The splashing sounds became louder as the stones landed closer to where they sat. One stone narrowly missed the lowest step of the stone-paved staircase.

"Who's there?" Tseng Chi-hsiang called out in a loud voice."Don't mind them."

"They're doing it on purpose."

"Today, even if it is the case, we will not mind them." A whistle blow was heard from the top of the river dike.

"A man and a woman together." It was the voice of a child. Another whistle blow sounded.

"Splash."

"A man and a woman together."

"White nose!"

"Bastard!" Tseng Chi-hsiang stood up angrily.

"Please! Chi-hsiang, don't!"

"Okay. But . . ."

"I promise."

"How about your parents?

"I'll convince them."

V.

"Japan has lost the war."

"Japan has lost the war."

In the beginning, people spoke secretly in subdued tones, their voices sounding incredulous. Everybody knew that Japan will not last the war. Japanese newspapers had earlier reported the fall of Okinawa. The Americans had dropped atomic bombs in the cities of Hiroshima and Nagasaki, making Japanese surrender imminent. But nobody expected the defeat to come so soon.

Today, everyone felt a bit strange. This morning, the sky was clear and bright but it was unusually silent. There were no alarms heard. The normal sound of airplanes flying was not heard today.

Inside the penitentiary, everyone was nervous and seemingly lost in thought.

Someone thought of placing a radio in the lobby of the penitentiary. At around noon, everyone was kneeling down as they listened to the voice of the Japanese emperor. The radio did not sound good. Reception was poor and there was too much interference. The emperor spoke with a trembling voice, almost unintelligible. He was obviously crying.

At the start, everyone knelt down silently. Then someone started to sob. Fists were tightly clenched and heads were bowed lower and lower. Someone pounded the floor with his fist.

Just like everybody else, Tseng Chi-hsiang knelt down listening. Today's events made him feel grief and bitter. He was kneeling down absentmindedly. Strangely, he felt as though this had nothing to do with him, but he also felt that Japan's defeat was of personal significance to him.

When the broadcast ended, everyone in the room bowed before the radio and remained kneeling for sometime.

"Japan has lost the war."

These same words took a different weight now. Tseng Chi-hsiang saw the Penitentiary Chief stood up, followed by the Street Chief, Section Chief. Director and the Investigation Chief. A few of them appeared dispirited. Some, however, looked as though they were quite resolute.

"Japan has lost the war!" By the time he was in the streets, people had started to speak louder and bolder.

"Japan has lost the war?" His wife asked when he showed up at the door. She helped remove his coat.

"Yes."

"What's going to happen in the future?"

"I do not know." All his life, he had never felt so unsure. "Will the Americans kill everybody?"

"Do you think so?"

"Of course not."

"Why do you ask?"

"The Japanese were good at propaganda. I could still remember what they said about the female students who committed suicide by jumping off the cliff in Okinawa. I mean those *himeyitri*."

"Why do you think of those things?"

"If you . . ."

"What about me?"

"If you make a command, I'll not be afraid to obey anything."

"We're different. We're not Japanese."

"I know. But you're a policeman working for the Japanese."

"At most, I'll throw these uniforms away."

"Can you do that?"

"Without a country, will the Japanese still care?"

"But . . ."

"The penitentiary has ordered locals to maintain peace and order."

"Yu-lan . . . Yu-lan . . ." Someone called at the door.

"It's you, sister. Come in."

"Your brother-in-law said that Chi-hsiang must leave this place immediately."

"Why?"

"People are still calm right now. The announcement came so suddenly and people don't know how to react. Tomorrow, next week, the situation will become dangerous. People can get killed."

"What about my son and me?"

"You can leave the boy with me for the meantime."

Tseng Chi-hsiang did not believe that people would do drastic things. He insisted that he had the duty to maintain peace and order in Old Town.

The day after, things started to happen.

First came the news of the Investigation Chief's suicide. On the day the emperor's message was broadcast, several Japanese officials committed suicide in the hinterland. It was like an epidemic. The newspapers reported suicides for days in succession. Although the chief was a lower level official, his suicide was big news in Old Town.

Old Town was a peaceful little town whose residents were law-abiding and disciplined. However, the atmosphere of revenge prevalent in other areas during the past few days soon also engulfed the town.

Some said that the first incident had involved the son of a dentist who was practicing without a license. During the war, another dentist, who was starting his practice, had testified against the unlicensed dentist who was subsequently arrested and jailed. As soon as the war ended, the dentist's son, who had learned judo in high school, went to his father's accuser to get even. In front of everybody, he flung the dentist on the pavement. Later, the son also confronted the policeman from Ryukyu who had arrested his father.

All of a sudden, these events awakened the people from their initial stupor over Japan's surrender. They each tried to look for their enemies to get even.

A few policemen were dragged to the temple square and forced to kneel down before gods as a punishment for their sins. A butcher, punished by policemen using the water engorgement method for illegal butchering during the war, held the two policemen at knife point and paraded them from Haishant'ou to Ts'aotianwei. The butcher appeared extremely pleased during the whole process.

However, most Taiwanese policemen were engaged in internal duties. For this reason, they normally did not have any problem with the public and were thus spared from reprisals. An exception was a policemen surnamed Lai who was dragged to the Tz'uyou Temple square.

"Beat him to death!" Someone shouted.

"Kill this running dog!" Someone added.

"Spare me. Spare me!" The man knelt down on the pavement, his head kowtowing ceaselessly. His wife also knelt down beside him.

"Kill him!" Someone again shouted angrily.

"Dog! Three-legged dog! You better die!" A man shouted as he kicked the policeman.

"Running dog! I'll kill you!" Another man hit him with a wooden pole.

"Ouch! Ouch!"

This policeman was only enemy No. 2, yet the mob still broke one of his legs.

Then someone in the crowd shouted. "Let's get White-nosed Raccoon." But nobody knew where Tseng Chi-hsiang had fled.

When the mob knocked at his door, Tseng Chi-hsiang quickly climbed to the roof top. On that same night, he fled the town in haste. He didn't have time to bring his wife and son along with him.

Yet the people didn't just give up. After destroying all his furniture, they took Yu-lan in custody.

"I don't have any idea where he is now. I am willing to do anything you want. Even if you kill me, I'll not resist."

They made a decision that she had to hire a theatrical group to perform at the temple square for three consecutive nights. During these three nights, she was required to arrange for an unlimited supply of cigarettes for all townsfolk.

At that time, local drama, which had long been suppressed by the Japanese, was slowly making a comeback. The sound of firecrackers had replaced gunshots. Everywhere, the sounds of cymbals and drums could be heard once again. People resumed their visits to temples and shrines, thanking their gods for bringing peace to the land.

A makeshift stage was made in front of Tz'uyou Temple, in a spot adjacent to the river dike. On the front awning of the stage were emblazoned large red characters that read "Compliments of the People's Sinner—Tseng Chi-hsiang." Between the stage and the temple, several baskets filled with cigarettes could be seen. This passageway was illumined by powerful light bulbs. Each of the baskets carried a red banner on which were written the same characters found on the stage. Tseng Chi-hsiang's wife, Yu-lan was kneeling in the temple as a punishment for his husband's sins.

"Come. Smoke a cigarette from White-nosed Raccoon," people invited each other as the crowd milled around the temple square in a festive mood."Let's watch the opera offered by White-nosed Raccoon."

The townspeople did feel regret that he had fled the town. But as days passed, they soon forgot everything about the affair.

VI.

"How old were you at that time?" the old man asked.

"Around twelve years old," I said after making some mental calculation.

"Do you still remember it?"

"It was a big issue."

"It's almost thirty-three years, wasn't it?"

"Yes. Thirty-three years now."

"Old Town . . . Old Town . . ."

"Did you ever return?"

"Return? How could I?" He slightly held his head to look at me, then lowered his gaze again. From where I stood, I could clearly see his nose. The passage of time had left its mark on his face but it could not conceal the starkly different color of his nose bridge.

"Old Town . . . It was my nightmare." Again he heaved a deep sigh, his eyes staring blankly at the wall. But his expression appeared as though he was seeing through the wall and looking at a distant point outside.

"I do not know what a nightmare is. Perhaps, my experience in Old Town was my nightmare. I have repeatedly tried to forget that place but failed each time. It's been quite a long time ago since I had left Old Town, but when I close my eyes, I still see the faces of those good-hearted but sometimes stupid people. I also remember your father. He had a small built and his feet extended outward. He's a good-hearted carpenter respected by the townsfolk. They call him uncle. Did you say he's already gone?"

"Yes, he's gone."

"I asked him to make an office table and he doubted for a while. For that, I slapped him. He was older than me but I still slapped him. At that time, I thought that I was carrying the country on my shoulder. I still remember the expression of his eyes. They were filled with hatred and contempt. But. I still thought that power was stronger than hatred.

"I also remember that woman everybody called Chai Pa-feng. She must have been one of your neighbors. She didn't queue up during meat rationing. I told her to kneel down before everybody with a pail of water on her head. Since it was a rationing, everybody had the chance to buy. But some still refused to fall in line. It was a small incident. I could have pretended not to know if I wished to. But I had previously heard the Japanese citing this point. They condemned the Taiwanese for their stupidity and lack of education in disrupting order in exchange for their own little vested interests. When I was small, my Japanese teachers looked at me that way. I also learned to look at my own people in the same way."

"I also remember Ah Chao, the butcher. Someone accused him of injecting water into the pork he sold. He denied the allegation and so I forced him to gulp down a lot of water. Now, I could still hear his pleas and screaming."

"It was a nightmare, a never-ending nightmare. I had good memory and excellent ability to judge. I used them as my tools to accomplish myself. I lorded it over Old Town the way a king would. I considered myself a tiger or a lion. Deep inside me. I was at best a cat or a dog. I learned how to capitalize on the power of the Japanese."

"I thought I was the king but people of the town considered me a plague. I knew they were avoiding me. But there were also those who tried to curry favor with me the way I did with the Japanese. Yu-lan used to dissuade me from overdoing it. Old Town was a small place and her family was one of the oldest in the town. About a third of the town's population were either relatives or family friends. But, how could I let go of my power? Anybody who enjoys power naturally immerses himself in it, even to the extent of forgetting himself."

"Yet, one day the Japanese were defeated. Frankly, the Japanese themselves had an inkling of what was to come but nobody ever thought that it would come so soon. Because it came so suddenly, before I could even react, Yu-lan's brother-in-law, the lawyer, tried to persuade me into fleeing the town."

"I didn't listen to him. I was convinced that I could still lead the townsfolk, until that day when I suddenly realized that the tame deer had turned into a fierce tiger. In haste, I fled the town alone and returned to my home town. This was the only place I could hide in. I never thought that my father would refuse to accept me. He said that I was no longer his son. I knew it was the wedding rite that infuriated him. I never expected such moral courage from a man who had lived in the rural area all his life. Fortunately, my mother pleaded with him. He agreed to let me stay temporarily in this small warehouse which was used to store farm implements. My father had some farm lands but he refused to let me plant on it. Actually, I couldn't plant. My mother secretly brought me food to eat."

"I silently waited for a reunion with Yu-lan. I had hoped that things would settle down and I could go look for her. After less than two months, she left this world after catching Typhoie fever. I couldn't believe it when word came."

"I remember having told that her house was sealed off. Everyone said that she died of a contagious disease and avoided getting close to her house."

"I suddenly felt that I was the most solitary person in this world. There is nothing in this world that could take her place. I could still vividly recall her poise as we played tennis. Soon after the war, she told me that if I commit suicide, she would not hesitate to follow me. I could almost imagine her on her knees as people milled around her at the temple square."

"I was told that facing the angry mob, she behaved with calmness and bravery. For my sake, a weak woman shouldered the burden of a people's sinner. When they cursed her, she pleaded for forgiveness, but not for herself. When someone spitted on her, she didn't brush it away. I am a man but I allowed my wife to suffer such a great humiliation."

"Didn't she have words of complaint at all? I couldn't even meet her for the last time before she died. Even if she wanted to pour out her protestations, there was nobody to turn to. How could have she died in peace?"

"I was fortunate to have had such a wife. Are my sins so unforgivable that I had to get her and lose her afterwards? When everybody, including my own family, despised me, only she silently tried to bear everything. Before I could even show my gratitude and remorse, she just left this world in silence."

"My heart died together with her. Actually, I should have died as soon as the Japanese surrendered. Many Japanese committed suicide then. I wasn't as brave. I said I wasn't a Japanese. I am a people's sinner. I should have died to gain forgiveness for my sins. But I didn't and instead, fled to the safety of the mountains. See how shameless I am. I escaped to this place so that she could ask forgiveness from the people. In my heart, I was still hoping that when things settled down. I could still return and become a policeman again."

"Her death totally changed the way I thought. From that day on, Tseng Chi-hsiang was no longer existing in this world. Actually, on that fateful day when the Japanese surrendered, he should have stopped existing. His people, his relatives and friends, his own parents, had all deserted him. But he shamelessly clung on."

"Ah . . . Yu-lan." he carefully picked up the photograph for a closer look. "Can't you really remember her?" His hands were trembling as he spoke. His eyes were blank and dry.

"I knew her. But because I was small then, it is difficult for me to recognize her now."

"You are not the only one who could not recognize her. If at your age you couldn't recognize her, then perhaps even the whole town wouldn't. You said a while ago that Old Town has progressed so rapidly and that you barely know the people in the street every time you return. I knew people will forget her quickly."

"Didn't you carve an image of her?"

"I did try but I couldn't. Although she was my wife and once very close to me, I couldn't carve an image of her. She's too far away from me now. I had once touched her body, but it didn't belong to me. Her heart used to belong to me but I couldn't grasp it. Her face, what was the expression on her face before she died? Somebody has yet to tell me."

"I knew she only had one wish. That was to die beside me and be buried beside me. I came to know that her parents died one after the other. I heard that Old Town had changed but I have never returned, not even once. I dared not go. First of all, I was afraid that those people still hated me. Then, I was afraid that my impurities would smear her land. I couldn't face her relatives. I also wished to bring her remains to this place but I was afraid that she'd find this place too unfamiliar, not having been here in her lifetime."

"Her son has grown up into a man. I say 'her son' because I am not qualified. He's now left Old Town for Taipei. I thought that when things had settled down, I would bring them here by my side. I never thought that she would leave us in a hurry. Her son was brought up by her older sister. He'd been here and asked me to live with him. But I couldn't bear to face him. Seeing him was more painful than anything else. He took after his mother. I wish that, like everybody else, he would despise me."

"I thought that I should tell him the story of Yu-lan and myself but I didn't know how to begin. Alone, I could talk to Yu-lan. But if she really appeared before me, I'm afraid I wouldn't be able to utter a word. This is perhaps one of the reasons why I couldn't carve an image of Yu-lan."

"You were blaming yourself when you carved those horses?" I asked him.

"In my time, the Taiwanese called the Japanese 'dogs', four-legged dogs. Those who worked for the Japanese were called 'three-legged dogs'."

"How come you only carve horses? Why not other animals?"

"That's because they wanted horses. I kept on carving horses, and all of a sudden one day, I saw myself in them. So, I included myself in my carvings."

I picked up the horses from the ground. Although their postures differed, they had a common point. Their expression and posture radiated pain and remorse.

"What do you plan to do with them?"

"I don't know," he hesitated, "perhaps I'll burn all of them one day."

"Burn them?"

"Because they have nothing to do with other people." he said with a feeble voice.

"Would you sell one to me?" I said with audacity. Actually, I was thinking that as long as I could afford them. I'll take all of them.

"Sell you one?" He again hesitated. Slowly, he turned his face towards me. "Okay, select one. During these past thirty-three years. I have not met anybody from Old Town except you. I had always wanted to but had been afraid all the time."

"But I've also left Old Town."

"At least, you still remember a policeman in Old Town by the name of White-nosed Raccoon."

I selected one horse. Three of its legs were kneeling on the ground and the only standing leg supported the weight of its body. The horse's head was slightly bent, its mouth wide open and its nostrils flaring out as if in the act of panting or neighing. Its mane was in disarray. I took a closer look. One of the hind legs had been broken and dragging on without power.

"That one is a gift for you." He said with hesitation.

"Why?"

"I was afraid you would choose that one. Usually, things you're afraid of come sooner than you expect them. One night, I dreamt of Yu-lan. I have not dreamt of her for a long time. I was afraid I had forgotten her. In the dream, I saw her kneeling before me with tears in her eyes. I was also crying. I have always thought that there wouldn't be tears anymore. But that night, my pillows were wet with tears. The next morning, I decided to stop all my work and concentrate on carving a horse. The result was that horse in your hand. If you look at horses, always look at their eyes. See those eyes for yourself."

I first looked at the wooden horse then turned my eyes on him. Then I noticed that his dry and lifeless eyes had suddenly turned moist.

I quickly turned my head away. Very slowly, I put down the wooden horse back where I had found it. Together with Lai Kuolin, I stepped out of the house in silence.

Translated by Carlos G. TEE 鄭永康

Authors & Translators

Selected from Summer 1984, Autumn 1996
YU Kwang-chung (余光中, 1928-2017) *was chair professor of English literature at National Sun Yat-sen University in Kaohsiung, Taiwan. A renowned poet and prolific writer, he has published over 70 volumes of poetry, prose, criticism and translation in Taiwan, Hong Kong, and Mainland China and is the recipient of a dozen major literary awards in Taiwan and Hong Kong. In 1991, he was conferred an honorary fellowship by the Hong Kong Translation Society. From 1990 to 1998 he served as President of the Taipei Chinese PEN Center. In 2000, Selected Poetry of Yu Kwang-chung was named one of The 100 Best Books in 20th-Century Chinese Literature in Beijing. He had spent lots of energy re-publishing his bilingual collection of poetry* The Night Watchman《守夜人》 *in 2017. He passed away in Kaohsiung at the age of 90.*

Selected from Summer 1988
Pai Chiu (白萩, 1937-2023), *born Ho Ching-jung* (何錦榮), *won the 1st National Literary Award for poetry in 1956. He was one of the founders of the Li Poetry Society and* Li Poetry《笠詩刊》. *Among his publications are collections of poetry* The Death of the Moth《蛾之死》, Rose of the Wind《風的薔薇》, Symbol of the Sky《天空象徵》, Chansons《香頌》, Poetry Square《詩廣場》, *and a critical review:* Critiques of Contemporary Poetry《現代詩散論》. *The well-respected poet passed away peacefully in Kaohsiung at the age of 87.*

Selected from Autumn 1987, Summer 1988, Autumn 1999

John J. S. BALCOM (陶忘機), *is a freelance writer, translator, and Professor at the Middlebury Institute of International Studies at Monterey, California, USA. He earned his Ph.D. in Chinese and comparative literature from Washington University in St. Louis and has translated many contemporary Taiwanese poems and novels as well as Buddhist literature into English, including former* Taipei Chinese PEN Quarterly *chief editor Chi Pang-yuan's best-seller* The Great Flowing River 《巨流河》.

Selected from Summer 1988

Lo Fu (洛夫, 1928-2018), *born Mo Lo-fu* (莫落夫), *was one of the founders of the* Epoch Poetry Quarterly *and served as its chief editor for many years. He received his B.A. in English Literature from Tamkang University and worked as an associate professor in the Foreign Language department at Soochow University. Lo Fu received several prestigious awards, including the National Culture and Arts Award, and was named as one of the ten leading poets of Taiwan. His acclaimed works, translated into languages such as English, French, Japanese, Korean, Dutch, and Swedish, include the poetry collection* Songs of a Wizard 《魔歌》 *(selected as one of the Taiwanese literary classics in 1999). In 2001, he published his long poem* Driftwood 《漂木》, *considered a significant masterpiece after his relocation to Canada. On March 19th, 2018, Lo Fu passed away at the Taipei Veterans General Hospital due to respiratory complications, reaching the age of ninety-one.*

Selected from Autumn 1993

Bai Ling (白靈), *born Chuang Tzu-hwang* (莊祖煌) *in Taipei. He received his M.S. in chemical engineering from the Stevens Institute of Technology, N.J. Having retired as Associate Professor from the National Taipei University of Technology, he now teaches Chinese literature at Soochow University in Taipei. Winner of many awards such as the National Culture and Arts Awards, he has been Editor-*

in-Chief of the Taiwan Poetry Quarterly, *and has published many volumes of poetry, including* Not A Single Cloud Needs A Boundary 《沒有一朵雲需要國界》 *and* The Gap Between Love and Death 《愛與死的間隙》, Pithy Poems by Bai Ling 《白靈截句》, *and* Flowing Faces: Bai Ling New Century Poetry 《流動的臉：白靈‧新世紀詩選》.

Selected from Autumn 1990, Winter 1992

Nancy CHANG ING (殷張蘭熙, 1920-2017) *was born in Beijing, China. She graduated from West China Union University in Chengtu with a B.A. in English literature and was an associate professor in the English Department of Soochow University for three years. In 1996 she attended the Harvard International Seminar at Cambridge. Her translations of Chinese short stories and poetry have been published in the collections:* New Voices, Green Seaweed and Salted Eggs, Ivory Balls and Other Stories, Black Tears. *Her book of poems,* One Leaf Falls, *was published in 1971. She translated six of the eight short stories in* The Execution of Mayor Yin 《尹縣長》, *a collection of short stories by Chen Jo-hsi, published by Indiana University Press, 1978. She used to be the publisher of THE CHINESE PEN Quarterly. She passed away on December 22, 2017, in Taipei at the advanced age of 98 .*

Selected from Summer 1994

Shang Qin (商禽, 1930-2010) *is the pen name of Lo Yen* (羅燕). *Born in 1930 in Sichuan, China, he followed the Nationalist army to Taiwan as a young soldier in 1949. He remained a soldier for 23 years before working as a longshoreman, a gardener, and a street peddler while writing poetry. He was a member of the* Epoch Poetry Quarterly *and has published* Dream or Dawn 《夢或者黎明》 *(and its revised and expanded edition),* Think with the Feet 《用腳思想》, *and finally poetry collections* Shang Qin—Century Poetry Anthology 《商禽‧世紀詩選》 *and* Shang Qin's Collected Poems 《商禽詩全集》.

Selected from Summer 1994

N. G. D. MALMQVIST (馬悅然, 1924-2019) *is Professor Emeritus at the University of Stockholm where he taught as Chair Professor of Chinese from 1965 to 1990. He was a member of the Swedish Academy, the Royal Swedish Academy of Science and Royal Swedish Academy of Letters, History and Antiquities. He has published extensively in the fields of Chinese linguistics and philology and has also translated many works of ancient, modern and contemporary Chinese literature into Swedish, such as Shuihu Chuan (水滸傳, the Chin Sheng-tan Version), the Hsi-yu-chi (西遊記), together with the works of Shen Ts'ung-wen (沈從文), etc.. The only Sinologist among the Nobel Literature Prize judges, he witnessed Mo Yan being rewarded in 2012. Passed away peacefully on 17th October 2019, his contributions in bridging Chinese literature to the world will be remembered forever.*

Selected from Autumn 1996

Lomen (羅門, 1928-2017), *a native of Hainan Island, was the pen name of HAN Jentsun (韓仁存). He was the author of 15 volumes of poetry and 7 volumes of essays, in addition to a 10-volume series. Lomen won many literary awards, including the Gold Medal from the President of the Philippines in 1965 with his poem* Fort McKinley 〈麥堅利堡〉 *and the Dr. Sun Yat-sen Award for Culture and Literature. His works have been translated into English, French, German, Swedish, Japanese, and Korean. He passed away peacefully at 6 a.m. on January 18th, 2017, at an elderly care center located in Beitou.*

Selected from Autumn 1999

Mei Hsin (梅新, 1937-1997), *also known as* Yuchuan (魚川), *was born I-hsin CHANG (章意新) in Zhejiang in 1937. His journey as a poet commenced during his teenage years while serving in the military, and in 1956, he joined the "Modernist" movement initiated by Ji Xian (紀弦). Mei Hsin made significant contributions to editorial work, playing a key role in the establishment of journals such as* Chung Wai Literary Quarterly《中外文學》, The World of Chinese Language and Literature《國文天地》, *and* UNITAS—A Literary Monthly 《聯合文學》. *He was involved in the planning of publications like* An Anthology of Contemporary Chinese Literature《中國現代文學大系》, Annual Selection of Modern Chinese Poetry《中國現代文學年選》, *and* Poetics《詩學》. *In 1982, he facilitated the revival of* Modern Poetry《現代詩》. *During his ten-year tenure as the editor of the supplement to* The Central Daily News《中央日報》, *Mei Hsin received the Government Information Office's Golden Tripod Award for Editorial Excellence four times. His literary achievements include the publication of 12 books, among them* The Reborn Tree《再生的樹》, From Beijing to Paris《從北京到巴黎》, Mei Hsin's Poems《梅新詩選》, *and* Curriculum Vitae《履歷表》.

Selected from Autumn 1993

Hsiang Ming (向明), *born in 1928 as Tung Ping* (董平) *from Changsha, Hunan, is a distinguished member of the Blue-star Poetry Club. He has held key roles as the editor-in-chief of the* Blue-star Poetry Quarterly《藍星詩刊》, *president of the* Taiwan Poetry Quarterly, *and chief editor for* The Best Taiwanese Poetry. *Over the years, he has been honored with awards such as the Chinese Literary Award, the Dr. Sun Yat-sen Award for Culture and Literature, and the National Award for Arts. Hsiang Ming has an extensive literary repertoire, including over fifty collections of poetry, essay poetry, essays, and fairy tales. His works have been translated into English, French, German, Dutch, Japanese, Korean, Slovak, and Malay. Even at the age of over 95, he continues his literary pursuits, with his latest work* Weed Discourse: Hsiang Ming Writing and Reading Poetry《野草說法：向明寫詩讀詩》.

Selected from Autumn 1993

Wai-Lim YIP (葉維廉) *was born in Guangdong in 1937 and grew up in Hong Kong. A graduate of National Taiwan University, he further obtained his Ph.D. at Princeton. He is also a Professor Emeritus of Chinese and Comparative Literature professor at the University of*

California at San Diego. His writings include Ezra Pound's Cathay, Modern Chinese Poetry, and Hiding in the Universe: Poems of Wang Wei (in English). He has also written many books of poems in Chinese and three collections of critical essays.

Selected from Spring 2015

Poet **CHEN I-Chih** (陳義芝) hails from Hualien and holds a Ph.D. in Chinese from National Kaohsiung Normal University. He retired from United Daily News《聯合報》 as Director of the Literary Supplement and from National Taiwan Normal University as Professor of Chinese. From 2010 to 2014 he was Secretary-General of the Taipei Chinese PEN. From 2019 to 2022, he served as Vice President of the Center. His many publications include 2 volumes of poetry The Boundary《邊界》 and Endless songs《無盡之歌》, as well as a collection of essays Songs Reaching Over The Hills《歌聲越過山丘》. He has won several major literary awards, including the China Times Literary Award and the Dr. Sun Yat-sen Culture and Literature Award.

Selected from Spring 2015, Summer 2016, Summer 2020

Yanwing LEUNG (梁欣榮), poet and translator, retired from the Department of Foreign Languages and Literatures of National Taiwan University in 2018. A Ph.D. in English from Texas A&M University, he has taught writing and translation both at NTU and at the Ministry of Foreign Affairs, R.O.C. He practices traditional Chinese poetry in his spare time and is the author of Poems Inspired by the Rubaiyat《魯拜新詮》and The Forgotten Rubaiyat: A Verse Interpretation in Chinese《魯拜拾遺》. He was the Editor-in-Chief of The Taipei Chinese PEN Quarterly.

Selected from Spring 2019

CHEN Yu-hong (陳育虹) was born in Kaohsiung, Taiwan. She holds a degree in English from Wenzao Ursuline College of Languages and lived in Vancouver, Canada, for over 10 years. She now resides in Taipei. Winner of the 2004 Annual Poetry Award, she is the author *of* Searching for the Metaphors《索隱》, Bewitchment《魅》 *and* In-between《之間》. *She has also published a series of Chinese translations of famous Western poets, including* Rapture *by Carol Ann Duffy,* Eating Fire *by Margaret Atwood, and* The Great Fires *by Jack Gilbert. Her* 2010 Chen Yu-hong's Diary《2010／陳育虹日記》*was very well received.*

Selected from Summer 2020

Hung Hung (鴻鴻) *is the pen name of Yen Hung-ya* (閻鴻亞). *Born in 1964 in Taiwan, he is an award-winning poet and author of poetry, short fiction, essays and theater criticism, chief editor of* Off the Roll Poetry+, *artistic director of Dark Eyes Performance Lab, which he founded in 2009, and director of more than forty plays, operas, and four films. He also served as curator of the Taipei Poetry Festival since 2004. Among his collections of poetry are* The Homemade Bomb《土製炸彈》 *and* Plowing the Earth on Renai Road《仁愛路犁田》.

Selected from Winter 2020

Hsu Hui-chih (許悔之) *was born Hsu Yu-chi* (許有吉) *in 1966.* A native of Taoyuan, he holds a B.S. in chemical engineering from National Taipei University of Technology (formerly National Taipei Institute of Technology). Formerly the chief editor of the literary supplement of The Liberty Times《自由時報》, UNITAS— A Literary Monthly《聯合文學》, *and UNITAS Publishing Co., he is currently running his own publishing house Unique Route Culture. His publications include* A Formosan Clan《家族》, Deer's Sorrow《有鹿哀愁》, *and* Do Not Go Gentle into That Sorrowful Night《不要溫馴地蹀入，那夜憂傷》. *In 2007, he published a collection of translated poems in Japanese titled* Deer's Sorrow《鹿の哀しみ》.

Selected from Summer 2004, Winter 2020

David VAN DER PEET (范德培) *was born to Dutch and German parents in Trier, Germany. He studied Chinese and Japanese at the University of Trier and received a B.A. in Chinese from National Cheng*

Kung University and an M.A. in Translation from Fu Jen Catholic University. He has been in Taiwan since 1989 and now resides in Tainan as a freelancer.

Selected from Autumn 1978

Yang Mu (楊牧) *is the pen name of Wang Ching-hsien* (王靖獻). *Born in Hualien, Taiwan in 1940, he graduated from Tunghai University and obtained a doctorate from the University of California at Berkeley. For about twenty years he taught at the University of Washington, where he was Professor Emeritus of Comparative Literature. From 1996 to 2001, he was Dean of the College of Humanities and Social Sciences at Dong Hwa University, Hualien, and from 2002 to 2006, he was Director of the Institute of Chinese Literature and Philosophy at the Academia Sinica. He was also Chair Professor of the Graduate Institute of Taiwan Literature at National Chengchi University. Yang Mu received numerous literary awards, including the China Times Prize for Literature, the Dr. Sun Yat-sen Award for Literature and Arts, the Wu Sanlian Literary Award, the National Culture and Arts Award, the Huazong International Chinese Literature Award, the Newman Prize for Chinese Literature, and the Cikada Prize. He authored over fifty works, spanning essays, poetry collections, plays, critiques, translations, and more. He co-founded Hongfan Bookstore with other writers, including Yaxian. On March 13, 2020, Yang Mu passed away at the National Taiwan Hospital in Taipei, at the age of 81.*

Selected from Autumn 1990

LUO Chih-cheng (羅智成), *born in Taipei in 1955, graduated from the Department of Philosophy at National Taiwan University. He holds degrees in Eastern Asian Studies from the University of Wisconsin, Madison. He has held various positions, including deputy editor and contributor at the China Times Human Supplement, deputy editor-in-chief and deputy chief editor at the China Times Evening News. He has founded several radio stations, magazines, and publishing houses. Luo*

Chih-cheng is the author of poetry collections such as The Sketch Book 《畫冊》, Book of Light《光之書》 *and* The Book of Slope《傾斜之書》. *His prose and critiques include works such as* Enlightenment of the Civilization《文明初啟》. *His latest work is the poetry collection* Prophecy Get In The Way《預言又止》.

Selected from Autumn 1992
LIN Wen-yueh (林文月, 1922-2023) *was born in the Japanese concession in Shanghai, and she received her early education in Japanese. Returning to Taiwan in the sixth grade, she began her Mandarin education. She received her M.A. in Chinese literature from National Taiwan University in 1959 and engaged in Chinese and Japanese literary translation since her university days. From 1958 to 1993, while teaching at the Department of Chinese Literature at National Taiwan University, she specialized in Six Dynasties literature and Chinese-Japanese comparative literature. She also taught courses on modern prose. Lin Wen-yueh received various accolades, including the China Times Prize for Literature, the National Culture and Arts Award for Essays and Translation, the Taipei Literary Award, and the 31st Executive Yuan Cultural Award. Her works primarily focus on essays and translations of classical Japanese literature, including* Notes on Nineteen Courses《飲膳札記》 *and* Genji Monogatari《源氏物語》 *by Murasaki Shikibu.*

Selected from Autumn 1992
Pang-yuan CHI (齊邦媛) , *an internationally recognized educator, scholar, and author, is Professor Emerita of English Literature at National Taiwan University in Taipei. A Fulbright scholar to University of Michigan and Indiana University, she was also a guest professor at the Free University of Berlin in 1985. She is the chief editor of* An Anthology of Contemporary Chinese Literature《中華現代文學大系》, *the first comprehensive anthology of modern Chinese literature from Taiwan. Among her collections of literary criticism are* Tears of a Thousand Years《千年之淚》 *and* A Day in the Life《一生中的一天》.

Her autobiography The Great Flowing River—A Memoir of China, from Manchuria to Taiwan《巨流河》 *is heralded as a literary masterpiece and a best-seller in the Chinese-speaking world. From 1992 to 1999, she served as the chief editor of* The Chinese PEN (Taiwan), *later renamed* The Taipei Chinese PEN.

Selected from Spring 2003
PAI Hsien-yung (白先勇), *one of the most accomplished of modern Chinese writers, was born in Guangxi Province in 1937. He graduated from the Department of Foreign Languages and Literature at National Taiwan University and earned his master's degree from the University of Iowa. He later taught at the University of California, Santa Barbara, in the Department of East Asian Languages and Cultural Studies. Pai Hsien-yung is a prolific novelist, essayist, critic, and playwright, with notable works such as* Taipei People《臺北人》, Crystal Boys《孽子》, *and* Even the Tree Isn't the Same《樹猶如此》. *In 1960, he founded the influential magazine* Modern Literature《現代文學》, *significantly impacting the literary scene. Following his retirement from the University of California, Pai Hsien-yung dedicated himself to AIDS prevention initiatives and the revival of Kunqu opera. He reproduced* The Peony Pavilion《牡丹亭》 *that toured extensively, receiving widespread acclaim. Transitioning from a "torchbearer of modern literature," he evolved into a "missionary of traditional opera."*

Selected from Spring 2003
David DETERDING (戴德巍) *was, until recently, Associate Professor at the Universiti Brunei Darussalam, where he taught phonetics and grammar. His wife,* **Ellen** (陳艷玲), *also an able translator, was born and raised in Taiwan.*

Selected from Autumn 2005
LIAO Yu-hui (廖玉蕙), *born in Taichung in 1950, received her Ph.D. in Chinese Literature from Soochow University. She has taught at Chung Cheng Institute of Technology, Soochow University, Shih Hsin*

University and is a retired professor in the department of Language and Creative Writing at National Taipei University of Education. She has won many literary awards, including Dr. Sun Yat-sen Award for Literature and Arts, the Chung Hsing Literary Award for Essays, the Wu Sanlian Literary Award, the National Culture and Arts Award, and the Lucian Wu Award for Essays. Her academic and popular publications include a collection of Tang Dynasty short stories The Tang Dynasty Legends《唐代傳奇》, A Fifty-year-old Princess 《五十歲的公主》, A Teacher Like Me《像我這樣的老師》 *and short lyrical essays, such as* If Memories Were Like the Wind《如果記憶像 風》.

Selected from Autumn 2005

May Li-ming TANG (湯麗明) *received her B.A. in Foreign Languages and Literatures from National Taiwan University and an M.A. in Translation and Interpretation Studies from Fu Jen Catholic University. She has retired from National Kaohsiung First University of Science and Technology and is currently a teacher, freelance translator and interpreter.*

Selected from Spring 2007

LUNG Yingtai (龍應台) *is a writer, literary critic and public intellectual. Lung not only has a large number of devoted readers in her native Taiwan, but her works also have great influence in the Chinese-language world in Hong Kong, China, and North America. Lung entered public service as Taipei City Government's first minister of culture in 1999 and served as Taiwan's inaugural Minister of Culture from 2012-2014. She is author of more than two dozen books, including essays, fiction, reportage, and literary criticism. Her 1985 book,* The Wild Fire《野火集》 *created a major cultural stir for its honest and introspective look at the social and political problems facing contemporary Taiwan society.* Big River, Big Sea: Untold Stories of 1949《大江大海一九四九》, *published in 2009, became a must-read in greater China even though it has been banned in China. She was Hung*

Leung Hao Ling Distinguished Fellow in Humanities at the University of Hong Kong from 2015-2020.

Selected from Spring 2007

Darryl STERK (石岱崙) *holds a Ph.D. in Taiwanese fiction and film from the University of Toronto, with a dissertation on the representation of inter-ethnic romance, and he is now studying translation between Mandarin and Indigenous languages, in particular Seediq. He has taught translation at the University of Alberta and National Taiwan University and is now at Lingnan University in Hong Kong.*

Selected from Spring 2015

Yin Dih (隱地) *was born Ko Ching-hwa* (柯青華) *in Shanghai in 1937 and moved to Taiwan in 1947. He was Editor-in-Chief of* Ching Shi Monthly《青溪雜誌》, New Literature and Arts《新文藝月刊》, *and* Book Review and Bibliography Monthly《書評書目》. *He founded the* Élite Publishing Co. *in 1975 and has been the publisher. He has initiated and edited the publication of* Annual Selections of Novel, Annual Selections of Poetry, *and* Annual Selections of Literary Criticism. *With a writing career spanning over seventy years, Yin Di has authored works such as* Tidal Days《漲潮日》, God-of-the-Day《一日神》, Sleeping Naked in French Style《法式裸睡》, *and* Yin Dih's Flash Fictions《隱地極短篇》, *covering various literary genres such as novels, essays, and poetry. His recent works include the* Thunder Trilogy, *written in the form of diary entries.*

Selected from Spring 2015

Michelle Min-chia WU (吳敏嘉) *was born in Taiwan and raised in New Zealand, Thailand and Korea. She holds an M.A. in translation and interpretation studies from Fu Jen Catholic University, and a B.A. in Foreign Languages and Literatures from National Taiwan University. She is currently Assistant Professor at the Department of Foreign Languages and Literatures at National Taiwan University and a professional conference interpreter who enjoys dabbling in literary* *translation. She is currently the Editor-in-Chief of The Taipei Chinese PEN Quarterly.*

Selected from Autumn 1973

Wen-hsing WANG (王文興, 1939-2023), *a native of Fujian, relocated to Taiwan in 1946. Holding a Master's degree of fine arts from the University of Iowa, he retired as Professor from the Department of Foreign Languages and Literatures of National Taiwan University in Taipei. He has published criticism, essays, and novels. He is best known for his unique and experimental use of words, which gives his writings a distinct artistic style. Among his novels,* Family Catastrophe《家變》 *and* Backed Against the Sea《背海的人》 *generated the most discussion. His latest novel is* Shearing Wings, a History《剪翼史》*. Wang was awarded an honorary doctorate by National Taiwan University in 2007 and received the prestigious Chevalier de la Legion d'honneur from France in 2011. He passed away peacefully at the age of 84, on September 27th, 2023.*

Selected from Autumn 1973

Chu-yun CHEN (陳竺筠) *is a native of Nanking. She received her M.A. degree in National Taiwan University. She is now an associate professor in the Department of Foreign Languages and Literature, National Taiwan University.*

Selected from Summer 1976

LIN Hwai-min (林懷民), *founder and Artistic Director of Cloud Gate Dance Theatre, and also founder of the Department of Dance, Taipei National University of the Arts, studied Chinese opera in his native Taiwan, modern dance in New York City, and classical court dance in Japan and Korea. An internationally renowned choreographer, he has won many awards, including the National Award for Arts, twice, from the National Culture and Arts Foundation, an Honorary Award of Fellowship from the Hong Kong Academy for Performing Arts, and a Lifetime Achievement Award from the Department of Culture of New*

York City. Among his publications is also a collection of short stories,
Cicada《蟬》.

Selected from Summer 1976
Yao-heng HU (胡耀恆)， *born in Hubei province in 1936, China,*
graduated from National Taiwan University with a B.A. in Foreign
Languages and Literatures of. A holder of master's degree from Baylor
University and Ph.D. from Indiana University in Theatre and Drama.
He was the professor at University of Michigan and University of
Melbourne, as well as the associate professor at University of Hawaii.
After returning to Taiwan, he lectured in the Department of Foreign
Languages and Literatures (DFLL) of National Taiwan University, and
the English department of Shih Hsin University. In 1995, he founded
The Graduate Institute of Drama and Theatre and the Department of
Drama and Theatre in National Taiwan University, and thus became
the Emeritus Professor of DFLL and the Department of Drama and
Theatre. Among his publications are History of Western Drama 《西
方戲劇史》， *translation of* Oedipus the King, Agamemnon, and The
Bacchae.

Selected from Winter 1995
CHENG Ching-wen (鄭清文, 1932-2017) *was born in Taoyuan and*
hailed from New Taipei City (formerly Taipei County). He graduated
from the Department of Business at National Taiwan University and
dedicated over 40 years to Hua-nan Commercial Bank, retiring in
1998. Cheng Ching-wen, a significant post-war second-generation
novelist, began his literary career in 1958. Throughout his prolific
writing journey, he contributed 223 short stories, 3 novels, 59 short
fairy tales, 1 long fairy tale, 3 poems, 457 reviews and essays, along
with 37 translated works. His notable publications include The Last
Gentleman《最後的紳士》, Short Stories By Cheng Ching-Wen《鄭
清文小說選》, *and the recipient of the Kiriyama Pacific Rim Book Prize,*
Three-Legged Horse《三腳馬》. *Cheng Ching-wen was honored with*
awards such as the Salinity Region Taiwan Literature Contribution

Award, the Wu Sanlian Literary Award, the National Culture and Arts Award, and the Tongshan Pacific Book Award. On November 4, 2017, Cheng Ching-wen passed away at the age of 85 due to a myocardial infarction.

Selected from Winter 1995

Carlos G. TEE (鄭永康) *is Associate Professor at the Graduate Institute of Translation & Interpretation, National Taiwan Normal University. A three-time recipient of the Liang Shih-chiu Literary Prize for Translation, he has a PhD in Comparative Literature (specialization in Literary Translation Studies, Narratology and James Joyce's Ulysses) from Fu Jen Catholic University. Before joining NTNU, he was full-time Asst. Professor at National Taiwan University and also taught in an adjunct capacity at Fu Jen's graduate program in T&I. He has published a number of translated books on Neoconfucian philosophy, Chinese archaic jade and porcelain as well as refereed monographic papers on Comparative literature, Translation Theory and the Chinese translation of stream of consciousness in James Joyce's Ulysses.*

主編序

　　筆會英譯季刊的出版已經堂堂進入第五十一年。在跨越五十年的這個歷史時間點上回顧，實覺得前人之耕耘誠可謂篳路藍縷。以一個民間團體而承擔起如此重大的文學外譯的文化輸出大任，前輩們若無理想前導、決心推助，實在很難想像如何能堅持五十年，且能持續推陳出新、出版不輟。

　　筆會季刊（曾有《台灣文譯》等名稱，並於2023年春季號改名《譯之華》）自五十一年前由殷張蘭熙女士創刊以來，皆邀請中英文造詣俱佳的優秀譯者，選譯台灣現代文學作品中之傑作出版，並對全球發行。本刊更是全球所有筆會中唯一此類刊物，其餘皆為會員通訊類刊物。季刊所選譯的詩文小說迄今已逾2789篇，篇篇皆為台灣現代文學具代表性的佳作。季刊的發行也涵蓋七洲五洋，廣為人知。若說筆會的季刊是五十年來台灣最重要的文學外譯與文化輸出管道，應當之無愧。

　　值此季刊初越五十周年的時刻，我們編譯了這本中英對照選集，讓讀者朋友們一方面能看到五十年來台灣現代文學演變的概貌，另一方面也能欣賞這些傑作經妙筆迻譯之後的另一種風味。很可惜因為篇幅有限，無法容納大量佳作，因此遺珠可謂散落各處。若欲一睹本刊過去五十年來對台灣文學的整理與譯介，歡迎讀者朋友們參考歷來季刊。

　　最後，特別感謝和碩聯合科技公司董事長　童子賢先生給予慷慨的挹助，讓筆會能夠重獲能量、再求精進。也要感謝老爺酒店集團執行長　沈方正先生對本紀念專書的鼎力資助，讓本書能及時問世，為歷史之見證。

會長　廖咸浩

於青田街星川浮舟

中華民國一一二年十一月十七日星期五

余光中

空山松子[*]

一粒松子落下來
沒有一點預告
該派誰去接它呢？
滿地的松針或松根？
滿坡的亂石或月色？
或是過路的風聲？
　說時遲
　那時快
一粒松子落下來
被整座空山接住

---

* 選自余光中，《余光中幽默詩選》，台北：天下遠見，2008年，頁60-61。

白萩

廣場[*]

所有的群眾一哄而散了
　　　　　　　　回到床上
　　去擁護有體香的女人

而銅像猶在堅持他的主義
對著無人的廣場
振臂高呼

只有風
頑皮地踢著葉子嘻嘻哈哈
在擦拭那些足跡

---
* 選自白萩，《詩廣場》，台中：熱點文化事業，1984年，頁25。

洛夫

寄鞋*

間關千里
寄給你一雙布鞋
一封
無字的信
積了四十多年的話
想說無從說
只好一句句
密密縫在鞋底

這些話我偷偷藏了很久
有幾句藏在井邊
有幾句藏在廚房
有幾句藏在枕頭下
有幾句藏在午夜明滅不定的燈火裡
有的風乾了
有的生霉了
有的掉了牙齒
有的長出了青苔
現在一一收集起來
密密縫在鞋底

---

* 選自洛夫，《因為風的緣故》，台北：聯經，2005年，頁64-67。

鞋子也許嫌小一點
我是以心裁量，以童年
以五更的夢裁量
合不合腳是另一回事
請千萬別棄之
若敝屣
四十多年的思念
四十多年的孤寂
全都縫在鞋底

白靈

風箏[*]

扶搖直上，小小的希望能懸得多高呢
長長一生莫非這樣一場遊戲吧
細細一線，卻想與整座天空拔河
上去再上去，都快看不見了
沿著河堤，我開始拉著天空奔跑

---

[*] 選自白靈，《五行詩及其手稿》，台北：秀威資訊科技，2010年，頁27。

商禽

電鎖[*]

這晚，我住的那一帶的路燈又準時在午夜停電了。

當我在掏鑰匙的時候，好心的計程車司機趁倒車之便把車頭對準我的身後，強烈的燈光將一個中年人濃黑的身影毫不留情的投射在鐵門上，直到我從一串鑰匙中選出了正確的那一支對準我心臟的部位插進去，好心的計程車司機才把車開走。

我也才終於將插在我心臟中的鑰匙輕輕的轉動了一下「卡」，隨即把這段靈巧的金屬從心中拔出來順勢一推斷然的走了進去。

沒多久我便習慣了其中的黑暗。

---

* 選自商禽，《用腳思想》，台北：漢光文化事業，1988年，頁12-13。

羅門

麥堅利堡*

超過偉大的
是人類對偉大已感到茫然

戰爭坐在此哭誰
它的笑聲　曾使七萬個靈魂陷落在比睡眠還深的地帶

太陽已冷　星月已冷　太平洋的浪被炮火煮開也都冷了
史密斯　威廉斯　煙花節光榮伸不出手來接你們回家
你們的名字運回故鄉　比入冬的海水還冷
在死亡的喧噪裏　你們的無救　上帝的手呢
血已把偉大的紀念沖洗了出來
戰爭都哭了　偉大它為什麼不笑
七萬朵十字花　圍成園　排成林　繞成百合的村
在風中不動　在雨裏也不動
沉默給馬尼拉海灣看　蒼白給遊客們的照相機看
史密斯　威廉斯　在死亡紊亂的鏡面上　我只想知道
　　　　那裏是你們童幼時眼睛常去玩的地方
　　　　　　那地方藏有春日的錄音帶與彩色的幻燈片

麥堅利堡　鳥都不叫了　樹葉也怕動
凡是聲音都會使這裏的靜默受擊出血

---

* 選自羅門，《麥堅立堡特輯》，台北：文史哲，1995年，頁3-5。

空間與空間絕緣　　時間逃離鐘錶
這裏比灰暗的天地線還少說話　　永恆無聲
美麗的無音房　　死者的花園　　活人的風景區
神來過　　敬仰來過　　汽車與都市也都來過
而史密斯　　威廉斯　　你們是不來也不去了
靜止如取下擺心的錶面　　看不清歲月的臉
在日光的夜裏　　星滅的晚上
你們的盲睛不分季節地睡著
睡醒了一個死不透的世界
睡熟了麥堅利堡綠得格外憂鬱的草場

死神將聖品擠滿在嘶喊的大理石上
給昇滿的星條旗看　　給不朽看　　給雲看
麥堅利堡是浪花已塑成碑林的陸上太平洋

一幅悲天泣地的大浮彫　　掛入死亡最黑的背景
七萬個故事焚毀於白色不安的顫慄
史密斯　　威廉斯　　當落日燒紅滿野芒果林於昏暮
神都將急急離去　　星也落盡
你們是那裏也不去了
太平洋陰森的海底是沒有門的

梅新

履歷表[*]

籍貫：
這一欄空著先別填
因我一時想不起來
但我確定我是有籍貫的
只是暫時忘了

出生年月日：
那年中國黃曆是閏十月
當兩個十月疊在一起時
也正是我誕生的時候
那年的天氣
母親的話竟成了傳說
她說，剪下的臍帶
立即被凍成了冰塊
落在地上還會擊出點點寒光

學歷：
私塾老師的戒尺下
現今仍壓著我一份證件

---

* 選自梅新，《履歷表》，台北：聯合文學，1997年，頁91-93。

經歷：
荷槍持望眼鏡
蹲在一棵百年的榕樹上
為一個新興豪華的賭場把風
由於寂寞
對空放了一槍
震驚了賭場內的人
我也就因此失了業

這分履歷表
我還沒有貼照片
你要也可以是你的

向明

湘繡被面*
——寄細毛妹

四隻蹁躚的紫燕
兩叢吐蕊的花枝
就這樣淡淡的幾筆
便把你要對大哥說的話
密密繡在這塊薄薄的綢幅上了

好耐讀的一封家書呀
不著一字
折起來不過盈尺
一接就把一顆浮起的心沉了下去

遲疑久久，要不把封紙拆開
一拆，就怕滴血的心跳了出來
最是展開觀看的 那
一床寬大亮麗的綢質被面
一展就開放成一朵花鳥夾道的路
仿佛走上去就可以回家
能這樣很快回家就好
海隅雖美，終究是失土的浮根
久已呆滯的雙目
真需放縱在家鄉無垠的長空

---

* 選自向明，《想回的水》，台北：九歌，1988年，頁165-167。

只是，這綢幅上起伏的褶紋
不正是世途的多舛
路的盡頭仍是海
海的面目，也仍
猙獰

後記：日前細毛三妹自湖南老家輾轉托人帶來親繡被面一
　　　幅，未附隻字說明，因有感而草此詩寄之。

陳義芝

尋淵明*

傳說他裹了頭巾
拄了手杖，越過一片野林
不知去到哪一個鄰家
有人撥開長草跨越桑麻
聽到狗吠雞鳴，看到榆槐桃李
卻找不到他虛掩的那扇門

遇見採薪的問
從前，他是住柴桑
大火燒了屋，現已搬去南村
遇見打漁的問
他酒藏詩書中，命藏琴弦裡
泛舟在平湖划槳在清溪

傳說他種過柳，修過籬
戴了冠冕穿了官袍
為釀酒，一心要種秫稻
巴望穀熟，卻不願為迎迓而折腰
秋來一片落葉飄下庭階
是他說不出口的那句話

---

* 選自陳義芝，《無盡之歌》，新北：INK印刻文學生活雜誌，2020年，頁94-97。

服食沾了露水的菊花
抬頭就看見時常相看的南山
近處有人語，遠處有風煙
更遠是隱隱的殺伐啊爭戰在翻騰
昏黃的天瀰漫無邊際的紅光
照映人心扭曲的溝壑

傳說他夢見一條無人知的河
沒有人跡，不知源自何處
彷彿是一處尚未呱啼的地方
或者竟是他中夜徘徊惆悵的所在
一千重山在霧裡放光
一萬棵樹開滿了桃花

我極目眺望不知名的遠處
孤鷹厲響在天空
一棵老松學他彎腰耕種
是貧士，曾乞食，終是讀書人啊
在動亂的時代我稱他安那其
一個無政府主義者

唉，在現代，不知誰能
與他談話為他斟酒
去哪裡找捕魚的武陵人
去哪裡找採藥的劉子驥
太元年間的桃源村早已消失千百年
這世上還有誰是問津的人

二〇一四年十一月

陳育虹

我叫你敘利亞*
——給 Alan Kurdi, 沙灘上的小男孩

你乖乖趴著睡
嘟著嘴或許想喝水
蹶起的屁股可能有尿兜
紅衫藍褲你睡在沙灘
穿著跑鞋鞋底許多細沙
你跑累了嗎
你在聽一波波浪嗎

（當你出發
前往綺色佳，希臘詩人說**
願你的旅程遙遠
充滿冒險，充滿發現……）

你要前往綺色佳
但沙灘冷冷，不是
你的家，波浪冷冷
沒有你的床
有人抱起你
像一隻祭獻羔羊
你三歲的身體直挺挺不動

---

* 選自李進文編，《創世紀詩雜誌》，185期，台北：創世紀詩雜誌社，2015年，頁29。
**希臘詩人 C.P.Cavafy 詩〈Ithaca 綺色佳〉首三句。

（前往綺色佳。有人
看見你迷航的身體
順著一波波浪
來到度假的博德魯姆）

至少這沙灘沒有戰火
你雙眼微闔，綺色佳仍然
遙遠，但天國很近並且
沒有國界，孩子
我叫你敘利亞
這時，你該在耶和華的懷裡
或者正奔向阿拉

鴻鴻

我現在沒有時間了*
——為抗議勞基法修惡的絕食勞工而作

我現在沒有時間了
時間在你們手裡
一週八天，一年六季
你們是上帝，而我的肋骨和脊椎
已經被你們統統收去

我現在沒有時間了
我會在駕駛的時候睡覺
看護的時候夢遊
蹲馬桶的時候吃便當
抽菸的時候抱小孩
而你們
在開會的時候數錢
度假的時候數錢
打砲的時候數錢
其實根本不用數
榨汁機的鉛管會直接通往
你們家裡的保險箱

---

* 選自凌性傑主編，《2018臺灣詩選》，台北：二魚文化，2019年，頁169。

我現在沒有時間了
鬧鐘在你們手裡
但我不打算交出我手裡的電池
我不打算交出我的脊椎
我不打算交出我的孩子和我自己的
那一點點抬頭看天空的時間
我不打算交出我的天空

土地需要時間才能肥沃
毛蟲需要時間才能變成蝴蝶
我需要時間才能呼吸
你也需要時間
才能認出鏡子裡的自己

許悔之

跳蚤聽法*

我的佛陀，當祢巍巍端坐
如蓄勢的海，不動的山
我卻只聽見蟬嘶盈耳
如浪奔來，淹沒我對祢的呼喚
呼喚祢，我的佛陀
我跟隨祢，聽祢說法四十年
早已知道祢實無一法可說
我也無一法可得
祢是那舟，帶我渡河
河既未渡，如何燒舟？

四十年來，我嗅祢的味
觀祢的形，見法如棄嬰長大
而祢，我的佛陀祢日益消瘦
我聽見祢的骸骨瞬間的崩落

我也有喜，不喜法喜
我是一隻跳蚤，被寬容地
可以活在祢的衣裡，懷抱之中
他們還在聽祢說法
或因羞慚而涕淚悲泣

---

* 選自許悔之，《不要溫馴地踱入，那夜憂傷》，台北：木馬文化，2020年，頁103-
105。

或因體解而讚嘆歡喜
只有我，只有我知道
祢是什麼都再也不能說了

四十年來，我將第一次
悲哀而無畏的
咬嚙祢，吸祢的血
我有法喜，這世界只有我
吮過祢的寶血
我有法悲，因為我吸的是
這世界最後一滴淚

楊牧

瓶中稿[*]

這時日落的方向是西
越過眼前的柏樹。潮水
此岸。但知每一片波浪
都從花蓮開始——那時
也曾驚問過遠方
不知有沒有一個海岸？
如今那彼岸此岸，惟有
飄零的星光

如今也惟有一片星光
照我疲倦的傷感
細問洶湧而來的波浪
可懷念花蓮的沙灘？

不知道一片波浪喧嘩
向花蓮的沙灘——迴流以後
也要經過十個夏天才趕到此？
想必也是一時介入的決心
翻身 那就已成型，忽然
是同樣一片波浪來了
寧靜地溢向這無人的海岸

---

[*] 選自楊牧，《楊牧詩集·I：1956-1974》，台北：洪範，1978年，頁467-470。

如果我靜坐聽潮
觀察每一片波浪的形狀
並 自己的未來寫生
像左手邊這一片小的
莫非是蜉生的魚苗？
像那一片姿態適中的
大概是海草，像遠處
那一片大的，也許是飛魚
奔火於夏天的夜晚

不知道一片波浪
湧向無人的此岸，這時
我應該決定做甚麼最好？
也許還是做他波浪
忽然翻身，一時迴流
介入寧靜的海
溢上花蓮的
沙灘

然則，當我涉足入海
輕微的質量不減，水位漲高
彼岸的沙灘當更濕了一截
當我繼續前行，甚至淹沒於
無人的此岸七尺以西
不知道六月的花蓮啊花蓮
是否又謠傳海嘯？

羅智成

父親*

「我一直想為您寫首詩，
　但是我們互愛的秘密
　是不容被揮霍的家當。」

有一天我們要走到大湖之濱
在祂忙於清點群魚時
幫祂清點香花和水鳥
當星星盥洗而昇
我們以顛沛的靈魂
幫祂測量土壤：
那時，我們蹲坐田壟
豐盛的眸光
和帶著風吹草動的寂靜
交談。安詳的笑容隨夜空緩轉
有一天我們將從子嗣們的
耕地裡出生
不再悲觀地歌詠肉體。
我們的福祐傳遞給後輩
頑強底額頭——
如果我們不曾阻止烈日
烈日鑄造他們的雙肩
如果我們不曾阻止洪水

---

* 選自羅智成《光之書》，台北：天下文化，2000年，頁172-173。

洪水給他們一箱箱
眉頭深鎖著的智慧

有一天有們將到天空去
屯墾
在星宿間圈我們的田
修我們的縣志。
修我們的菜園。
此刻，請看我
我銀色的額頭因熟睡而，融化

牲畜們在我枕邊飲水
村婦以波光編結魚網
在大湖之濱
再緊繡的夜幕也不能籠蓋的
這曠沃之土，您看
遠處的黎明，就是夜他捉襟見肘的地方

父親，而我們的家族
將蔚為森林
像在時間之海裡高舉的机檣

林文月

溫州街到溫州街*

　　從溫州街七十四巷鄭先生的家到溫州街十八巷的臺先生家，中間僅隔一條辛亥路，步調快的話，大約七、八分鐘便可走到，即使漫步，最多也費不了一刻鐘的時間。但那一條車輛飆馳的道路，卻使兩位上了年紀的老師視為畏途而互不往來頗有年矣！早年的溫州街是沒有被切割的，臺灣大學的許多教員宿舍便散布其間。我們的許多老師都住在那一帶。閒時，他們經常會散步，穿過幾條人跡稀少的巷弄，互相登門造訪，談天說理。時光流逝，臺北市的人口大增，市容劇變，而我們的老師也都年紀在八十歲以上了，辛亥路遂成為咫尺天涯，鄭先生和臺先生平時以電話互相問安或傳遞消息；偶爾見面，反而是在更遠的各種餐館，兩位各由學生攙扶接送，筵席上比鄰而坐，常見到他們神情愉快地談笑。

　　三年前仲春的某日午後，我授完課順道去拜訪鄭先生。當時《清畫堂詩集》甫出版，鄭先生掩不住喜悅之情，叫我在客廳稍候，說要書房去取一本已題簽好的送給我。他緩緩從沙發椅中起身，一邊念叨著：「近來，我的雙腿更衰弱沒力氣了。」然後，小心地蹭蹭地在自己家的走廊上移步。望著那身穿著中式藍布衫的單薄背影，我不禁又一次深刻地感慨歲月擲人而去的悲哀與無奈！

　　《清畫堂詩集》共收鄭先生八十二歲以前的各體古詩千餘首，並親為之註解，合計四八八頁，頗有一些沈甸甸的重量。我從他微顫的手

＊ 選自林文月，《作品》，台北：九歌，1993年，頁139-148。

中接到那本設計極其清雅的詩集，感激又敬佩地分享著老師新出書的喜悅。我明白這本書從整理，謄寫，到校對、殺青，費時甚久；老師是十分珍視此詩集的出版，有意以此傳世的。

是我也掩不住興奮地翻閱書頁，鄭先生用商量的語氣問我：「我想親自送一本給臺先生。你哪天有空，開車送我去臺先生家好嗎？」封面有臺先生工整的隸書題字，鄭先生在自序末段寫著：「老友臺靜農先生，久已聲明謝絕為人題寫書簽，見於他所著《龍坡雜文》〈我與書藝〉篇中，這次為我破例，尤為感謝。」但我當然明白，想把新出版的詩集親自送到臺先生手中，豈是僅止於感謝的心理而已；陶潛詩云：「奇文共欣賞，疑義相與析。」何況，這是蘊藏了鄭先生大半生心血的書，他內心必然迫不及待地要與老友分享那成果的吧。

我們當時便給臺先生打電話，約好就在那個星期日的上午十時，由我駕車接鄭先生去臺先生的家。其所以挑選星期日上午，一來是放假日子人車較少，開車安全些；再則是鄭先生家裏有人在，不必擔心空屋無人看管。

記得那是一個春陽和煦的星期日上午。出門前，我先打電話給鄭先生，請他準備好。我依時到溫州街七十四巷，把車子停放於門口，下車與鄭先生的女婿顧崇豪共同扶他上車，再繞到駕駛座位上。鄭先生依然是那一襲藍布衫，手中謹慎地捧著詩集。他雖然戴著深度近視眼鏡，可是記性特別好，從車子一發動，便指揮我如何左轉右轉駛出曲折而狹窄的溫州街；其實，那些巷弄對我而言，也是極其熟悉的。在辛亥路的南側停了一會兒，等交通號誌變綠燈後，本擬直駛到對面的溫州街，但是鄭先生問：「現在過了辛亥路沒有？」又告訴我：「過了辛亥路，你就右轉，到了巷子底再左轉，然後順著下去就可以到臺先生家了。」我有些遲疑，這不是我平常走的路線，但老師的語氣十分肯定，就像許多年前教我們課時一般，便只好依循他的指示駕駛。結果竟走到一個禁止左轉的巷道，遂不得不退回原路，重新依照我所認識的路線行駛。鄭先生得悉自己的指揮有誤，連聲向我道歉。「不是您的記性不好，是近年來臺北的交通變化太大。您說的是從前的走法；如今許多巷道都有限制，不準隨便左轉或右轉的。」我用安慰的語氣說。「唉，好些年沒來看臺先生，路竟然都不認得走了。」他有些感慨的樣子，習慣地用右手掌摩挲光禿的前額說。「其實，是您的記性太好，記得從前的路啊。」我又追添一句安慰的話，心中一陣酸楚，不知這樣的安慰妥當與否？

崇豪在鄭先生上車後即給臺先生打了電話，所以車轉入溫州街十八巷時，遠遠便望見臺先生已經站在門口等候著。由於我小心慢駛，又改道耽誤時間，性急的臺先生大概已等候許久了吧？十八巷內兩側都停放著私家小轎車，我無法在只容得一輛車通行的巷子裏下車，故只好將右側車門打開，請臺先生扶鄭先生先行下車，再繼續開往前面去找停車處。車輪慢慢滑動，從照後鏡裏瞥見身材魁梧的臺先生正小心攙扶著清癯而微傴的鄭先生跨過門檻。那是一個有趣的形象對比，也是頗令人感覺溫馨的一個鏡頭。臺先生比鄭先生年長四歲，不過，從外表看起來，鄭先生步履蹣跚，反而顯得蒼老些。

待我停妥車子，推開虛掩的大門進入書房時，兩位老師都已端坐在各自適當的位置上了——臺先生穩坐在書桌前的籐椅上，鄭先生則淺坐在對面的另一張籐椅上。兩人夾著一張寬大的桌面相對晤談著；那上面除雜陳的書籍、硯臺、筆墨，和茶杯、菸灰缸外，中央清出的一塊空間正攤開著《清晝堂詩集》。臺先生前前後後地翻動書頁，急急地誦讀幾行詩句，隨即又看看封面看看封底，時則又音聲宏亮地讚賞：「哈啊，這句子好，這句子好！」鄭先生前傾著身子，背部微駝，從厚重的鏡片後瞇起雙眼盯視臺先生。他不大言語，鼻孔裏時時發出輕微的喀嗯喀嗯聲。那是他高興或專注的時候常有的表情，譬如在一篇學生的佳作時，或聽別人談說一些趣事時；而今，他正十分在意老友臺先生對於他甫出版詩集的看法。我忽然完全明白了，古人所謂「奇文共欣賞」，便是眼前這樣一幕情景。

我安靜地靠牆坐在稍遠處，啜飲杯中微涼的茶，想要超然而客觀地欣賞那一幕情景，卻終於無法不融入兩位老師的感應世界裏，似乎也分享得他們的喜悅與友誼，也終於禁不住地眼角溫熱濕潤起來。

　　日後，臺先生曾有一詩讚賞《清畫堂詩集》：

　　千首詩成南渡後，精深雋雅自堪傳。
　　詩家更見開新例，不用他人作鄭箋。

　　鄭先生的千首詩固然精深雋雅，而臺先生此詩中用「鄭箋」的典故，更是神來之筆，實在是巧妙極了。

　　其實，兩位老師所談並不多，有時甚至會話中斷，而呈現一種留白似的時空。大概他們平常時有電話聯繫互道消息，見面反而沒有什麼特別新鮮的話題了吧？抑或許是相知太深，許多想法盡在不言中，此時無聲勝有聲嗎？

　　約莫半個小時左右的會面晤談。鄭先生說：「那我走了。」「也好。」臺先生回答得也簡短。

　　回鄭先生家的方式一如去臺先生家時。先請臺先生給崇豪、秉書夫婦打電話，所以開車到達溫州街七十四巷時，他們兩位已等候在門口；這次沒有下車，目送鄭先生被他的女兒和女婿護迎入家門後，便踩足油門駛回自己的家。待返抵自己的家後，我忽然冒出一頭大汗來。覺得自己膽子真是大，竟然敢承諾接送一位眼力不佳，行動不甚靈活的八十餘歲老先生於擁擠緊張的臺北市區中；但是，又彷彿完成了一件大事情而心情十分輕鬆愉快起來。

　　那一次，可能是鄭先生和臺先生的最後一次相訪晤對。

　　鄭先生的雙腿後來愈形衰弱；而原來硬朗的臺先生竟忽然罹患惡疾，纏綿病榻九個月之後，於去秋逝世。

　　公祭之日，鄭先生左右由崇豪與秉書扶侍著，一清早便神色悲戚地坐在靈堂的前排席位上。他是公祭開始時第一位趨前行禮的人。那原本單薄的身子更形單薄了，多時沒有穿用的西裝，有如掛在衣架上似的鬆動著。他的步履幾乎沒有著地，全由女兒與女婿架起，危危顛顛地挪移至靈壇前，一路慟哭著，涕淚盈襟，使所有在場的人倍覺痛心。我舉首望見四面牆上滿布的輓聯，鄭先生的一副最是真切感人：

六十年來文酒深交弔影今為後死者

八千里外山川故國傷懷同是不歸人

　　那一個仲春上午的景象，歷歷猶在目前，實不能相信一切是真實的事情！

　　臺先生走後，鄭先生更形落寞寡歡。一次拜訪之際，他告訴我：「臺先生走了，把我的一半也帶走了。」語氣令人愕然。「這話不是誇張。從前，我有什麼事情，總是打電話同臺先生商量；有什麼記不得的事情，打電話給他，即使他也不記得，但總有些線索打聽。如今，沒有人好商量了！沒有人可以尋問打聽了！」鄭先生彷彿為自己的詩作註解似的，更為他那前面的話作補充。失去六十年文酒深交的悲哀，絲毫沒有掩飾避諱地烙印在他的形容上、迴響在他的音聲裏。我試欲找一些安慰的話語，終於也只有惻然陪侍一隅而已。腿力更為衰退的鄭先生，即使居家也須倚賴輪椅，且不得不雇用專人伺候了。在黃昏暗淡的光線下，他陷坐輪椅中，看來十分寂寞而無助。我想起他〈詩人的寂寞〉啟首的幾句話：「千古詩人都是寂寞的，若不是寂寞，他們就寫不出詩來。」鄭先生是詩人，他老年失友，而自己體力又愈形退化，又豈單是寂寞而已？近年來，他談話的內容大部分圍繞著自己老化的生理狀況，又雖然緩慢卻積極地整理著自己的著述文章，可以感知他內心存在著一種不可言喻的又無可奈何的焦慮。

　　今年暑假開始的時候，我因有遠行，準備了一盒鄭先生喜愛的鬆軟甜點，打電話想徵詢可否登門辭行。豈知接電話的是那一位護佐，她勸阻我說：「你們老師在三天前突然失去了記憶力，躺在牀上，不方便會客。」這真是太突然的消息，令我錯愕良久。「這種病很危險嗎？可不可以維持一段時日？會不會很痛苦？」我一連發出了許多疑問，眼前閃現兩周前去探望時雖然衰老但還談說頗有條理的影像，覺得這是老天爺開的玩笑，竟讓記性特好的人忽然喪失記憶。「這種事情很難說，有人可以維持很久，但是也有人很快就不好了。」她以專業的經驗告訴我。

旅次中，我忐忑難安，反覆思考著：希望回臺之後還能夠見到我的老師，但是又恐怕體質比較薄弱的鄭先生承受不住長時的病情煎熬；而臺先生纏綿病榻的痛苦記憶又難免重疊出現於腦際。

七月二十八日清晨，我接獲中文系同事柯慶明打給我的長途電話。鄭先生過世了。慶明知道我離臺前最焦慮難安的心事，故他一再重複說：「老師是無疾而終。走得很安詳，很安詳。」

九月初的一個深夜，我回來。次晚，帶了一盒甜點去溫州街七十四巷。秉書與我見面擁泣。她為我細述老師最後的一段生活以及當天的情形。鄭先生果然是走得十分安詳。我環顧那間書籍整齊排列，畫畫垂掛牆壁的客廳。一切都沒有改變。也許，鄭先生過世時我沒有在臺北，未及瞻仰遺容，所以親耳聽見，也不能信以為真。有一種感覺，彷彿當我在沙發椅坐定後，老師就會輕咳著、步履維艱地從裏面的書房走出來；雖是步履維艱，卻不必倚賴輪椅的鄭先生。

我辭出如今已經不能看見鄭先生的溫州街七十四巷，信步穿過辛亥路，然後走到對面的溫州街。秋意尚未的臺北夜空，有星光明滅，但周遭四處飄著悶熱的暑氣。我又一次非常非常懷念三年前仲春的那個上午，淚水便禁不住地婆娑而往下流。我在巷道中忽然駐足。溫州街十八巷也不再能見到臺先生了。而且，據說那一幢日式木屋已不存在，如今鋼筋水泥的一大片高樓正在加速建造中；自臺先生過世後，實在不敢再走過那一帶地區。我又緩緩走向前，有時閃身讓車輛通過。

不知道走了多少時間，終於來到溫州街十八巷口。夜色迷濛中，果然矗立著一大排未完工的大廈。我站在約莫是從前六號的遺址。定神凝睇，覺得那粗糙的水泥牆柱之間，當有一間樸質的木屋書齋；又定神凝睇，覺得那木屋書齋之中，當有兩位可敬的師長晤談。於是，我彷彿聽到他們的談笑親切，而且彷彿也感受到春陽煦暖了。

白先勇

樹猶如此[*]
——紀念亡友王國祥君

我家後院西隅近籬笆處曾經種有一排三株義大利柏樹。這種義大利柏樹（Italian Cypress）原本生長於南歐地中海畔，與其他松柏皆不相類。樹的主幹筆直上伸，標高至六、七十呎，但橫枝並不恣意擴張，兩人合抱，便把樹身圈住了，於是擎天一柱，平地拔起，碧森森像座碑塔，孤峭屹立，甚有氣勢。南加州濱海一帶的氣候，溫和似地中海，這類義大利柏樹，隨處可見。有的人家，深宅大院，柏樹密植成行，遠遠望去，一片蒼鬱，如同一堵高聳雲天的牆垣。

我是一九七三年春遷入「隱谷」這棟住宅來的。這個地區叫「隱谷」（Hidden Valley），因為三面環山，林木幽深，地形又相當隱蔽，雖然位於市區，因為有山丘屏障，不易發覺。當初我按報上地址尋找這棟房子，彎彎曲曲，迷了幾次路才發現，原來山坡後面，別有洞天，谷中隱隱約約，竟是一片住家。那日黃昏驅車沿著山坡駛進「隱谷」，迎面青山綠樹，只覺得是個清幽所在，萬沒料到，谷中一住迄今，長達二十餘年。

巴塞隆納道（Barcelona Drive）九百四十號在斜坡中段，是一幢很普通的平房。人跟住屋也得講緣分，這棟房子，我第一眼便看中了，主要是為著屋前屋後的幾棵大樹。屋前一棵寶塔松，龐然矗立，頗有年分，屋後一對中國榆，搖曳生姿，有點垂柳的風味，兩側的灌木叢又將鄰舍完全隔離，整座房屋都有樹蔭庇護，我歡這種隱遮樹叢中的房

* 選自白先勇，《樹猶如此》，台北：天下遠見，2008年，頁12-34。

屋，而且價錢剛剛合適，當天便放下了定洋。

房子本身保養得還不錯、不須修補。問題出在園子裡的花草。屋主偏愛常春藤，前後院種滿了這種藤葛，四處竄爬。常春藤的生命力強韌驚人，要拔掉煞費工夫，還有雛菊、罌粟、木槿都不是我喜愛的花木，全部根除，工程浩大，絕非我一人所能勝任。幸虧那年暑假，我中學時代的至友王國祥從東岸到聖芭芭拉來幫我，兩人合力把我「隱谷」這座家園，重新改造，遍植我屬意的花樹，才奠下日後園子發展的基礎。

王國祥那時正在賓州州立大學做博士後研究，只有一個半月的假期，我們卻足足做了三十天的園藝工作。每天早晨九時開工，一直到傍晚五、六點鐘才鳴金收兵，披荊斬棘，去蕪存菁，清除了幾卡車的廢枝雜草，終於把花園理出一個輪廓來。我與國祥都是生手，不慣耕勞，一天下來，腰痠背痛。幸虧聖芭芭拉夏天涼爽，在和風煦日下，胼手胝足，實在算不上辛苦。

聖芭芭拉附近產酒，有一家酒廠釀製一種杏子酒（Aprivert），清香甘洌，是果子酒中的極品，冰凍後，特別爽口。鄰舍有李樹一株，枝椏一半伸到我的園中，這棵李樹真是異種，是牛血李，肉紅汁多，味甜如蜜，而且果實特大。那年七月，一樹纍纍，掛滿了小紅球，委實誘人。開始我與國祥還有點顧忌，到底是人家的果樹，光天化日之下，採摘鄰居的果子，不免心虛。後來發覺原來加州法律規定，長過了界的樹木，便算是這一邊的產物。有了法律根據，我們便架上長梯，國祥爬上樹去，我在下面接應，一下工夫，我們便採滿了一桶殷紅光鮮的果實。收工後，夕陽西下，清風徐來、坐在園中草坪上，啜杏子酒，啖牛血李，一日的疲勞、很快也就恢復了。

聖芭芭拉（Santa Barbara）有「太平洋的天堂」之稱，這個城的山光水色的確有令人流連低徊之處，但是我覺得這個小城的一個好處是海產豐富：石頭蟹、硬背蝦、海膽、鮑魚，都屬本地特產，尤其是石頭蟹，殼堅、肉質細嫩鮮甜，而且還有一雙巨螯，真是聖芭芭拉的美味。那個時候美國人還不很懂得吃帶殼螃蟹，碼頭上的魚市場，生猛螃蟹，團臍一元一隻，尖臍一隻不過一元半。王國祥是浙江人，生平就好這一樣東西，我們每次到碼頭魚市，總要攜回四、五隻巨蟹，蒸著吃。蒸蟹第一講究是火候、過半分便老了，少半分又不熟。王國祥蒸螃蟹全憑直覺、他注視著蟹殼漸漸轉紅叫一聲「好！」將螃蟹從鍋中一把提起，十拿九穩，正好蒸熟。然後佐以薑絲米醋，再燙一壺紹興酒，那便是我們的晚餐。那個暑假，我和王國祥起碼饕掉數打石頭蟹。那年我剛拿到終身教職，《台北人》出版沒有多久。國祥自加大柏克萊畢業後，到賓州州大去做博士後研究是他第一份工作，那時他對理論物理還充滿了信心熱忱、我們憧憬，人生前景是金色的，未來命運的凶險，我們當時渾然未覺。

　　園子整頓停當，選擇花木卻頗費思量。百花中我獨鍾茶花。茶花高貴，白茶雅潔，紅茶穠麗，粉茶花俏生生、嬌滴滴，自是惹人憐惜。即使不開花，一樹碧亭亭，也是好看。茶花起源於中國，盛產雲貴高原，後經歐洲才傳到美國來。茶花性喜溫濕，宜酸性土，聖芭芭拉恰好屬於美國的茶花帶，因有海霧調節，這裡的茶花長得分外豐蔚。我們遂決定，園中草木以茶花為主調，於是遍搜城中苗圃，最後才選中了三十多株各色品種的幼木。美國茶花的命名、有時也頗具匠心：白茶叫「天鵝湖」，粉茶花叫「嬌嬌女」，有一種紅茶名為「艾森豪威爾將軍」——這是十足的美國茶，我後院栽有一棵，後來果然長得偉岸嶔奇，巍巍然有大將之風。

　　花種好了，最後的問題只剩下後院西隅的一塊空地，屋主原來在此搭了一架鞦韆，架子撤走後便留空白一角。因為地區不大，不能容納體積太廣的樹木，王國祥建議：「這裡還是種Italian Cypress吧。」這倒是好主意，義大利柏樹占地不多，往空中發展，前進無量。我們買了三株幼苗，沿著籬笆，種了一排。剛種下去，才三、四呎高，國祥：「這三棵柏樹長大，一定會超過你園中其他的樹！」果真，三棵義大利柏樹日後抽發得傲視群倫，成為我花園中的地標。

　　十年樹木，我園中的花木，欣欣向榮，逐漸成形。那期間，王國祥已數度轉換工作，他去過加拿大、又轉德州。他的博士後研究並不順遂，理論物理是門高深學問，出路狹窄，美國學生視為畏途，念的人少，教職也相對有限，那幾年美國大學預算緊縮，一職難求，只有幾家名校的物理系才有理論物理的職位，很難擠進去，亞利桑拿州立大學曾經有意聘請王國祥，但他卻拒絕了。當年國祥在台大選擇理論物理，多少也是受到李政道、楊振寧獲得諾貝爾獎的鼓勵。後來他進柏克萊，曾跟隨名師，當時柏克萊物理系竟有六位諾貝爾獎得主的教授。名校名師，王國祥對自己的研究當然也就期許甚高。當他發覺他在理論物理方面的研究無法達成重大突破，不可能做一個頂尖的物理學家，他就斷然放棄物理，轉行到高科技去了。當然，他一生最高的理想未能實現，這一直是他的一個隱痛。後來他在洛杉磯休斯（Hughes）公司找到一份安定工作，研究人造衛星。波斯灣戰爭，美國軍隊用的人造衛星就是休斯製造的。

那幾年王國祥有假期常常來聖芭芭拉小住，他一到我家，頭一件事便要到園中去察看我們當年種植的那些花木。他隔一陣子來，看到後院那三株義大利柏樹，就不禁驚嘆：「哇，又長高了好多！」柏樹每年升高十幾呎，幾年間，便標到了頂，成為六、七十呎的巍峨大樹。三棵中又以中間那棵最為茁壯，要高出兩側一大截，成了一個山字形。山谷中，濕度高，柏樹出落得蒼翠欲滴，夕照的霞光映在上面，金碧輝煌，很是醒目。三四月間，園中的茶花全部綻放，樹上綴滿了白天鵝，粉茶花更是嬌艷光鮮，我的花園終於春意盎然起來。

一九八九年，歲屬馬年，那是個凶年，那年夏天，中國大陸發生了天安門「六四」事件，成千上百的年輕生命瞬息消滅。那一陣子天天看電視全神貫注事件的發展，很少到園中走動。有一天，我突然發覺後院三棵義大利柏樹中間那一株，葉尖露出點點焦黃來。起先我以為暑天乾熱，植物不耐旱，沒料到才是幾天工夫，一棵六、七十呎的大樹，如遭天火雷殛，驟然間通體枯焦而亡。那些針葉，一觸便紛紛斷落，如此孤標傲世風華正茂的常青樹，數日之間竟至完全壞死。奇怪的是，兩側的柏樹卻好端端的依舊青蒼無恙，只是中間赫然豎起槁木一柱，實在令人觸目驚心，我只好教人來把枯樹砍掉拖走。從此，我後院的兩側，便出現了一道缺口。柏樹無故枯亡，使我鬱鬱不樂了好些時日，心中總感到不祥，似乎有甚麼奇禍即將降臨一般，沒有多久，王國祥便生病了。

那年夏天，國祥一直咳嗽不止，他到美國二十多年，身體一向健康、連傷風感冒也屬罕有。他去看醫生檢查，驗血出來，發覺他的血紅素竟比常人少了一半，一公升只有六克多。接著醫生替他抽骨髓化驗，結果出來後，國祥打電話給我：「我的舊病又復發了，醫生說，是『再生不良性貧血』。」國祥說話的時候，聲音還很鎮定，他一向臨危不亂，有科學家的理性與冷靜，可是我聽到那個長長的奇怪病名，就不由得心中一寒，一連串可怕的記憶，又湧了回來。

許多年前，一九六〇年的夏天，一個清晨，我獨自趕到台北中心診所的血液科去等候化驗結果，血液科主任黃天賜大夫出來告訴我：「你的朋友王國祥患了『再生不良性貧血』。」那是我第一次聽到這個陌生的病名。黃大夫大概看見我滿面茫然，接著對我詳細解說了番「再生不良性貧血」的病理病因。這是一種罕有的貧血症，骨髓造血機能失調，無法製造足夠的血細胞，所以紅血球、血小板、紅血素等統統偏低。這種血液病的起因也很複雜，物理、化學、病毒各種因素皆有可能。最後黃大夫十分嚴肅的告訴我：「這是一種很嚴重的貧血症。」的確，這棘手的血液病，迄至今日，醫學突飛猛進，仍舊沒有發明可以根除的特效藥，一般治療只能用激素刺激骨髓造血的機能。另外一種治療法便是骨髓移植，但是台灣那個年代，還沒有聽說過這種事情。那天我走出中心診所，心情當然異常沉重，但當時年輕無知，對這種症病的嚴重性並不真正了解，以為只要不是絕症，總還有希望治癒。事實上，「再生不良性貧血」患者的治癒率，是極低極低的，大概只有百分之五的人，會莫名其妙自己復元。

王國祥第一次患「再生不良性貧血」時在台大物理系正要上三年級，這樣一來只好休學，而這一休便是兩年。國祥的病勢開始相當險惡，每個月都需到醫院去輸血，每次起碼五百CC。由於血小板過低，凝血能力不佳，經常牙齦出血、甚至眼球也充血，視線受到障礙。王國祥的個性中，最突出的便是他爭強好勝，永遠不肯服輸的戇直脾氣，是他倔強的意志力，幫他暫時抵擋住排山倒海而來的病災。那時我只能在一旁替他加油打氣，給他精神支持。他的家已遷往台中，他一個人寄居在台北親戚家養病，因為看醫生方便。常常下課後，我便從台大騎了腳踏車去潮州街探望他，那時我剛與班上同學創辦了《現代文學》，正處在士氣高昂的奮亢狀態，我跟國祥談論的，當然也就是我辦雜誌的點點滴滴。國祥看見我興致勃勃，他是高興的，病中還替《現代文學》拉了兩個訂戶，而且也成為這本雜誌的忠實讀者。事實上國祥對《現代文學》的貢獻不小，這本賠錢雜誌時常有經濟危機，我初到加州大學當講師那幾年，因為薪水有限，為籌雜誌的印刷費，經常捉襟見肘。國祥在柏克萊念博士拿的是全額獎學金，一個月有四百多塊生活費。他知道我的困境後，每月都會省下一兩百塊美金寄給我接濟《現文》，而且持續了很長一段時間。他的家境不算富裕，在當時，那是很不小的一筆數目。如果沒有他長期的「經援」，《現代文學》恐怕早已停刊。

我與王國祥十七歲結識，那時我們都在建國中學念高二，一開始我們之間便有種異姓手足禍福同當的默契。高中畢業，本來我有保送台大的機會，因為要念水利，夢想日後到長江三峽去築水壩，而且又等不及要離開家，追尋自由，於是便申請保送台南成功大學，那時只有成大才有水利系。王國祥也有這個念頭，他是他們班上的高材生，考台大，應該不成問題，他跟我商量好便也投考成大電機系。我們在學校附近一個軍眷村裡租房子住，過了一年自由自在的大學生活，後來因為興趣不合，我重考台大外文系，回到台北。國祥在成大多念了一年，也耐不住了，他發覺他真正的志向是研究理論科學，工程並非所好，於是他便報考台大的轉學試，轉物理系。當年轉學、轉系又轉院，難如登天，尤其是台大，王國祥居然考上了，而且只錄取了他一名。我們正在慶幸，兩人懵懵懂懂，一番折騰，幸好最後都考上與自己興趣相符的校系。可是這時王國祥卻偏偏遭罹不幸，患了這種極為罕有的血液病。

西醫治療一年多，王國祥的病情並無起色，而治療費用的昂貴已使得他的家庭日漸陷入困境，正當他的親人感到束手無策的時刻，國祥卻遇到了救星。他的親戚打聽到江南名醫奚復一大夫醫治好一位韓國僑生，同樣也患了「再生不良性貧血」，病況還要嚴重，西醫已放棄了，卻被奚大夫治癒。我從小看西醫，對中醫不免偏見。奚大夫開給國祥的藥方裡，許多味草藥中，竟有一劑犀牛角，當時我不懂得犀牛角是中藥的涼血要素，不禁嘖嘖稱奇，而且小小一包犀牛角粉，價值不菲。但國祥服用奚大夫的藥後，竟然一天天好轉，半年後已不需輸血。很多年後，我跟王國祥在美國，有一次到加州聖地牙哥世界聞名的動物園去觀覽百獸，園中有一群犀牛族，大大小小七隻，那是我第一次真正看到這種神奇的野獸，我沒想到近距離觀看，犀牛的體積如此龐大，而且皮之堅厚，似同披甲帶鎧，鼻端一角聳然，如利斧朝天，神態很是威武。大概因為犀牛角曾治療過國祥的病，我對那一群看來兇猛異常的野獸，竟有一分說不出的好感，在欄前盤桓良久才離去。

我跟王國祥都太過樂觀了，以為「再生不良性貧血」早已成為過去的夢魘，國祥是屬於那百分之五的幸運少數。萬沒料到，這種頑強的疾病，竟會潛伏二十多年，如同酣睡已久的妖魔，突然甦醒，張牙舞爪反撲過來。而國祥畢竟已年過五十，身體抵抗力比起少年時，自然相差許多，舊病復發，這次形勢更加險竣。自此，我與王國祥便展開了長達三年，共同抵禦病魔的艱辛日子，那是一場生與死的搏鬥。

鑒於第一次王國祥的病是中西醫合治醫好的，這一次我們當然也就依照舊法。國祥把二十多年前奚復一大夫的那張藥方找了出來，並託台北親友拿去給奚大夫鑑定，奚大夫更動了幾樣藥，並加重分量；黃芪、生熟地、黨參、當歸、首烏等都是一些補血調氣的草藥，方子中也保留了犀牛角。幸虧洛杉磯的蒙特利公園市的中藥行這些藥都買得到。有一家叫「德成行」的老字號，是香港人開的，貨色齊全，價錢公道。那幾年，我替國祥去檢藥，進進出出，「德成行」的老闆夥計也都熟了。因為犀牛屬於受保護的稀有動物，在美國犀牛角是禁賣的。開始「德成行」的夥計還不肯拿出來，我們懇求了半天，才從一隻上鎖的小鐵匣中取出一塊犀牛角，用來磨些粉賣給我們。但經過二十多年，國祥的病況已大不同，而且人又不在台灣，沒能讓大夫把脈，藥方的改動，自然無從掌握。這一次，服中藥並無速效。但三年中，國祥並未停用過草藥，因為西醫也並沒有特效治療方法，還是跟從前一樣，使用各種激素；我們跟醫生曾討論過骨髓移植的可能，但醫生認為，五十歲以上的病人，骨髓移植風險太大，而且尋找血型完全相符的骨髓贈者，難如海底撈針。

那三年，王國祥全靠輸血維持生命，有時一個月得輸兩次。我們的心情也就跟著他血紅素的數字上下而陰晴不定。如果他的血紅素維持在九以上，我們就稍寬心，但是一旦降到六，就得準備，那個週末，又要進醫院去輸血了。國祥的保險屬於凱撒公司（Kaiser Permanente），是美國最大的醫療系統之一。凱撒在洛杉磯城中心的總部是一連串延綿數條街的龐然大物，那間醫院如同一座迷宮，進去後，轉幾個彎，就不知身在何方了。我進出那間醫院不下四、五十次，但常常闖進完全陌生地帶，跑到放射科、耳鼻喉科去。因為醫院每棟建築的外表都一模一樣，一整排的玻璃門窗反映著冷冷的青光。那是一座卡夫卡式超現代建築物，進到裡面，好像誤入外星。

因為輸血可能有反應，所以大多數時間王國祥去醫院，都是由我開車接送。幸好每次輸血時間定在週末星期六，我可以在星期五課後開車下洛杉磯國祥住處，第二天清晨送他去。輸血早上八點鐘開始，五百CC輸完要到下午四、五點鐘了，因此早上六點多就要離開家。洛杉磯大得可怕，隨便到哪裡，高速公路上開一個鐘頭車是很平常的事，尤其在早上上班時間，十號公路塞車是有名的。住在洛杉磯的人，生命大部分都耗在那八爪魚似的公路網上。由於早起，我陪著王國祥輸血時，耐不住要打個盹，但無論睡去多久，一張開眼，看見的總是架子上懸掛著的那一袋血漿，殷紅的液體，一滴一滴，順著塑膠管往下流，注入國祥臂彎的靜脈裡去。那點點血漿，像時間漏斗的水滴，無窮無盡，永遠滴不完似的。但是王國祥躺在床上卻能安安靜靜的接受那八個小時生命漿液的挹注。他兩隻手臂彎上的靜脈都因針頭插入過分頻繁而經常瘀青紅腫，但他從來也沒有過半句怨言。王國祥承受痛苦的耐力驚人，當他喊痛的時候，那必然是痛苦已經不是一般人所能負荷的了。我很少看到像王國祥那般能隱忍的病人，他這種斯多葛（Stoic）式的精神是由於他超強的自尊心，不願別人看到他病中的狼狽。而且他跟我都了解到這是一場艱鉅無比的奮鬥，需要我們兩個人所有的信心、理性，以及意志力來支撐。我們絕對不能向病魔示弱，露出膽怯，我們在一起的時候，似乎一直在互相告誡：要挺住，鬆懈不得。

事實上，只要王國祥的身體狀況許可，我們也盡量設法苦中作樂，每次國祥輸完血後，精神體力馬上便恢復了許多，臉上又浮現了紅光，雖然明知這只是人為的暫時安康，我們也要趁這一刻享受一下正常生活。開車回家經過蒙特利公園時我們便會到平日喜愛的飯館去大吃一餐，大概在醫院裡磨了一天 ，要補償起來，胃口特別好。我們常去「北海漁邨」，因為這家廣東館港味十足，一道「避風塘炒蟹」非常道地。吃了飯便去租錄影帶回去看，我一生中從來沒看過那麼多中港台的「連續劇」，幾十集的《紅樓夢》、《滿清十三皇》、《嚴鳳英》，隨著那些東扯西拉的故事，一個晚上很容易打發過去。當然，王國祥也很關心世界大勢，那一陣子，東歐共產國家以及「蘇維埃社會主義聯邦共和國」土崩瓦解，我們天天看電視，看到德國人爬到東柏林牆上喝香檳慶祝，王國祥跟我都拍手喝起采來，那一刻，「再生不良性貧血」，真的給忘得精光。

王國祥直到八八年才在艾爾蒙特（El Monte）買了一幢小樓房，屋後有一片小小的院子，搬進去不到一年，花園還來不及打點好，他就生病了。生病前，他在超市找到一對醬色皮蛋缸，上面有薑黃色二龍搶珠的浮雕，這對大皮蛋缸十分古拙有趣，國祥買回來，用電鑽鑽了洞，準備作花缸用。有一個星期天，他的精神特別好，我便開車載了他去花圃看花。我們發覺原來加州也有桂花，登時如獲至寶，買了兩棵回去移植到那對皮蛋缸中。從此，那兩棵桂花，便成了國祥病中的良伴，一直到他病重時，也沒有忘記常到後院去澆花。

王國祥重病在身，在我面前雖然他不肯露聲色，他獨處時內心的沉重與懼恐，我深能體會，因為當我一個人靜下來時，我自己的心情便開始下沉了。我曾私下探問過他的主治醫生，醫生告訴我，國祥所患的「再生不良性貧血」，經過二十多年，雖然一度緩解，已經達到末期。他用「End Stage」這個聽來十分刺耳的字眼，他沒有再說下去，我不想聽也不願意他再往下說。然而一個令人不寒而慄的問題卻像潮水般經常在我腦海裡翻來滾去：這次王國祥的病，萬一恢復不了，怎麼辦？事實上國祥的病情，常有險狀，以至於一夕數驚。有一晚，我從洛杉磯友人處赴宴回來，竟發覺國祥臥在沙發上已是半昏迷狀態，我趕緊送他上醫院，那晚我在高速公路上起碼開到每小時八十英哩以上，我開車的技術並不高明，不辨方向，但人能急中生智，平常四十多分鐘的路程，一半時間便趕到了。醫生測量出來，國祥的血糖高到八百MC/DL，大概再晚一刻，他的腦細胞便要受損了。原來他長期服用激素，引發血糖升高。醫院的急診室本來就是一個生死場，凱撒的急診室比普通醫院要大幾倍，裡面的生死掙扎當然就更加劇烈，只看到醫生護士忙成一團，而病人圍困在那一間間用白幔圈成的小隔間裡，卻好像完全被遺忘掉了似的，好不容易盼到醫生來診視，可是探一下頭，人又不見了。我陪著王國祥進出那間急診室多次，每次一等就等到天亮才有正式病房。

自從王國祥生病後，我便開始到處打聽有關「再生不良性貧血」治療的訊息。我在台灣看病的醫生是長庚醫學院的吳德朗院長，吳院長介紹我認識長庚醫院血液科的主治醫生施麗雲女士。我跟施醫生通信討教並把王國祥的病歷寄給她，與她約好，我去台灣時，登門造訪。同時我又遍查中國大陸中醫治療這種病症的書籍雜誌。我在一本醫療雜誌上看到上海曙光中醫院血液科主任吳正翔大夫治療過這種病，大陸上稱為「再生障礙性貧血」，簡稱「再障」。同時我又在大陸報上讀到河北省石家莊有一位中醫師治療「再障」有特效方法，並且開了一家專門醫治「再障」的診所。我發覺原來大陸上這種病例並不罕見，大陸中西醫結合治療行之有年，有的病療效還很好。於是我便決定親自往大陸走一趟，也許能夠尋訪到能夠醫治國祥的醫生及藥方。我把想法告訴國祥聽，他說道：「那只好辛苦你了。」王國祥不善言辭，但他講話全部發自內心。他一生最怕麻煩別人，生病求人，實在萬不得已。

一九九〇年九月，去大陸之前，我先到台灣，去林口長庚醫院拜訪了施麗雲醫師。施醫生告訴我她也正治療幾個患「再生不良性貧血」的病人，治療方法與美國醫生大同小異。施醫生看了王國祥的病歷沒有多說甚麼，我想她那時可能不忍告訴我，國祥的病，恐難治癒。

我攜帶了一大盒重重一疊王國祥的病歷飛往上海，由我在上海的朋友復旦大學陸士清教授陪同，到曙光醫院找到吳正翔大夫。曙光是上海最有名的中醫院，規模相當大。吳大夫不厭其詳以中醫觀點向我解說了「再障」的種種病因及治療方法。曙光醫院治療「再障」也是中西合診，一面輸血，一面服用中藥，長期調養，主要還是補血調氣。吳大夫與我討論了幾次王國祥的病況，最後開給我一個處方，要我與他經常保持電話聯絡。我聽聞浙江中醫院也有名醫，於是又去了一趟杭州，去拜訪一位輩分甚高的老中醫，老醫生的理論更玄了，藥方也比較偏。有親友生重病，才能體會得到「病急亂投醫」這句話的真諦。當時如果有人告訴我喜馬拉雅山頂上有神醫，我也會攀爬上去乞求仙丹的。在那時，搶救王國祥的生命，對於我重於一切。

我飛到北京後的第二天，便由社科院袁良駿教授陪同，坐火車往石家莊去，當晚住歇在河北省政協招待所。那晚在招待所遇見了一位從美國去的工程師，原本也是台灣留美學生，而且是成大畢業。他知道我為了朋友到大陸訪醫特來看我。我正納悶，這樣偏遠地區怎會有美國來客，工程師一見面便告訴了我他的故事：原來他太太年前車禍受傷，一直昏迷不醒，變成了植物人。工程師四處求醫罔效，後來打聽到石家莊有位極負盛名的氣功師，開診所用氣功治療病人。他於是辭去了高薪職位，變賣房財，將太太運到石家莊接受氣功治療。他告訴我每天有四、五位氣功師輪流替他太太灌氣，他講到他太太的手指已經能動，有了知覺，他臉上充滿希望。我深為他感動，是多大的愛心與信念，使他破釜沉舟，千里迢迢把太太護運到偏僻的中國北方去就醫。這些年來我早已把工程師的名字給忘了，但我卻常常記起他及他的太太，不知她最後恢復知覺沒有。幾年後我自己經歷了中國氣功的神奇，讓氣功師治療好暈眩症，而且變成了氣功的忠實信徒。當初工程師一番好意，告訴我氣功治病的奧妙，我確曾動過心，想讓王國祥到大陸接受氣功治療。但國祥經常需要輸血，而且又容易感染疾病，實在不宜長途旅行。但這件事我始終耿耿於懷，如果當初國祥嘗試氣功，不知有沒有復原的可能。

次晨，我去參觀那家專門治療「再障」的診所，會見了主治大夫。其實那是一間極其簡陋的小醫院，有十幾個住院病人，看樣子都病得不清。大夫很年輕，講話頗自信，臨走時，我向他買了兩大袋草藥，為了便於攜帶，都磨成細粉。我提著兩大袋辛辣嗆鼻的藥粉，回轉北京。那已是九月下旬，天氣剛入秋，是北京氣候最佳時節。那是我頭一次到北京，自不免到故宮、明陵去走走，但因心情不對，毫無遊興。我的旅館就在王府井附近，離天安門不遠。晚上，我信步走到天安門廣場去看看，那片全世界最大的廣場，竟然一片空曠，除了守衛的解放軍，行人寥寥無幾。相較於一年前「六四」時期，人山人海，民情沸騰的景象，天安門廣場有一種劫後的荒涼與蕭殺。那天晚上，我的心境就像北京涼風習習的秋夜一般蕭瑟。在大陸四處求醫下來，我的結論是，中國也沒有醫治「再生不良性貧血」的特效藥。王國祥對我這次大陸之行，當然也一定抱有許多期望，我怕又會令他失望了。

回到美國後，我與王國祥商量，最後還是決定服用曙光醫院吳正翔大夫開的那張藥方，因為藥性比較平和。石家莊醫生的兩大袋藥粉我也扛了回來，但沒有敢用。而國祥的病，卻是一天比一天沉重了。頭一年，他還支撐著去上班，但每天來回需開兩小時車程，終於體力不支，而把休斯的工作停掉。幸虧他買了殘障保險，沒有因病傾家蕩產。第二年，由於服用太多激素，觸發了糖尿病，又因長期缺血， 影響到心臟，發生心律不整，逐漸行動也困難起來。

　　一九九二年一月，王國祥五十五歲生日，我看他那天精神還不錯便提議到「北海漁邨」，去替他慶生。我們一路上還商談著要點些甚麼菜，談到吃我們的興致又來了。「北海漁邨」的停車場上到飯館有一道二十多級的石階，國祥扶著欄杆爬上去，爬到一半，便喘息起來，大概心臟負荷不了，很難受的樣子，我趕忙過去扶著他，要他坐在石階上休息一會兒，他歇了口氣，站起來還想勉強往上爬，我知道，他不願掃興，我勸阻道：「我們不要在這裡吃飯了，回家去做壽麵吃。」我沒有料到，王國祥的病體已經虛弱到舉步維艱了。回到家中，我們煮了兩碗陽春麵，度過王國祥最後的一個生日。星期天傍晚，我要回返聖芭芭拉，國祥送我到門口上車，我在車中反光鏡裡，瞥見他孤立在大門前的身影，他的頭髮本來就有少年白，兩年多來，百病相纏，竟變得滿頭蕭蕭，在暮色中，分外怵目。開上高速公路後，突然一陣無法抵擋的傷痛，襲擊過來，我將車子拉到公路一旁，伏在方向盤上，不禁失聲大慟。我哀痛王國祥如此勇敢堅忍，如此努力抵抗病魔咄咄相逼，最後仍然被折磨得形銷骨立。而我自己亦盡了所有的力量，去迴護他的病體，卻眼看著他的生命一點一滴耗盡，終至一籌莫展。我一向相信人定勝天，常常逆數而行，然而人力畢竟不敵天命，人生大限，無人能破。

　　夏天暑假，我搬到艾爾蒙特王國祥家去住，因為隨時會發生危險。八月十三日黃昏，我從超市買東西回來，發覺國祥呼吸困難，我趕忙打九一一叫了救護車來，用氧氣筒急救，隨即將他扛上救護車揚長鳴笛往醫院駛去。去醫院住了兩天，星期五，國祥的精神似乎又好轉了。他進出醫院多次，這種情況已習以為常，我以為大概第二天，他就可以出院了。我在醫院裡陪了他一個下午，聊了些閒話，晚上八點鐘，他對我說道：「你先回去吃飯吧。」我把一份《世界日報》留給他看，說道：「明天早上我來接你。」那是我們最後一次交談。星期六一早，醫院打電話來通知，王國祥昏迷不醒，送進了加護病房。我趕到醫院，看見國祥身上已插滿了管子。他的主治醫生告訴我，不打算用電擊刺激國祥的心臟了，我點頭同意，使用電擊，病人太受罪。國祥昏迷了兩天，八月十七星期一，我有預感恐怕他熬不過那一天。中午我到醫院餐廳匆匆用了便餐，趕緊回到加護病房守著。顯示器上，國祥的心臟愈跳愈弱，五點鐘，值班醫生進來準備，我一直看著顯示器上國祥心臟的波動，五點二十分，他的心臟終於停止。我執著國祥的手，送他走完人生最後一程。霎時間，天人兩分，死生契闊，在人間，我向王國祥告了永別。

一九五四年，四十四年前的一個夏天，我與王國祥同時匆匆趕到建中去上暑假補習班，預備考大學。我們同級不同班，互相並不認識，那天恰巧兩人都遲到，一同搶著上樓梯，跌跌撞撞，碰在一起，就那樣，我們開始結識，來往相交，三十八年。王國祥天性善良，待人厚道，孝順父母，忠於朋友。他完全不懂虛偽，直言直語，我曾笑他說謊舌頭也會打結。但他講究學問，卻據理力爭，有時不免得罪人，事業上受到阻礙。王國祥有科學天才，物理方面應該有所成就，可惜他大二生過那場大病，腦力受了影響。他在休斯研究人造衛星，很有心得，本來可以更上一層樓，可是天不假年，五十五歲，走得太早。我與王國祥相知數十載，彼此守望相助，患難與共，人生道上的風風雨雨，由於兩人同心協力，總能抵禦過去，可是最後與病魔死神一搏，我們全力以赴，卻一敗塗地。

我替王國祥料理完後事回轉聖芭芭拉，夏天已過。那年聖芭芭拉大旱，市府限制用水，不准澆灑花草。幾個月沒有回家，屋前草坪早已枯死，一片焦黃。由於經常跑洛杉磯，園中缺乏照料，全體花木黯然失色，一棵棵茶花病懨懨，只剩得奄奄一息，我的家，成了廢園一座。我把國祥的骨灰護送返台，安置在善導寺後，回到美國便著手重建家園。草木跟人一樣，受了傷須得長期調養。我花了一兩年工夫，費盡心血，才把那些茶花一一救活。退休後時間多了，我又開始到處蒐集名茶，愈種愈多，而今園中，茶花成林。我把王國祥家那兩缸桂花也搬了回來，因為長大成形，皮蛋缸已不堪負荷，我便把那兩株桂花移到園中一角，讓它們入土為安。冬去春來。我園中六、七十棵茶花競相開發，嬌紅嫩白，熱鬧非凡。我與王國祥從前種的那些老茶，二十多年後，已經高攀屋簷，每株盛開起來，都有上百朵。春日負暄，我坐在園中靠椅上，品茗閱報，有百花相伴，暫且貪享人間瞬息繁華。美中不足的是，抬望眼，總看見園中西隅，剩下的那兩棵義大利柏樹中間，露出一塊楞楞的空白來，缺口當中，映著湛湛青空，悠悠白雲，那是一道女媧煉石也無法彌補的天裂。

齊邦媛

一生中的一天[*]

　　那個六月的早晨，我凝神靜氣地走進二十四教室，習慣性地先拿起一根粉筆，再打開《英國文學史》課本，開始我一生所授的最後一課。不久前，我們師生都很艱辛地跋涉出艾略特一九二二年的〈荒原〉，行經兩次世界大戰後由驚駭、頹喪，到復甦的半世紀，驀然到了一九八三年，即將繼任桂冠詩人休斯（Ted Hughes, 1930-1998）的〈河〉。休斯寫了半生猙獰生猛的自然詩，由鳥獸、爬蟲的微觀到自然景物的宏觀，而以「從天上墜落，躺臥在大地之母懷中」的河述志：

　　河水源源不絕由天上來，洗淨了一切死亡。

　　在此恆久不變的希望中，我闔上了課本。接著把十世紀至今的英國文學發展再作一遍回溯，與一年前開課時的緒語作個完整的呼應。下課鐘響時，我向這幾十張仰起的年輕的臉道別，祝福他們一生因讀書而快樂。三言兩語，平靜地走下講台。為了維持自己教書的風格，不在教室中說課外的話，更不願將個人的喜、怒、哀、樂帶上講台，我終於無淚地作了這一場割捨。

　　由教室走到迴廊時，手上是捧著一大把花的，淺紫、粉紅和白色的孔雀花。每一朵都是語言的延長，向我說著再見。再見了，老師！有

---

* 選自齊邦媛《一生中的一天》，台北：爾雅出版社，民國九十三年。

許多美好的早晨，我們被你那厚重，有時深奧難解的文學史拴在座位上，傾聽你的聲音由一個年代飄進另一個年代，眼睛望向窗外的樹與天空。再見了，老師。也許在未來的歲月裡，我會記起你讀的一兩行詩，你說的一兩句話，有關文學的，有關人生的。

我抱著花走在陳舊斑駁的迴廊裡，突然憶起第一次走進這迴廊時的長髮和青春，不禁百感交集。提前退休也是退了、休了麼？由這裡我將走向怎樣的人生呢？

這一天下午排了研究所學生的期考。倚在十六教室的窗邊看著校園漸漸沉寂的午後景象。天空湛藍，疏疏落落的一些腳踏車匆匆騎過，一些捧著書的學生走向圖書館……不久一輛長長的車子駛來，停在傅鐘前面，裡面走出穿著飄拂白紗的新娘，開始擺著各種姿勢照像。是在投入真正的人生前來此作一番回顧吧。許多年前，自己也幾乎是由這座老樓嫁出去又回來的，這些年中，生活的長河波濤洶湧，白紗心情已難於記憶了。

當我回答了學生的問題再回到窗前，晴朗的天空幾乎已全為低垂的黑雲遮蓋，新娘正收攏長裙跑回紮了綵帶的汽車。雨點大滴驟落，迅速密集成為雨幕，隱隱悶擊的雷電由遠方移近，漸漸好似集中在校園裡，不留喘息餘閒地急擂猛擊。閃電有時似乎穿窗而入，由另一面窗出去，到小方院中爆炸。這時學生們由考卷上抬頭看我，看到我在台前鎮靜地站著，似乎安心地又俯首疾書。雷聲連續地震動心肺，窗外那棵隨著季節變色的欖仁樹的闊葉上雨水傾注而下，雨幕密織，霎時已全看不到對面的行政紅樓。在瀑布傾瀉似的雨聲中，我與這二十多位學生形成了休戚與共的孤島，我更不知此時應怎樣說才是最適當的告別。告別的不祇是這一班學生，告別的還有數十年間共同經過的生長、驟變與激盪！

雷雨和來時一樣，驟然停止。收了考卷，我站在迴廊窗前等待積水消退，知道此時校門外的新生南路也沒有我能走的空間。躊躇間，幾位學生前來陪伴。我們決意涉一小段水去後樓咖啡店小坐。在笑話簇擁中，我們踩過了大大小小的水窪，似乎聽得見沙土急渴吸水的聲音。陽光由雲縫閃射下來，闊葉樹上金光閃耀，積水上映出漸漸擴大的藍天和飛馳的白雲……在這樣的天象中，我又建新緣。

這樣的壯麗天象，莫非即是造物主給我最慷慨明白的啟示麼？它用這樣強烈豐沛的語言告訴我：黑髮與白髮是多麼渺小的瞬間萬變的現象！你既無能為力，且歡唱前行吧！雷電雨雪會隨著你，陽光也會隨著你。

廖玉蕙

如果記憶像風[*]

　　我的女兒上國中，除了學校課業不甚理想外，她開朗、乖巧、體貼且善解人意，我們雖然偶爾在思及「優勝劣敗」的慘烈升學殺伐時，略微有些擔心外，整體而言，我們對她相當滿意，尤其在聽到許多同輩談及他們的女兒如何成天如刺蝟般地和父母唱反調、鬧彆扭時，外子和我都不禁暗自慶幸。

　　去年暑假，考高中的兒子從學校領回了聯考成績單，母子倆正拿著報紙上登載的分數統計表，緊張地核算著可能考上的學校，女兒從學校的暑假輔導課放學，朝我們說：

　　「事情爆發了！」

　　女兒每天放學總是一放下書包便跟前跟後的和我報告學校見聞，相干的、不相干的。這時候，大夥兒可沒心情聽這些，我說：

　　「別吵！先自己去吃飯，我們正在找哥哥的學校。」

　　飯後，核算的工作終告一個段落。長久以來，因為家有考生的緊繃情緒，總算得到釋放。我在書房裡和兒子談著新學校的種種，女兒又進來了，神色詭異地說：

　　「事情爆發了！老師要你去訓導處一趟。」

　　才剛放鬆下來的心情，在聽清楚這句話後，又緊張了起來。在印象中，要求家長到訓導處，絕非好事，我差點兒從椅子上跳起來，問：

　　「什麼事爆發了？為什麼要去訓導處？」

---

* 選自廖玉蕙《新世紀散文家：廖玉蕙精選集》，台北：九歌出版社，民國九十一年。

女兒被我這急慌慌的表情給嚇著了，她小聲地說：

「我在學校被同學打了，那位打人的同學另外還打了別人，別人的家長告到學校去……反正，我們老師說請你到訓導處去一趟。你去了，就知道了啦！」

這下子，更讓我吃驚了！一向彬彬有禮且文弱的女兒，怎麼會捲入打架事件？又是什麼時候的事，怎麼從來沒聽她提起？我們怎麼也沒發現？

「是前一陣子，你到南京去開會的時候。有一天，我和爸爸一起在和式房間看書，爸爸看到我的腳上烏青好幾塊，問我怎麼搞的，我騙他說跌倒的，其實就是被同學打的，我怕他擔心，沒敢說。」

「同學為什麼要打你呢？你做了什麼事？」

「我也不知道！」

怎麼讓人給打了，還不知道原因。事有蹊蹺，當天傍晚，我在電話中和導師溝通，更震驚地發現，毆打不止一回，女兒共被打了四次。據導師說，這是群毆事件，領導者有三位，三位都是家庭有問題的女孩子。其中一位經常扮演唆使角色的R，與外婆同住，外婆當天被請到訓導處時，還拍案怒斥訓導人員污衊她的孫女。遭受不同程度威脅或毆打的女孩有數位，其中，以我的女兒最慘，十天之內，被痛打四回，導師希望我到訓導處備案，以利訓導作業。放下電話，我覺得自己的手微微發抖，我不知道，一向聒噪且和我無話不說的女兒，在我遠遊回來多日中，怎能忍住這麼殘酷悲痛的事件而不透露半點風聲。我因之確信她一定遭遇到極大的壓力，果然不出所料，在外子和我款款導引下，她痛哭失聲，說：

「K威脅我，如果我敢向老師和爸媽告狀，她會從高樓上把我推下去，讓我死得很難看！」

我聽了，毛骨悚然。女兒接著補充說：

「何況，我也怕爸、媽擔心。」

我止不住一陣心酸。平日見她溫順、講理，不容易和別人起衝突，也忽略了和她溝通類似的校園暴力的應變方法，總以為這事不會臨到她頭上。沒想到溫和的小孩，反倒成了暴力者覬覦的目標。而最讓人傷心的，莫過於沒讓小孩子對父母有足夠的信任。

和外子商量過後，我們決定暫緩去訓導處備案，因為，除了增加彼此的仇視外，我們不太相信，對整個事件會有任何幫助，我們決定自力救濟。當然，這其中最重要的關鍵是我們都不認為十三、四歲的孩子會真的壞到哪裡去，多半是一時糊塗。尤其是知道這些孩子全是出自問題家庭，想來也是因為缺乏關愛所致，亦不免讓人思之心疼。於是，我想法子找到了主事的三位學生中的兩位T、R學生的電話號碼，K同學並非女兒的同班同學，據云居無定所，且早在警局及感化院多次出入。當我在電話中客氣地說明是同學家長後，接電話的R的祖母，隨即開始破口大罵訓導人員的無的放矢，任意污衊，足足講了數分鐘，言辭之中充滿了敵意。我靜靜聆聽了許久後，才誠懇地告訴她，我並非前來指責她的孫女，只是想了解一下狀況，祖母猶豫了一會兒，大聲呵斥她的孫子說：

「人家的家長找到家裡來了啦！」

電話那頭傳來了模糊的聲音，似乎是女孩不肯接電話，祖母粗暴地說：

「沒關係啦！人家的媽媽很客氣的啦！」

小女孩自始至終否認曾動手打人，我原也無意強逼她認錯，只是讓她知道，家長已注意及此事，即使未親自參與毆鬥，每次都在一旁搖旗吶喊也是不該。

第二位的T在電話中振振有辭的說：

「她活該。為什麼她功課不好，我功課也不好，可是，老師每次看到她都笑瞇瞇的，看到我卻板著臉孔，我就不服氣。」如此的邏輯，著實教人啼笑皆非。我委婉的開導她：

「你如果看我女兒不順眼，可以不跟她一起玩；如果我女兒有任何不對的地方，你可以直接告訴她改進，或者告訴老師或我。不管如何，動手打人都不好，阿姨聽說了女兒挨打好心疼，換做是你挨揍，你爸媽是不是也很捨不得的呀！」

T倔強地回說：

「才不哪！我爸才不會心痛，我爸說，犯錯就該被狠揍一頓。」後來，我才知道，T在家動輒挨打，她爸打起她來，毫不留情。當我在和兩位女孩以電話溝通時，女兒一旁緊張地屏息聆聽，不時地遞過小紙條提醒我：

「拜託！不要激怒她們，要不然我會很慘。」我掛了電話，無言以對。

兩位女孩都接受了我的重託，答應我以後不但不再打女兒，而且還要善盡保護的責任。我相信這些半大不小的孩子是會信守承諾的，她們有她們的江湖道義，何況，確實也沒有什麼嫌隙。

事隔多日的一個中午，女兒形色倉皇的跑回家來，說是那位神龍見首不見尾的K，在逃學多日後，穿著便服在學校門口出現，並揚言要再度修理女兒，幸賴T通風報信並掩護由校園後門逃出，才倖免於難。看著女兒因過度緊張而似乎縮小了一圈的臉，我不禁氣憤填膺。這是什麼世界，學校如果不能保護學生的安全，還談什麼傳道、授業、解惑！

我撥電話到學校訓導處，訓導主任倒很積極，他說：「我剛才在校門口看到K，我再下去找她，找到人後，再回你電話。」

過了不到十分鐘，電話來了。我要求和K說話。我按捺住胸中怒火，K怯生生地叫「蔡媽媽」，我心腸立刻又軟了下來。這回，我不再問她為什麼要打人了，我慢慢了解到這些頭角崢嶸的苦悶小孩打人是不需要有什麼理由的，瞄一眼或碰一下都可以構成導火線。我問她：

「聽說，你一直沒到學校上課，大夥兒都到校，你一個人在外面閒逛，心裡不會慌慌的嗎？」女孩低聲說：

「有時候會。」

「為什麼不到學校和同學一起玩、一起讀書呢？」

「我不喜歡上課。」

「那你喜歡什麼呢？……喜歡看小說嗎？」

「喜歡。」

我誠懇地和她說：

「阿姨家有很多散文、小說的，有空和我女兒一起來家裡玩，不要四處閒逛，有時候會碰到壞人的。」

女孩子乖乖地說了聲「謝謝！」我沉吟了一會兒，終究沒提打人的事。歎了口氣，掛了電話，眼淚流了一臉。是什麼樣的環境把孩子逼得四處為家？是什麼樣的父母，忍心讓孩子流落街頭？我回頭遵照訓導主任的指示，叮嚀女兒：

「以後再有類似狀況，就跑到訓導處去，知道嗎？」女兒委屈地說：

「你以為我不想這樣做嗎？他們圍堵我，我根本去不了。」過了幾天，兒子從母校的操場打球回來，邊擦汗邊告訴我：

「今天在學校打球時，身後有人高喊K的名字，我回頭看，遜斃了！又瘦又小，妹妹太沒用，是我就跟她拚了。」女兒不服氣地反駁說：

「你別看她瘦小，那雙眼睛瞪起人來，教人不寒而慄，好像要把人吃掉一樣，嚇死人哪！」

事情總算解決了，因為據女兒說，從那以後，再沒人找過她麻煩，我們都鬆了口氣，慶幸漫天陰霾全開。

今年年初，時報舉辦兩岸三邊華文小說研討會，一邊兩天，我在誠品藝文空間參與盛會。那天，回到家，外子面露憂色說：

「很奇怪哦！女兒這個星期假日，成天埋首寫東西，畫著細細的格子，密密麻麻的，不知寫些什麼，不讓我看。」夜深了，孩子快上床，我進到女兒房裡和她溝通，我問她是不是有什麼事要和我說，她起先說沒有，我說：

「我們不是說好了，我們之間沒有祕密嗎？」

女兒從書包裡掏出那些紙張，大約有五、六張之多，前後兩面都寫得滿滿的，全是她做的噩夢和那回被打的經過，像是在警察局錄口供似的，我看了不禁淚如雨下，差點兒崩潰。原先以為不過是小孩之間的情緒性發洩，沒想到是如此血淋淋的校園暴力。

女兒細細的小字寫著：

「第一次：那一天是星期五，十五班的K跑來，叫我放學後在校門口等她。下課後，她打扮得花枝招展在門口等我，還噴了香水。她把我騙到隔壁××國宅二樓，我才放下書包，一轉身，她就變了一個臉，兇狠地問我一個我聽不懂的問題，我還來不及回答，她就打了我好幾個耳光，我楞了一下，她打我？我真是不敢相信？我和她無怨無仇，她為什麼打我？我跟她扭打在一起，她拉我的頭髮，我扯她衣服，她抓住我的頭髮把我丟出去，我整個跪到地下，也就是所謂的『一敗塗地』。她把我從地上拉起來恐嚇我『你要是敢講出來，我就把你從樓上推下去』，我怕得要命，因為氣喘病發，正喘著氣，突然從圍觀的人群中跑出來一個年約二十左右的女人對我吼：『你還喘！喘死啊！』說完，又給我一個耳光，我整個人又跪到地上去。我因為害怕，什麼都聽她的，出了國宅，我真的忍不住哭了！我哭的原因是因為我好膽小，而且我不甘心啊！我竟然就這樣傻傻地被她打！她還說我說話很ㄅㄧㄠˇ，ㄅㄧㄠˇ是什麼意思啊？我從來沒有這樣屈辱過，連爸媽都從來沒有打過我啊！她憑什麼打我？我恨死她了，我生平沒恨過什麼人，我發誓與她勢不兩立。」「第二次：暑期輔導中午，K突然從校外跑來（她沒有參加輔導），約我去國宅十二樓talk talk，我很膽小，不敢反抗，只好乖乖地跟她去，一到十二樓，她就說：『上次你扯我衣服，害我整個曝光，你今天是要裸奔回去？還是被我打？』她看起來很生氣的樣子，我考慮了一下，就選擇挨打。她打人很奇特，不只是打臉，連後腦勺一起打，我被她打得臉熱辣辣的，腫得像豬頭皮似的，我實在痛得受不了了，請她等一下。我用手往牙齒一摸，手上都是血！她兇狠地說：『今天饒了你，算你走狗運！』走的時候，又恐嚇我不准講，要不然會死得很難看……」

「第三次：這一次本來是要找班上另一位同學的麻煩的，那位同學跑了，所以就找我。她們又問我一些莫名其妙的問題，問一句，揍我一下，這一次真的很慘，T、K二人連打帶踢地弄得我全身是傷，膝蓋上一大塊青腳印，久久不消，這次，嘴巴又流了好多血，啊！我真是沒用啊……

「第四次：這次是在參觀資訊大樓時，T把我堵到廁所裡，又是拳打腳踢……」

「K：我到底是哪裡讓你看不順眼，為什麼一定要動手打人呢？這樣你又有什麼好呢！這樣打人是要被……」

「有一天我夢到我當上了警察，我們組長要我去××國宅抓兩名通緝犯，一是K，一是T。我到××國宅時，果然看到她們又在打人，我立刻上前制止，乘機從背後將K的雙手反扣，交給同事帶回局裡；再轉身冷冷地朝T說：『我這一次放你走，希望你改過，別讓我再抓住，不要讓我失望。』她問我：『你到底是誰？』我把證件拿給她看，她嚇了一跳，馬上向我下跪。……」

「前兩天我又夢到K，她完全失去了兇狠的眼神，變得脆弱不堪，我勸她：『回家去吧！再不回家，妳媽媽要得相思病了！』K問我是誰？我告訴她，我就是以前被她打三次的人，我勸她改進向善，並幫她找回了媽媽，她高興地流下了眼淚……」

「……」

我一邊看，一邊流淚，這才知道，我們的一念之仁是如何虧待了善良的女兒，那樣的暴行對她造成的傷害遠遠超過我們的想像，而那些施暴的孩子的行徑，著實可用「可恨」或「可惡」來形容，我必須慚愧的承認，如果我早知道那些孩子是如此殘忍地對待我的女兒，我是絕不會那樣委曲求全地去和行兇者打交道的，我也深信，沒有任何一個母親會加以容忍的，我是多麼對不起女兒呀！可是，事隔半年，為什麼會突然又舊事重提呢？

「不是答應過媽媽，把這件事徹底忘掉嗎？」

「最近考試，老師重新排位置，那兩位曾經打我的T、R同學，一位坐我左邊，一位坐我前面，我覺得好害怕！雖然她們已經不再打我了，可是，我想到以前的事，就忍不住發抖。……」我摟著女兒，心裡好痛好痛，安慰她：

「讓我去和老師商量，請老師調換一下位置好嗎？」女兒全身肌肉緊縮，緊張地說：

「不要！到時候她們萬一知道了，我又倒楣了。我答應你不再害怕就是了！」

外子和我徹夜未眠，不知如何是好。女兒柔弱，無法保護自己，強硬的手段，恐怕只會給她帶來更大的傷害，我們第一次認真地考慮到轉學問題。一連幾天，我打電話問了幾間私立教會學校，全說轉學得經過學科考試，篩選十分嚴格。想到女兒不甚理想的學科成績，只好快快然打退堂鼓，上帝原來也要揀選智慧高的子民，全不理會柔弱善良的百姓。我在從學校回家的高速公路上，望著前面筆直坦蕩的公路，覺得前途茫茫，一時之間，悲不自勝，竟至涕泗滂沱。

正當我們幾乎是心力交瘁時，女兒回來高興地報告：

「老師說，下禮拜又要重新排位置。媽媽不要再擔心了。……媽媽，真是對不起。」

那夜，我終於背著女兒和導師聯絡，請她在重換位置時，注意一下，是不是能儘量避免讓她們坐在一塊兒。老師知道情況後連連抱歉，並答應儘快改進，臨掛電話前，導師說：

「你那女兒實在可愛，她一點兒也不記仇，上次班際拔河比賽，她拚命為T加油，我一旁看著她喉嚨都喊啞了，臉紅嘟嘟的……我有時候上了一天課，好辛苦，偶爾上課時，朝她的方向望過去，她總不忘給我一個甜甜的笑容。蔡太太，你也是當老師的，應該會知道，那種窩心的感覺，當老師的快樂不就是這樣嗎？真是讓人心疼的孩子！」

第二天傍晚，孩子放學回來，我聽從導師的建議，和女兒一起到七樓陽台上把她寫的那些密密麻麻的紙條全燒光，希望這些不愉快的記憶隨著燒光的紙片兒灰飛煙滅。

紙片兒終於燒成灰燼！我轉過身拿掃把想清掃灰燼時，突然一陣風吹過來，把紙灰一古腦全吹上了天空，女兒惘然望著蒼天，幽幽地說：

「如果記憶像風就好了。」記憶真的會像風嗎？

龍應台

在紫藤廬和Starbucks之間*

台灣的內向性

一位居龍頭地位的電子企業家告訴我，一九六八年，他曾經陪同他的美國企業總裁來台灣考察，思索是否要把他們第一個亞洲分廠設在台北。考察結果卻是把分廠設到新加坡去。原因？當時的台北顯得很閉塞，對國際的情況很生疏，普遍的英語能力也差。換言之，國際化的程度太低。

二〇〇二年，孤星出版社（Lonely Planet）出版了專門介紹台灣的英語版旅遊書。作者用功不深，對台北市的新發展似乎沒什麼概念，但是整體印象他是有的。台北，他寫著，是亞洲最難接近的城市之一。意思是說，台北顯得閉塞，與國際不太接軌，英語能力也差，以至於，國際的旅遊者很難在這個城市裡悠遊自在。

三十五年過去了，台灣還是一個閉塞、國際化不足的地方？

是的。有經驗的人一眼就可以看出台灣的內向性。中正機場裡外國旅客非常少。首都的英語街道標示一團混亂。報紙的國際新聞五分鐘就可以讀完，有線電視的新聞報導更像是一種全國集體懲罰：小孩吞下釘子的報導時間十倍於伊索匹亞百萬人餓死的消息，南投的一隻狗吃檳榔的鏡頭比阿根廷的總統大選更重要。八國領袖舉行高峰會議，示威者的裸體大大地刊出，但是示威者究竟為了什麼理念而示威？不

---

* 選自顏崑陽主編之《92年散文選》，台北：九歌出版社，民國九十三年。

置不詞。一天二十四小時，這個國家的人民被強灌影像，政客的嘴臉、口沫、權力鬥爭的舉手投足，鉅細靡遺地注入，就像記憶影片植入動物體內一樣。國際間所重視的問題——戰爭、生態、貧窮、飢餓、新思潮的出現、舊秩序的突變、大危機的潛伏等等，在這裡，彷彿都不存在。

不對呀，你辯駁，台北是很國際化的。Starbucks咖啡館的密度居世界第一，二十四小時便利商店佔據每一個街角。最流行的嘻哈音樂和服飾到處可見，好萊塢的電影最早上市。生活的韻律也與國際同步；二月十四日買花過情人節，十月底戴上面具參加「萬聖節」變裝遊行，十一月有人吃火雞過感恩節，十二月市府廣場上萬人空巷載歌載舞慶祝耶誕節；年底，則總統府都出動了，放煙火、開香檳，倒數時，親吻你身邊的人。

民選的新政府甚至要求政府公文要有英文版，公務員要考英文，全民學英語，而最後的目標則是：把英語變成正式的官方語言。

誰說台灣閉塞？

變得跟誰一樣？

究竟什麼叫「國際化」呢？如果說，「現代化」指的是，在傳統的文化土壤上引進新的耕法——民主制度、科學精神、工業技術等等，從而發展出一種新的共處哲學與生活模式。如果說，「全球化」指的是，隨著科技與經濟的跨越國界，深層的文化體系，始料所未及地，也衝破了國家與民族的傳統界線。原來沿著那條線而形成的千年傳統——種種律法、信仰、道德、價值，面對「全球化」，不得不重新尋找定義。「現代化」是很多開發中國家追求的目標；「全球化」是一個正在急速發生的現實，在這個現實中，已開發國家盤算如何利用自己的優勢，開發中國家在趁勢而起的同時暗暗憂慮「自己不見了」的危險。

那麼，「國際化」是什麼呢？按照字義，就是使自己變得跟「國際」一樣，可是，誰是「國際」呢？變得跟誰一樣呢？把英語變成官方語言，是要把台灣變成英國美國，還是印度菲律賓？還是香港新加坡？當執政者宣布要將別國的語言拿來作自己的官方語言時，他對於自己國家的安身立命之所在、之所趨，有沒有認真地思考過呢？

牧羊人穿過草原

一九七八年我第一次到歐洲；這是啟蒙運動、工業革命的發源地，先進國家的聚集處，我帶著滿腦子對「現代化」的想像而去。離開機場，車子沿著德法邊境行駛。一路上沒看見預期中的高科技、超現實的都市景觀，卻看見他田野依依，江山如畫。樹林與麥田盡處，就是村落。村落的紅瓦白牆起落有致，襯著教堂尖塔的沈靜。斜陽鐘聲，雞犬相聞。綿延數百里，竟然像中古世紀的圖片。

車子在一條鄉間小路停下。上百隻毛茸茸圓滾滾的羊，像下課的孩子一樣，推著擠著鬧著過路，然後從草原那頭，牧羊人出現了。他一臉鬍子，披著簑衣，手執長杖，在羊群的簇擁中緩緩走近。夕陽把羊毛染成淡淡粉色，空氣流動著草汁的酸香。

我是震驚的；我以為會到處看見人的「現代」成就的驕傲展現，但是不斷撞見的，卻是貼近泥土的默不作聲的「傳統」。穿過濃綠的草原，這牧羊人緩緩向我走近，就像舊約聖經裡的牧羊人走近一個口渴的旅人。

爾後在歐洲的長期定居，只是不斷見證傳統的生生不息。生老病死的人間禮儀——什麼時辰唱什麼歌、用什麼顏色、送什麼花，對什麼人用什麼遣詞與用句，井井有條。春夏秋冬的生活韻律——暮冬的化裝遊行以驅鬼，初春的彩繪雞蛋以慶生，夏至的廣場歌舞以休憩，耶誕的莊嚴靜思以祈福。千年禮樂，不絕如縷，並不曾因「現代化」而消失或走樣。至於生活環境，不論是羅馬、巴黎還是柏林，為了一堵舊時城牆、一座破敗教堂、一條古樸老街，都可能花大成本，用高科技，不計得失地保存修復，為了保留傳統的氣質氛圍。

傳統的「氣質氛圍」，並不是一種膚淺的懷舊情懷。當人的成就像氫氣球一樣向不可知的無限的高空飛展，傳統就是綁著氫氣球的那根粗繩，緊連著土地。它使你仍舊樸實地面對生老病死，它使你仍舊與春花秋月冬雪共同呼吸，使你的腳仍舊踩得到泥土，你的手摸得到樹幹，你的眼睛可以為一首古詩流淚，你的心靈可以和兩千年前的作者對話。

傳統不是懷舊的情緒，傳統是生存的必要。

我發現，自己原來對「現代化」的預期是片面的。先進國家的「現代化」是手段，保護傳統是目的。譬如在環境生態上所做的鉅額投資與研發，其實不過是想重新得回最傳統最單純的「小橋流水人家」罷了。大資本、高科技、研究與發展，最終的目的不是飄向無限，而是回到根本——回到自己的語言、文化，自己的歷史、信仰，自己的泥土。

文化的進退失據

於是我看見：越先進的國家，越有能力保護自己的傳統；傳統保護得越好，對自己越有信心。越落後的國家，傳統的流失或支離破碎就越厲害，對自己的定位與前景越是手足無措，進退失據。

台灣的人民過西洋情人節但不知道Valentine是什麼；化裝遊行又不清楚Carnival的意義何在；吃火雞大餐不明白要對誰感恩；耶誕狂歡又沒有任何宗教的反思。凡節慶都必定聯繫著宗教或文化歷史的淵源；將別人的節慶拿來過，有如把人家的祖宗牌位接來祭拜，卻不知為何祭拜、祭拜的是何人。節慶的熱鬧可以移植，節慶裡頭所蘊含的意義卻是移植不來的。節慶變成空洞的消費，而自己傳統中隨著季節流轉或感恩或驅鬼或內省或祈福的充滿意義的節慶則又棄之不顧。究竟要如何給生活賦予意義？說得出道理的人少，手足無措的人，多。

台灣的領導人要把英語變成官方語言，更是真正的不知所云。語言難道是一支死的木棍，伸手拿來就可以使？

語言不是木棍，語言是活生生的千年老樹，盤根錯節、深深扎根在文化和歷史的土壤中。移植語言，就是移植文化和歷史，移植價值和信念，兩者不可分。殖民者為了更改被殖民者的價值觀，統治的第一步就是讓被殖民者以殖民者的語言為語言。香港和新加坡就這樣成為英語的社會。嫻熟英語，通曉英語世界的價值觀與運作模式，固然使新加坡和香港這樣的地方容易與國際直接對話，但是他們可能要付出代價，文化的代價。英語強勢，可能削弱了本土語言文化——譬如漢語或馬來語——的發展，而英語文化的厚度又不足以和紐約或倫敦相提並論，結果可能是兩邊落空，兩種文化土壤都可能因為不夠厚實而無法培養出參天大樹。

國際化，是知識

本國沒有英語人口，又不曾被英語強權殖民過，為什麼宣稱要將英語列為官方語言？把英語列為官方語言在文化上意味著什麼後果？為政者顯然未曾深思。進退失據，莫此為甚。

不是移植別人的節慶，不是移植別人的語言，那麼「國際化」是什麼？

它是一種知己知彼。知己，所以要決定什麼是自己安身立命、生死不渝的價值。知彼，所以有能力用別人聽得懂的語言、看得懂的文字、講得通的邏輯詞彙，去呈現自己的語言、自己的觀點、自己的典章禮樂。它不是把我變得跟別人一樣，而是用別人能理解的方式告訴別人我的不一樣。所以「國際」是要找到那個「別人能理解的方式」，是手段，不是目的。

找到「別人能理解的方式」需要知識。不知道非洲國家的殖民歷史，會以為「台灣人的悲哀」是世界上最大的悲哀。不清楚國際對中國市場的反應，會永遠以政治的單一角度去思考中國問題。不了解國際的商業運作，會繼續把應該是「經濟前鋒」的台商當成「叛徒」看待。不了解美伊戰爭後的歐美角力，不了解聯合國的妥協政治，不了解俄羅斯的轉型，不了解開放後的中國在國際上的地位，不了解全球化給國家主權和民族文化帶來的巨大挑戰……不了解國際，又如何奢談找到什麼對話的語言讓國家了解台灣呢？

越是先進的國家，對於國際的知識就越多。知識的掌握，幾乎等於國力的展示，因為知識，就是權力。知道越多，掌握越多。如果電視是一種文化指標，那麼台灣目前二十四小時播報國內新聞，把自己放大到鋪天蓋地的肚臍眼自我耽溺現象，不只是國家落後的象徵，已經是文化的變態。人們容許電視台徹底剝奪自己知的權力，保持自己對國際的淡漠無知，而同時又抱怨國際不了解台灣的處境，哀嘆自己是國際孤兒，不是很矛盾嗎？

Starbucks還是紫藤廬

我喜歡在Starbucks買咖啡。不見得因為它的咖啡特別好，而是因為，你還沒進去就熟悉它的一切了。你也許在耶路撒冷，也許在倫敦，在北京，或者香港，突然下起雨來，遠遠看見下一個街角閃著熟悉的燈，你就知道在那裡可以點一大杯拿鐵咖啡加一個bagel麵包，雖然這是一個陌生的城市。

「全球化」，就是使你「客舍似家家似寄」。

我更喜歡在紫藤廬喝茶，會朋友。茶香繚繞裡，有人安靜地回憶在這裡聚集過的一代又一代風流人物以及風流人物所創造出來的歷史，有人慷慨激昂地策畫下一個社會改造運動；紫藤花閒閒地開著，它不急，它太清楚這個城市的身世。

台北市有五十八家Starbucks，台北市只有一個紫藤廬。全世界有六千六百家Starbucks，全世界只有一個紫藤廬。

「國際化」不是讓Starbucks進來取代紫藤廬；「國際化」是把自己敞開，讓Starbucks進來，進來之後，又知道如何使紫藤廬的光澤更溫潤優美，知道如何讓別人認識紫藤廬──「我」──的不一樣。Starbucks越多，紫藤廬越重要。

隱地

一日神*

一日喜，一日怒……一日甜，一日苦……。創造神、破壞神、保護神……人，誰能擺脫這些神？祂們在天地之間形成一面天羅地網。

看起來是三分天下，世界之大，豈止此三神？三神各有兵馬，這些兵馬其實就是大大小小的宇宙諸神，祂們掌控著萬物的命運，人想創造生命，走出一條康莊大道，諸神聽了，只在我們背後偷偷竊笑。

話說有一個最不為人知的一日之神，祂在一年三百六十五天之中，只和我們相處一日，就離我們而去，所以，從來也不為我們發現，因而輕忽了祂的存在。

一日神身輕如燕，祂天明來，夜半去，悄悄相處一日，就和我們說拜拜，何日再相逢，祂不知道，每一個我們，誰也不知道。

不知道祂在哪裡，但知道祂在，也知道祂已經走了。

一日神和一日神何時交換衛兵？我們完全無法察覺，只是一日之隔，喜訊已成惡耗，為何天差地遠？

昨日明明好好的一個人，怎麼只是睡了一覺，清晨醒來，世界彷彿全變了樣。

不對，就是不對，一大清早照鏡子，出現一個看了好讓人討厭的糟老頭，昨天還老得滿帥氣的，怎麼一下子就醜了？此刻瞧著，就是不舒服。他拿起梳子梳啊梳的，怎麼梳也梳不服貼，頭髮就是不聽話，

---

* 選自隱地，《一日神》，台北：爾雅出版社，頁9-16。

更尋不到一絲光澤，繼續梳，仍然梳不出一個樣子來，有的，只是溢滿腦際的懊惱。

俱往矣，生命就這麼萎縮了嗎？六十年，整整一甲子，應當是無限長的生命，看來好日子都過去了。春花、秋月，全成了過去式。而夏日的燦爛，怎麼我從未感受過，卻已經成了杳不可及的夢？

他戰戰兢兢的度著他的一日。一日之計在於晨，他最擔心一早起來惡兆臨頭——果然，整日的不順心，從自己的頭髮引起。快樂總是如白駒過隙，而鬱悶卻經常如漫漫長夜無邊無際，啃蝕得他連胃都翻騰著痛，一旦胃不適，食慾全無，一天也就自然報銷了。

噢，今天的一日神，看來並非是凶戾的煞星，一定是一位懨懨之神，把我弄得一天都無精打采——趕快用柔和之心來擋袒，千萬不要和袛發生磨擦。講理要和講理的人講，神鬼更如此，一旦來了不講理的神，你就快閃，閃過這一天，天下太平，閃不過，會死人的，人死了，你就和鬼一樣，也成了鬼。

「我就是閃躲不過嘛！」所以囉，這世上早已鬼多於人。你就得更加小心地過日子。幸好保護神永在，一日煞星也只能糾纏你一天，明天會有一個吉祥的微笑之神向你迎面走來。

人間多麼好，只要黑夜之後的黎明你醒得過來，樹在、花在，雲飄在藍藍的天空，一輪旭日正冉冉上升，這人世間多美好，鳥正為你歌唱之際，你還可為自己煮杯咖啡，巴哈的無伴奏大提琴樂聲更讓他感覺幸福已團團圍成一個圓圈，在蕩漾開來……

二十歲的時候，他像一架上升的飛機。世界在他面前都是會飛的、上揚的，連他小小的陽具，也都經常往上抬著頭；四十歲的時候，他讀《如何在四十歲前成功》，書上竟然這樣寫著：「四十歲不健康，健康不起來，四十歲不成功，成功不起來，四十歲沒有錢，有錢不起來……」到了六十歲，原先無神論的他，變成一個多神論者，且處處感覺與神同在。甚至，他認為，每一日，都有一個「一日神」陪伴著……創造神創造了他，人人都該感謝自己的創造神；我的創造神是誰？有一天，突然他這麼問自己，他要用溫柔的感恩之眼，向他的神膜拜。「你不用向我膜拜，重要的是，請不要激怒你的『破壞神』就好了！」一種遙遠的聲音彷彿來自天際，他看不到「保護神」的臉，卻清楚聽到一種來自祂的關懷聲音，原來「創造神」創造了他，最怕自己的作品不能長長久久的存活於世。「破壞神」無所不在，但只要不去惹祂，破壞神有祂自己忙不完的工作，「對，」保護神微笑著說：「你不惹是生非，我的日子也可過得輕鬆自在。」

自從感悟有諸神存在，如今他凡事小心翼翼，可「一日神」中搗蛋鬼特多，常來尋他開心，讓他經常有虛幻之感。

他有兩串鑰匙，一串用來開辦公室的各種門鎖，一串用來開家裡的門鎖，除了鑰匙，還有眼鏡和錢包，也是他經常在尋找的，愛捉弄他的「一日神」，經常喜歡和他玩躲迷藏，總以他身邊的這幾樣東西逗著他玩──靜物是沒有腳的，卻怎麼老是跑來跑去，「明明記得放在桌上」，桌上就是尋不到他要找的；「一日神啊一日神，我是有些年紀了，開始記不住這樣那樣東西放在確切的位置，請不要天天和我過不去，一定是你偷偷移動，讓我總是不停地尋找。」

有一天社區開住戶大會，三十二戶人家互相怪來怪去，彼此說話都毫不客氣，左鄰右舍都有院子，院子裡家家都種著花樹，樹長高了，難免枝葉會伸展到隔壁人家，於是起了糾紛，根據一種說法，你的樹枝進到我家院子，我就有權把它剪除，結果是你剪我家的樹，我當然同樣可剪你家伸延過來的樹枝，如此剪來剪去，鄰居自然成了冤家。

這是什麼神嘛！讓鄰居和鄰居都不得安寧。如果是「一日神」還好，臉紅耳赤吵一架，第二日彼此若肯反省，雙方說聲對不起，一笑泯恩仇。可惜這不是「一日神」能解決的，「一日神」之上還有一位「月神」，「月神」的上司是「年神」，啊，有人為了一棵樹，變成一輩子的世仇，年神也不得不退在一旁，只好讓破壞神親自出征，從此隔鄰兩家成了世仇，吵到後來，刀啊槍啊全部出籠，結果出了人命，好好的人不做，全去做了鬼！

「我不惹破壞神，讓我心平氣和的過日子！」他在心底祈求「一日神」。是的，就算只有一天，也是好的，有了一日的平平順順，明天就算有煞星登門，我也會低頭忍著，吃苦、受氣，本來都是人生免不了的運命啊！

「真的嗎？」躲在門角的「氣神」顯然不信，祂是一個讓人從早氣到晚的神。只要祂和你纏上，包你氣鼓鼓的板著一張臉，也說不出什麼原因，全身上下就是有氣。不想還好，越想越氣，好像全世界的人都欠著自己什麼。想起往事，更是件件讓人生氣。氣自己那麼容易生氣，為何別人的臉上能經常掛著笑容。可我就做不到，晚上睡在床上翻過來轉過去就是睡不著，當然也為睡不著生氣，徹夜翻騰到天明。容易生氣的人，還在為一整天氣鼓鼓的自己生著氣。

明日復明日，明日何其多。「一日神」啊！今天我的氣生得夠多了，我不喜歡生氣的自己，明天給我一個心平氣和的日子，至於明日的明日的明日，「一日神」，我是子民，在天地間，我已看盡人生百態，嘗盡人生酸甜苦辣滋味，在我離開人世之前，我只求能平凡的呼吸於凡人之間。

喜怒哀樂傷身，我只要平心靜氣過日子。「一日神」，請多派些老派且溫和之神保護我，那些古靈精怪、頑皮透頂的一日神，讓祂們和青少年去周遊，少年人精力旺盛，也喜歡刺激，就讓他們一塊去攪和吧！

王文興

欠缺[*]

　　那年我大概十一歲，因為我剛剛考進了師院附中的初中部。那時節我們的家還住在同安街；這是我們在臺北的最早居處；還不曾搬到後來的通化街，通化街以後又曾搬到過連雲街，但似乎在我的印象中還是每一先住的地方較以後的為好，每遷移一次便降差一等。也許是對愈遠童年的偏愛造成的這個錯覺。

　　同安街是一條安靜的小街，住著不滿一百戶人家，街的中腰微微的收進一點彎曲，盡頭通到灰灰的大河那裏。其實若從河堤上看下來，同安街上沒有幾個行人，白的街身，彎彎的走向，其實也是一條小河。這是我十一歲那年的安靜相貌，以後小型的汽車允許開到這一條街中來了，便失去這份寂寞了。我現在回憶的還是通行汽車以前的時代。

　　總之，在那個時候的同安街，可以看到花貓遊在短墙頭孄孄的散著步，從一家步到另一家。街中是滿眼的綠翠，清芬的花氣撲鼻，因為在人家的短墙背後植滿了花木，其中包含百里香、杜鵑、木芙蓉、夾竹桃、金雀花等等。花是最愛同安街的「居民」了，春天時開花，秋天也開花。而尤教人無從忘懷的還是那小街的夜晚，當黑暗的街衙點上靜穆的路燈的時候。夜晚似乎更靜了一些。賣雜貨的小舖子，不一樣的鬧市裏的商店，九點半鐘便打烊了。子夜從九點半鐘開始了。夜在這一條街上有著極安穩的睡眠；且有著最長久的睡眠。風搖動著蕭

* 選自王文興，《十五篇小說》，台北：洪範書店，1979年，頁163-176。

蕭的夾竹桃尖葉，天空裏細小星辰映眨著眼睛，幾個時辰以後，黑夜過去，黎明到來。在早霧中，仍不同於鬧市裏的商店，小雜貨舖子的頭家便卸下門板了。

一個少婦，在那一年的春天，在靠近大河的街尾的地段，開出一家裁縫店來。那時正是樸素淡雅的臺北市開始步向經濟繁榮的初期，一些三層樓臺的洋樓可以在這裏那裏看到疊落起來。從前一個冬季開始，我們小孩子便有趣的看著我們家對面的空地上築疊起一座洋樓了，我們那時覺得心中又興奮又悲哀，興奮是孩童的我們對一切新奇的經驗，新的聲音，新的顏色，新的物體，新的遭遇，均感到是對無任大的胃納的一種滿足，悲哀的是一塊可以踢球的臺芟空地從此失落掉了。樓房在春天蓋成，婦人便搬遷進來。這是一座橫三間，高三層的房子，婦人和她的家佔右邊的一組，上中下都歸他們，樓下便是開店，二樓和三樓住家。據說這一個少婦是這幢高樓的房主，整幢的房屋都屬於她的，我們小孩子都以為房主便要將整個的樓上下都拏來自己住，但她只住它的一部份，泰半租出去給別人。租出去後不滿一個星期，她又將那泰半轉售給別人。我們心中難免不覺地為她只住到一部份感到惋惜。

我那時候是一個早熟的孩子，雖然我的個子看起來較我的年齡還低兩歲。但正如一般普通發育不全的孩子樣，心智在另方面做著脫鏃的補償，比年齡還高兩歲。有一天，我發現我愛上這一個婦人了。發現的時節是在春假裏，綿延不息的春雨過後，百花競開的四月。

我是一個敏感而又內向的孩子，對於冶豔妖嬈的女人，心中存著懼怕的心念，只喜歡那容貌善良的女人（唉，到今天還是這樣），裁縫店的這位女主人便是我最易傾心的那類。

她大約三十五六模樣，不大愛打扮（這點很重要），臉上不抹胭脂也不搽粉，只在嘴唇上塗一層唇膏。那一張唇又是經常咧開露出雪白和懇切笑容的。還有她的一對眼睛，不僅美麗，露出的善良更重要。我對於她的愛不僅出於對她風姿的讚歎，也誠出於對她美德的一份景慕之忱。

　　愛在一個早熟的孩子身上，髣髴一朵過重的花開在一枝太纖細的梗莖下，不勝其負荷。我纔體味到愛原來是一種燃燒，光亮的火光如果是愛的快樂，造成這火光的卻是燃料牠自己的燒灼。我實在不能相信這種用燒灼自己來換取快樂的自虐狀的倒錯是種快樂。我雖則那時的人生體驗還不足短短的十一年，但我已經從若許過往的微細痛苦裡得出一條躲避苦痛的方法，便是你若歡喜上某件東西，或某個人，你即刻尋出他的缺點來，這樣你便能不再愛他，減卻你的負重。我在往後的幾天，便時常潛伏在她的店鋪的對面，極為冷酷地，想要看出她的醜貌來。然而我察看的愈久，愈覺得她的容貌美麗。因是我知道愛已陷進體內得更深，已經無能起出它，只有聽任它留在身體內了。

　　春假已經是最後一天，我預備著要盡這一天在外邊把假期玩滿。一早我便到新的踢球場那裏（改在雜貨店旁邊的垃圾堆前面），去等候其他孩子的聚集。我們這一天玩得比平時提早得多，那時大概纔八點鐘不到，我們吵鬧的尖亮嗓音吵醒了一座木樓上的一個公務員，他打開小窗子，身穿睡衣，探出頭來大聲的罵，我們的皮球又不時打到垃圾堆旁邊擺著煙攤的窮老太婆頭上，她提著一柄掃把想打走我們，但因為她老得實在沒有追上我們的氣力，只有像個衛兵一樣橫著掃把站在煙攤的前面，誰要跑那裏過的就吃她的一槍，但大家都不小心的不跑那裏過。阿久的小狗也跟瘋了似的跟著我們亂跑，牠不知為甚麼更是要跟定了我，不斷的跳到我身上，害我絆倒了好幾跤。直玩到阿久的媽媽出來將他們五個兄弟喊回家吃燒餅，我們纔把遊戲結束，悻悻然的散了開去。那時好太陽已經照了一街，人家墻頭的樹叢綠蔭蔭的，買菜去的媽媽們已打著接近夏天的遮陽傘，因為幾天以來陽光已增加了好一些熱度，熱得已經把打蕾的金雀花和夾竹桃都提早熱開了。我覺得口乾，便鑽到劉小冬家的院子裏，到他們的水龍頭上去喝水。水流得我一臉一脖子都是，我就讓陽光去自行的曬乾它。我走那裁縫店經過，看見那婦人在店門口和一位太太在聊天，並在逗弄太太手中的孩子玩。我爬上同安街尾的斜坡，下了臺階，到大河去。

　　這河在陽光下閃出粼粼的波光，像有千萬個圖釘在一上一落。河的對岸，兩輛牛車在沙灘上緩緩的爬著。站在一棵新纔吐芽的小樹底下，我聞到岸上烘乾了的泥土的香味，吹到還涼冷著的河風。從小樹下走開時，我不禁拉開了喉嚨，高聲的唱起：「夏天裡過海洋」。我邊唱著歌，手裡邊打著拍子，向河的上游走去。我走到一片竹林子裡，找到了一塊較平坦的地方，躺了下去。

前面是竹葉間閃閃發光的河流，後面是織錦得像波斯地毯的河邊農地，上面大塊大塊的翠綠是稻秧；大塊的鷿褐是新翻未種的春土；小長條的淺綠，像那醫生用的玻璃試片的，是豆苗；金黃的方塊是油菜花。這一切都在春風裡跋動。農夫的短小黑影，可以看見到在遠處工作中。田中不時傳來一陣陣輕糞的薄味。

我靜靜的躺著，想著各式不著實際的事情，但都是快樂的事情，讓幻想跟著天上被輕風吹送的白雲跑。我翻過一個身，把下頰枕在交疊的雙肘上，凝望著竹葉隙縫外頭的河。我想到那裁縫店中的婦人身上。我的愛情找不到任何的人可以告訴，只有向河訴說。後來這條河又成為我後一年學習游泳的痛苦所在，現在想起來，我的童年是可以說是在這一條河的旁邊長大的。我後來瞞著我的母親，一人到暑日下的河水中，懷著對溺斃的恐懼，獨自去尋求浮在水面的技術，但終未成功。從此我未有再學，因為失去了去掙扎的勇氣。

河流似也不懂回答我的細訴，我翻回原來仰臥的姿勢，用一面手帕蓋起了臉。

直到日頭行到當午的時候，我纔揭開手帕坐起來。我想起我的母親在家中等我吃飯，便離身站起，走回家去。這時田中的農夫都已不在，大概也都回家吃飯去了。

我在家裏遇到那個臺灣的莰芭尚，她還沒有走，仍在替我們熨燙衣服。莰芭尚看到我便問：「少爺，你看到我的春雄了沒有？」

我說沒有。

「你不是在外面和他一同玩的麼？」

我說不是。

「不曉得死那裏去了，我叫他快點來幫我拖地板的，可一直就沒看到他的影。我的春雄遠比不上你們的少爺呵，太太，你們少爺又聰明，又用功，小小的年紀就唸初中了，以後就唸高中了，唸完高中就做大官了。」她抖著一件父親的白襯衫說。

莪芭尚時常這樣的讚譽我，說我唸完了初中便唸高中，高中唸完了後她不知道尚有大學，所以唸完高中，就做大官了。

母親打著生硬的臺灣話回答她道：

「你還不也是一樣，春雄將來也唸書，也掙錢給你用，孝順著你。」

「多謝，多謝。可是我苦命人啊，太太，春雄的爹早早死了，剩下我一個人來帶著春雄，是，我別的都不希望了，只希望春雄也跟你們的少爺一樣，好好唸書，以後考進初中，進完初中高中——我可是怎麼的苦，洗衣服洗到了老，也要掙殼讓他讀書。」

「他會好好的唸書的，」母親說。

莪芭尚喟然歎了一口氣。

啊，這善良的老婦人，我還能記得她那深褐寬大的臉龐，像一塊黑麵包，溫軟而又光澤，那一種單純的善和純正的愛的糅合。後來她不知到哪裏去了，沒有人曉得。像這一種類型的溫良人物，隨著我年齡的逐見長大，愈見愈減少了。我想他們是不易生存在日趨工業化的社會裏的。關於她我記得清楚的還有另一件細事，那是出於童年時的怪異的觀察力：我常常注意到她的一雙光腳板，那是踏在我們家的油亮亮的地板上的，十個肥腳趾趵踪開來。我注意到這件事大概是因為家裏的人都穿拖鞋，我們放在玄關的門口也有許多雙請別人穿的拖鞋。莪芭尚大約還不習慣我們這種外省人的習慣，所以總是不穿。那時我在小小腦筋裏想，就是我們的莪芭尚肯穿上拖鞋了，我們又上哪裏去找那樣大的一雙送給她穿呢？

那春假的最後一天，我記得的另一件事是，下午我去買回了一本日記。某種對周圍的新奇，對自身內心生活的興趣，對於新萌芽的愛，以及未始不對春天，使我想到要模仿劉小冬的大哥的模樣，存一本日記。以上所回憶的當日舊事，便記在我當夜的頭篇日記裏。

　　春假過後，愛情痛苦着我，似乎在催促着我要去做一件甚麼事，一件能使我，至少感覺上，更接近她一步的事。我便想到要拿一件衣服到她的店裏去補（一種可悲的求愛方式，我承認），但她的店又是只收女裝的。我想不出其他的辦法，一天，（當一切都無辦法時，唯一想就的辦法便成為可行的辦法）我終於拿了一件童軍的上裝，脫了隻扣子的，到她的店裏。

　　她的店內擺設得十分雅致，四面的牆上貼著日本女裝雜誌上的婦人照片，牆角的几上並設著鮮紅的玫瑰花，店中坐著四個少女，低著頭踏車，並說笑著，彩色炫麗的衣料舖在機車上。

　　「你要做甚麼，小弟弟？」一個圓臉孔，掛著假珠項圈的少女抬起頭問我。

　　「我要縫扣子，」我說，轉向那一個婦人，她正站在一張長桌邊尺量衣服，「妳會縫麼？」

　　這婦人便過來接過了我的衣服，然後她說：

　　「阿秀，你現在給他縫一下，」說畢她就將衣服交給了那圓臉的少女，然後轉回身繼續尺量她的衣服。

　　我覺得被冷待的悲傷。

　　「哪一個扣子？」那圓臉的少女問我。

　　我告訴了她，眼睛望著那婦人。

　　「多少錢？」我問那婦人。

　　「一塊，」那少女說。

　　婦人似乎沒有聽見我問她的話，因為她連頭都沒有抬。我的悲傷遂種到心的根底裏去。但過了一會，我看到這個婦人戴起了一副眼鏡，於是我的悲哀便逐漸被我漸高的好奇心代替了。我奇怪她居然也戴眼鏡，彷彿這是一件最不可能的事。我不歡喜她戴了眼鏡的模樣，那似乎不再像她，她的眼鏡戴得太低，看起來太老，而且有一種貓頭鷹的表情。

　　然後我驀然覺得自己在店裏獃望得太久，於是便問那圓臉的少女：

　　「我等一下來拿好嚜？」

「不，就好了，你再等一會兒。」

我便不安地站在店中等她縫好。我又看了看掛在四壁的日本婦人，他們都很美麗，露著皓齒巧笑著，但奇怪為何她們的眼皮都是單眼皮。我又看了看那瓶放在牆角的玫瑰花，牠們仍是那樣的鮮紅，我覺得似乎比普通的玫瑰花還要鮮紅些，於是仔細的再看一下，發見原來是一瓶假花。

不久，一個男孩子從店後的樓梯上下來，一邊走，一邊的咬嚼一隻楊桃。他的個子比我高，也穿著童子軍制服，鼻樑上還架一付眼鏡。我突然領悟，這是她的孩子。我見過她有兩個纔學步的小孩，但直未見到過這一個：平時又不見他出來和我們玩的；新搬來的孩子都如此。萬分驚愕中，我，私戀他母親的人，目送他提著一隻水瓶上樓。

縫好了鈕扣後我便不多逗留的挾了衣服走出門。在門口我遇見莪芭尚正也跨步進來，我因為怕她告母親知道，我是瞞著母親出來縫鈕扣的，便一溜煙從她的身邊溜掉。

雖然我覺得在她的店裏受冷待了，雖然我看見她的遠比我還大的兒子，我的愛情仍舊沒有蛻變，一個孩子的愛是不易變更的。我仍舊把我十一歲時心中的少年全部的愛情熱烈獻送給她。

於是我便忠心的繼續這件無希望，無發展，也無人知道的愛情。這種絕望，反而替我的愛情染上了一層憂鬱的美。實在的說，我分不清楚當初這絕望到底是給了我苦惱，還是快樂。然而我能確定一件事情，便是在這樣的愛情裏，有一件我比成年人的快樂，我可以不必作無謂的擔憂，不必像成年人一樣無時地起杞憂它一日會突時告結；我劫免了這層憂慮，只要一日我的思慕存在，愛也便存在。現在看起來，那時候應當算作為十分快樂。

那一次到她的店鋪裏去，我記得，是我惟一去她店鋪中的一次。此後我尋不到其他的機會，而且，我不知道甚麼原因，我變得十分膽小起來，我並且為那一次的到她店中感覺無比的羞赧。想到只是藉著縫一顆鈕扣的藉口去她店中，我的羞赧愈回想愈增多，終而那一次的事情變成為一件恐怖一般呈現在眼前，使我出汗。勇氣是一件奇怪的東西。第一次不應當算作勇氣，第二次以後方纔能算。

我雖然未去她的店中，但我時常去她的店前。她的正對面是一家雜貨店，那裏賣孩子們吃的零食的，我時常到那裏去眺望她了。每每是我啣著半塊餅乾，望著她在她的店裏走動。有時我也看到她的丈夫，一個卅多歲的男人，騎著機器腳踏車，據說是在一家商業銀行裏做事。奇怪的一件事是，我竟然對這個男人了無妒意。從這點大約便可以知道我離成長還差得甚遠。我似乎不大明瞭丈夫的意義，以為他只是她的家中的一份子，定義就跟她的哥哥，她的叔叔，她的姐夫等一樣。但是假如她和一個別的男人談話，譬如她和隔壁的理髮匠閒聊一會，我的妒嫉會使我看到這個理髮匠倒在地上，胸口插一把刀。

於是日子便一天又一天的這樣過下去，像我的一頁翻過一頁的日記簿一樣。不久盛夏蒞至，學期的結束眼看就在前面了。我開始為我的功課擔心，因為我的代數唸得非常之糟，我非常憂慮我能不能在大考考得及格。代數的老師已經向我幽默的威脅過，說下學期他還要和我碰頭。我受驚得發抖，因為我讀書以來還沒有留過級，但這一年似乎留級的常數很大。然而即便是憂慮，也含著無限的期望，期望那自由並快樂，海闊天空的暑假的解脫。大考的烏雲便如是籠陰著我，我鎮日的手中捧拿代數，但我並沒有去看他，只是端著牠憂慮著。我變得蒼白復消瘦了。

終於那沉重的，壓迫人的大考過去了。所有的學生都像小鳥一樣逃出了囚籠，奔向自由的暑假的天空。快樂的我只是他們之中的一個，多少的孩子受到考試的折磨，多少的孩子等待他們的暑假，等待之中他們都以為暑假不會實現，或者所受的磨難將那期望時的快樂都銷盡了——噢，考試，噢，暑假。

那頭一天的假期的早上，我睜開了十一歲的眼睛，聽著好鳥的亂唱，看這個陽光燦爛的世界。考試已經丟在背後了，不管考得多麼壞，我已經完全忘記；也許孩子都沒有替過去擔憂的能力。坐在小床上，我能殼感覺到「這」是暑假，不是日曆上得來的指示，是一陣聲音，一道氣味，一片陽光，與以前不同的，提出來的暗示。我聽到蟬的知了知了，我發見天花板上印著洗臉盆的水影，聞到昨夜母親打開冬衣皮箱準備拿出來「過」日的樟腦丸的香味——我知道這是暑假。快樂是那一個孩子，他從床上跳下來。

年年到覺醒暑期的時候，也就是提醒我們該整理釣魚竿的時候。這時矮小的我們便到廚房的舊炭簍裏，把那曾被母親扔擲在裏面的一根細竹竿找出（那是我們自己做的），將牠拿到洗澡間裏，費了很大的一番功夫洗乾淨牠，以為今年又可以用牠釣到大魚了，雖則以後多半都是用牠釣田雞。

這一天我同樣的尋出了「釣竿」，洗好了牠，但拿在手上時，我突然覺得牠太不中看了。這曾是我矜傲過的，金色過的手藝，今年我看出牠的粗陋來。我覺得我需要一枝新的釣竿，而且須是一枝真的釣竿，不能再是這樣自個兒手削的彆腳一枝。我要一枝裝輪子的，有鈴鐺的，細軟得像鞭子的，揮出去時呼的一聲的——要問父親去買。我有希望得到這樣的一枝，因為我可以告訴他那最充足的理由，我十一歲了。

我依舊把這枝「釣竿」丟進舊炭簍裏。

我便去垃圾場尋找我的夥伴，我們都已經隔了兩週，為因大考，未出來踢球過了。我們的媽媽禁止我們。

我走裁縫店經過，希望看到她的臉，但今天她的店鋪沒有開門。想是她和一家出去玩了。我有些悵然若失，雖然每一天我都看到她，只一天未看也令我悵惘。

我的夥伴們早已經玩起來了，我急忙加入了進去，捲進了吵聲動天的戰團。我們快樂地直玩到日近旁午時方散。我的那一邊輸了，他們怪我不好，我怪加錯了這邊。但我們都驕勇十足的決定明天再來，一定要打敗他們。走回家去時，裁縫店依舊關著門，我又覺得了一次惆悵。

我回家時我的母親正在抱怨著說為甚莪芭尚今天不來洗衣服，有事情也應該叫春雄過來通知一聲。然後她便說看我一上午像撒放出了的鴿子一樣，玩得沒有了影子，本想叫我去找莪芭尚的，但找我先就找不到了；說我這樣會把心玩野掉的，不要以為是暑假便貪玩哩。這些當然是我最不愛聽的。

午日過後，我十分的瞌睡，外邊的太陽白亮得睜不開眼，屋子裏幾隻蒼蠅在沒有抹淨的餐桌面上停停歇歇地飛。我約莫盹了十分鐘，自己還不知道。醒覺來時，望着窗外的烈陽和屋內桌上的蒼蠅，一種很熟悉的感覺回到我的心臆。我為甚麼早先忘記了牠呢？原來暑假原都是煩悶的。

這時隔壁的劉伯母又慣例的來找媽媽聊天來了。她頂著滿頭像蛋捲似的髮捲子跨進門來，問我說：

「你媽媽在家嚜，小弟？」

「我在廚房裏啊，劉太太，」媽媽應道，「妳坐就來。」

劉伯母已經尋着聲音到廚房裏去了。

不一忽兒她們從廚房裏出來，媽媽的手上被滿了胰子的泡沫，找了一塊布來揩拭着。

「要死，妳怎麼自己洗衣服了呢？」劉伯母坐了下來說。

「不是啊，今天那個莪芭尚不曉得為甚麼沒有來，只好先自個兒洗一下囉。」

「就是嚜，我就要告訴妳的，」劉伯母說，搖着她一頭花枝亂顫的髮捲，「妳知道莪芭尚怎麼了罷？她的錢全部倒光了。一共兩萬塊錢的積蓄，全部倒的光光的。這回子她病了哩。」

「哦？是嚜？我都不知道她有積蓄，」母親說，覺得很詫異。

「是她辛辛苦苦洗衣服積起來的呵，她都說是積了給她的孩子以後唸書用的。真作孽哦，倒了她的。不過，這一回我們街上吃虧的人也多著哩。葉太太就倒了一萬，聽說還是大前天剛剛放進去的，且還是葉先生辦公廳裏的煤球代金哩。吳太太也埋了三千下去。哼，那個害人的妖怪女人呵，現在一家都逃了。」

「誰啊？」

「那個開裁縫店女人啊！妳不知道她好厲害，一倒就是十五萬。誰也沒有想到她會來上這樣一手。人家都是看她店業好，信用她，也貪她的利息不弱，哪知她噗突倒了。」

「真沒有想到，」母親說，「看她平時人滿好的嚜，哎，那莪芭尚這回也怪可憐的……」

我已經沒有聽清楚是母親下面說的甚麼。我轉過身跑出了屋子，向著那一家裁縫店跑。

裁縫店仍然關閉著門，門口多了幾個抱臂站在那閒聊天的婦人，我望著那店鋪，發獃了半晌。那幾個婦人的談話我能殼聽得到。

「昨天晚上溜走的啊，不曉得現在哪裏。」

「可以去告訴警察嚜，捉她回來。」

「沒有用處的，捉到了後她只需宣告一聲破產，便甚麼責任也沒有了。況且她有了錢，官司就吃不到頭上。」

「是早就有計劃的啊，」一個說，「你看她來這裏不到一個月就急著把大半個樓先賣出去。」

「聽說留下的這片店面子上一個星期也變賣掉了。」

有幾個下女站在店的右邊向內中張望，我也過去張望了一下，從一塊小玻璃窗望進去，裏邊已經空無一物了，縫紉機和桌椅都已經搬走了。

「真是的，連那幾個女工的工錢都不發就溜走了，真是好意思！」

聽到這一句話，我的耳朵也突然忿怒的發熱起來。

我回到家裏，劉伯母已經走掉了。母親看見我進來便喃聲說道：

「真是沒有想到，真是沒有想到。人心一年不如一年。市上發財的人多了，詐財欺騙的事也多了。市面的景象固鬧熱，但要人心壞了，要這樣的鬧熱做甚麼？這回幸虧得我們是沒有錢的人家，否則也放了進去，不也吃了她的虧！」

我們是沒有錢的人家，我的父親那時在一所中學裏教書，教書在臺灣，是應當歸為清貧的一類的。但莪芭尚又是有錢的人家嚜？我這麼想。為何也倒她錢？還有那幾個未領到工資的女工，為甚麼吞她們的？

那一天的傍晚，我拿了一本書登到屋頂的晒衣場陽臺上，我預備聽從我母親的話溫一點功課了。天空是寧謐的柔藍色，我頭倚著陽臺的欄杆，坐在灰格子的磚地上。

樓底下街的斜對面，我能殼瞥得見那家裁縫店，仍掩閉著門，但門口聊天的婦人已經離散了。

想起這一個婦人，想起她那一張美麗而慈善的臉，我一時還不能相信這一個婦人是一個騙子。但她委確是一個騙子。每想到這，我的心便忍受一遍陣痛的痙攣。

我還眷戀著我對她的愛情，我期望保存住牠。我閉攏上眼瞼，想像她的那張如白蘭花一般的面貌──然而每次我都會想起她的這一件缺憾；我便在那一張臉上看出醜惡來；花便枯萎的拘下了頭。

暮靄已漸漸的合上了同安街，人家的煙囪頂已繚起了淡白的炊煙，我發覺眼前的景緻漸漸地模糊了，原來我的眼中盛滿了盈盈的淚水。

呵，少年，也許那時我悲傷的不純是一個女人的失望我，而是因為感悲於發現生命中有一種甚麼存在欺騙了我，而且長久的欺騙我，發現的悲傷和忿怒使我不能自已。

自那一天以後，彷彿我多懂了一些甚麼，我新曉得了生活中攙雜有「欠缺」這回事，同時曉得以後還需面對更多「欠缺」的來臨。自那一天以後，我忘卻了那一個女人的美麗，雖然我直未能忘卻這一件事故的前後和始末。難怪的，那是我最初一次的戀情。

林懷民

穿紅襯衫的男孩[*]

第一次看到小黑，我並不喜歡他。

也許因為他頭髮太長，百結蛇纏的，兩道髮腳直拖腮邊。也許因為衣服太紅、太髒——我一向看不慣男孩子穿紅戴綠，何況那麼鮮明，帶有侵略意味的紅。

也許全不是，而是為了他那滿不在乎，彷彿天塌下來，也不會眨一下眼睛的態度。似乎他是另一個種族，我生活圈子以外的陌生的種族。

出了馮家，嘉克點上一根菸，開始抱怨，說馮師母想兒子想瘋了，連這種大保似的浪兒也往家裡迎。

太保？或者不至於那麼糟。但小黑那副模樣，在馮老師雅緻的客廳中，的確顯得格格不入。

這不過是我們的感覺，他可自在得像在自己家裡。這本書翻翻，那個花瓶摸摸，沙發上一坐，抓根菸，蹺起二郎腿，悠閒地吞煙吐霧起來。

那天小黑是到馮家修電唱機。馮師母直誇他行，抽水馬桶不通，自來水管漏水，什麼壞了，他三下兩下就弄好。前院葡萄架也是小黑搭的。不像我們這群大學生，除了讀死書，光會玩。有一晚大家聊天，聽唱片、燒咖啡、烤麵包，叭的一聲保險絲斷了，一屋子黑，沒人會修。

---

[*] 選自國立編譯館編，《青少年台灣文庫——小說讀本1：穿紅襯衫的男孩》，台北：五南，2006年，頁164-189。

小黑咧著嘴傻笑，露出一口參差不齊的白牙，右腳一挑一挑地玩弄那隻破得可以丟進垃圾桶的拖鞋，活像他真的行得不得了，真的比我們強。

馮老師握住他那根出名的菸斗，望著小黑，一個縱容的笑把臉上的皺紋拉得好柔好柔，跟在課堂上的神情儼然兩個人。

嘉克是個受不了冷落的人，聽見馮師母左一句小黑，右一句小黑，再也坐不住，要請馮老師寫推薦信的事也不提了，拖著彬美和我告辭。

彬美一肚子不高興，等到嘉克嚕囌起來，立刻開口頂他：

「少說兩句吧。你只是嫉妒。人家什麼地方得罪你啦？看多了你們這些自以為了不起、裝模作樣的臭男生，倒覺得他很可愛，要笑就笑，自自然然的。」

嘉克總算吃了一驚，托了托眼鏡，還未回嘴，彬美意猶未盡又加上一句：

「有時，我覺得像小黑這種人才是真真正正的在活著。不像我們──」

「媽的！」嘉克一氣急起來，粗話就出了口：「妳去追他好了，沒人攔著妳！」

我最怕他們吵架，夾在中間，不知幫誰才好，萬一鬧翻了，我又有幾天好看嘉克那份又悔又急、又硬著嘴巴不肯道歉的難過相，所以趕快說，我要先走一步，回去趕讀書報告。

或許以前也見過小黑，因為不認識也就沒注意。那夜之後，他倒像突然由哪個角落跳出來似的，一個禮拜內總有兩三回碰到他在學校附近晃來晃去，或在「山東味」看到他埋頭猛吃放了好多辣椒的大碗陽春麵，大半穿著那件火一樣紅的襯衫，和磨得發白的牛仔褲。

一天晚上，從圖書館出來，又在麵店遇上了他，吃完兩人一道走。

馮師母說他是高中畢業的。我沒話說，就問他，幹麼不上大學？這樣混日子有什麼意思？

小黑一揚眉，反問我，讀大學有什麼用？如果不愛讀書，只是看人家念，自己也跟著念，又算什麼？

他說，他從小就對書本沒興趣，他老子怎麼打他，也沒「屁用」。好容易高工畢業，當完兵，他老子說他是老大，應該留在家幫忙種地。他不幹，一個人跑出來討生活。

「做些什麼呢？」

「啊，多了。起初上山當測量員，我在學校學礦冶，別的沒學好，簡單的測量倒會了。那個測量工作結束後，回台南畫電影廣告，後來又在一家水電行做，做了四個月吧，跟老板兒子打了一架……」

「怎麼回事？」

「幹，那傢伙不是東西，把一個店員睡大了肚子，哄她到高雄冰果室當侍女，把孩子打掉，就不睬人家了。」

「就為這件事？怎麼啦？你喜歡那個女孩子？」

「沒這回事，」小黑把手一揮：「那女的長得根本不登樣！是後來他一天到晚折磨一個國小畢業的小學徒，我看不過，和他吵起來，他以為自己是少東可以揍人，刮我一記耳光，媽的，我就幹啦！」

「哦。」

「剛好那時候一位同學來找我上船打魚，我就出海啦。不過也沒幹好久，我好容易厭煩，什麼都做不長。」他一縮肩膀：「乾脆跑到台北打零工。」

「為什麼不回家呢？」

「不是說種地有什麼不好，只是我待不住，天天守著那幾分地，好沒意思！我喜歡打零工，你高興接多少就接多少，不高興幹就不幹，不必看人臉色。我喜歡台北，讓你覺得只要你肯拚命苦幹，有一天，你也能有那許多東西，許多錢。」

他說得那樣起勁，我不得不承認彬美是對的，她說小黑有那麼點逗人喜歡的地方──有股子勁兒，而那是我身上最缺少的。

冷不防，小黑問我：

「你將來幹什麼呢？夏天你就要畢業了。」

「當兵啊。」

「我是說當完兵以後。」

我自然明白他是問當完兵以後做什麼。可是，我不知道我要幹什麼。

「你也要去美國留學嗎？」

我想我是有點想出去的，大家都出去。大家都說，成績這麼好，不出去實在可惜。嘉克和彬美是說什麼也要走的，正緊鑼密鼓地申請學校。可是，芸康已經跟我攤牌了：「要走你自己走！」

她一天到晚說，看那些小說，留學生日子是怎麼過的！我說小說大半是假的。她馬上又說，她一個遠房堂姐去了三年，倒有一年住在精神病療養院，還是她同學寄信回來講開，家人才知道，還以為她在新大陸享福呢。

「留在國內，一樣可以發得起來的。」芸康振振有詞：「如果你那麼想出去，等將來有錢出去玩一趟，環遊世界什麼的，還不是一樣。我們可以努力賺錢，賺夠了，去玩一趟，回來再從頭幹起。」

至於她自己，她才不在乎不出去。她最大的願望是：有一天能拋開一切，到陽光下，舒舒服服地打一場高爾夫球；那片草地看起來好迷人，在上邊走一定好安逸……

那麼，就不出去吧。倒不是非留著陪芸康打高爾夫球不可，說實話，我也不懂出去幹麼。不過，不出去又幹什麼呢？教書吧，我這麼懶散的人教教書最好。

我便對小黑說：

「也許教書吧。」

「教書有什麼好？苦巴巴的，一個月就拿那麼兩三千塊，現在我就能掙那麼多，如果運氣好一點的話。」

「可是，你難道不覺得這種生活不太穩定，太沒有保障了嗎？」

「誰管那些！我喜歡這樣自由自在。死不了的！」他的口氣大得可以喝下一整個太平洋的水，聳聳肩又說：

「咦，你的口氣倒跟馮太太一個調調，她一有機會就勸我安定下來，成家立業。哈，成家立業——我剛從教授家來的。你曉得我去幹

麼？替他們釘雞舍。馮太太說她要開始養雞了，真是活見鬼。他們家
又不少這兩個錢。兒子養大了，一個個出去了都不回來，這會兒又要
養雞！」

　我曉得馮師母為什麼要養雞。每次去他們家，總看到她在打毛線，
打了一件又一件。馮老師說美國東西多得很，用不著她費心。師母才
不聽他的，照打不誤。帽子、圍巾、襪子。只是從前替兒子女兒打，
現在也給三個孫子打。馮老師自己雖不打毛衣，卻也無所事事，躺椅
上一倒，咬著菸斗看少林門徒與武當派爭霸，看膩了，站起來，背著
手，在客廳裡，踱過來，踱過去。

　我自然不會告訴小黑這些事，說不定他知道的比我更多。剛好到了
我住處，我隨口說，我住二樓，沒事來玩。

　過了十天左右，小黑真的來了，不過不是來看我。房東找他來油漆
新翻修的幾個房間。

　一連兩天，整個房子瀰漫著刺鼻的新油漆味，以及小黑圓潤宏亮的
口哨——成曲成曲的流行歌。連嘉克也說，想不到這小子吹得這麼一
口好口哨。

　九月底的週末，和幾個同學去爬觀音山，回到家，帶著一身臭汗，
衝上樓，急著洗個澡。

　門半開，嘉克不在，小黑枕著我心愛的War and Peace，縮著長長的
腳，半開口，睡得爛熟，依然是那件紅襯衫，不知幾天沒換，變成黯
黯的醬色，滿身油漆顏彩，一腮幫子的鬍髭。

　我洗過澡回來，他已坐起，翻著一本畫報。見我進來，掀著白牙一
笑，好像不告而入並不是什麼了不起的事。他抓抓蓬草似的亂髮，
說：

　「幹了三天兩夜的活，幹，真能叫人垮下來。」東摸摸西摸摸，摸
出一包壓得扁扁的新樂園，又開始找火柴。

　「幹什麼去了？」我在桌上找到嘉克的火柴，遞給他。

　「畫招牌，國慶日用的小牌坊。我一個人包，兩千五，不過錢還要
等兩天才拿得到。」

「哦。」我不得不欽佩他，我當家教，被那個小鬼氣得半死，一個月才四百五。

他點上菸，深深吸一口，吐出來，舒展一下身子，說回來累得要死，下了車，懶得再走回他那個「狗窩」，就近上我這兒「休息一下」。

他那個「狗窩」，我去過一回，幫馮師母找他去漆雞舍。馮老師說雞舍漆個什麼勁兒，她一定要，要綠的，真虧她想得出來。

那回去，小黑不在，他的「狗友」在。狗友，那是他自己說。那地方，在一條拐彎抹角的深巷裡，又髒又黑，白天也要點燈。不過他不在乎：「反正只是個睡覺的地方。」四個榻榻米大，常常擠四個人，有時六七個。那批「狗友」都是打工的小伙子，有工作互通信息，分著做，大夥兒彼此照應。

「剛剛你進來時，嘉克在吧？」

小黑搖搖頭，說門根本沒鎖，就算鎖了，他照樣可以進來。

「你會開鎖？」

「不！」他夾著菸的手做了一個爬的姿勢，說他可以從走道上的氣窗爬進來，他知道我們上面的窗向來不上鎖。

「哦！」

「我是最會爬了，知道我為什麼被人叫小黑？我們在高中時，常常看白戲，沒錢買票，翻電影院的圍牆進去，我爬得最快，總是在上邊把那些爬不上來的小子拉上來，這叫『提拔後進』。有回看了部非洲打獵的電影，有一隻小黑猿，鬼靈精，爬上爬下的，他們就叫我小黑猿。後來覺得麻煩，叫著叫著，後邊的猿字乾脆丟了，叫我小黑！」

「你簡直可以去拍武俠片了嘛。」

小黑翻翻眼皮，笑嘻嘻地說：

「還有一年夏天，在台南畫廣告時，一家運河邊的飯店找我畫招牌，畫在三樓外邊牆上，好叫人老遠就看得見。我搭了個架子，搞了四五天才弄好。」

「畫完了那天，我錢也用完了，可是飯店的人一定要等經理看過，才肯給錢。我餓得發昏，只好去找那個在船上做的同學，剛好他也沒有錢，在餓肚子。他是活該，賭三色牌輸光了。我們兩個人口袋的錢加起來，也不夠喝冰水，坐在船上，看著運河裡紅一塊綠一塊的燈光，聽到那家飯店傳出熱鬧的笑聲，只能不住嚥口水。」

「我說，這樣坐下去也不是辦法，讓我上去弄點東西下來吧。誰叫他們不付工錢！等到打烊，我藉口把刷子忘在架上，一直跑上三樓廚房，趁著一個師傅出去倒冰水喝，抓了三隻烤鴨往下扔，那個朋友在後邊巷子接。誰知他笨得一隻沒接著，全在泥沙裡滾了好幾趟。怎麼洗也洗不乾淨，不過總比沒吃強。我們拿回船上吃，一面吃一面說，這烤鴨是沾過胡椒鹽的。把每根骨頭部啃得乾乾淨淨，躺在甲板上，兩個人聊著聊著，不知怎的，都睡著了。」

我聽得一楞一楞的，這是怎麼的生活呵！而小黑卻在氤氳煙霧中，拿來當笑話講。

「你常偷嗎？」

「不！」他皺起眉頭，彷彿奇怪我有此一問：「只有這一次，再也沒偷過，真的。我是氣昏了，氣他們不給錢。」

有些人騙起人來是臉不變色的，而我相信小黑說的是實話。我們坐得這樣近，我可以看到他的眼睛在說他沒扯謊。

「不談這個了！」小黑把菸蒂扔到地板上，用腳搓熄，衝著我喊：

「喂！」他似乎永遠學不會叫我的名字：「這張給我好嗎？」

他把畫報送到我胸前，是一頁機車廣告：「You meet the nicest people on Hondas，你在本田機車上遇見最好的人」。一大隊人馬騎著本田小機車，有帶鬖毛狗的胖太太，帶著女朋友的小伙子，帶花的家庭主婦⋯⋯

我說：「你要就拿去吧。」

他刷的一聲，撕下來，折進襯衣口袋：

「我搜集機車廣告。我要買一部摩托車。」

「本田？像廣告上的？」

「啊！」他皺鼻、咧嘴，一副鄙夷不屑的神情：「那種小機車只是給娃娃玩的——我要買一百二十西西的，還沒決定要什麼牌子。不過要紅的。」

「為什麼一定要紅的？」

「不為什麼。一個人總要有屬於自己的東西，自己的顏色。」小黑垂下頭，望著雙手，慢慢地說。

我第一次注意到，他這一個看起來並不碩壯的人，竟有那麼一雙厚實、寬闊、修長的巨掌，上面顏彩斑斑，錯雜地割著大大小小的疤痕和厚繭。一雙生活過的手。

「我高中起，就喜歡穿紅衣服，」他輕輕笑起來，「我老子最討厭我穿，說什麼家門不幸，出了個流氓，他愈恨，愈不許我穿，我愈要穿！」

小黑猛然抬頭：

「憑什麼我要穿得和別人一樣，穿得討人喜歡？名字是父母取的，你沒有選擇的餘地。名字是給人叫的，而衣服是穿著叫自己快活。我喜歡紅色。紅衣服讓我感覺到自己，走進人群中，還認得出自己；鮮紅的顏色提醒你，你還活著，要幹下去！不要睡覺！」

「有些時候，我打不起精神，就希望生點小病，甚至受傷、流血，這兒痠、那兒疼的。這些感覺都可以告訴你，你還活著。這是很要緊的：讓自己知道還活著！不然你什麼事也做不成。」

我捏著一把剛由浴室帶回來的溼毛巾，怔在椅子上。

從不知穿衣服還有這套大道理——要有屬於自己的顏色！我忽然感到自己好可憐，我沒有自己的顏色！什麼顏色都無所謂。」

如果要我由繽紛多彩的顏色中，挑一種給自己，我一定會茫茫然，無從選擇——說不定我也和小黑挑相同的顏色吧。我怎能斬釘截鐵地肯定自己真正討厭紅衣服呢？我壓根兒沒好好想過這問題啊。我又怎麼曉得，那夜在馮家，我看不順眼小黑的紅襯衫，會不會是因為自己心底也想穿而不敢穿，才討厭他。

如果世界上每個人都像小黑那麼「勇敢」，穿著各人喜好的顏色，世界一定會比現在更熱鬧更漂亮！

　　我站起來，把毛巾掛起來，決定不再中小黑的毒，胡思亂想。因為我居然有了個不倫不類的聯想：照小黑的說法，彷彿我這種情形不僅沒有個性，甚至與人盡可夫的女人沒兩樣！

　　小黑掏出那頁廣告，認真看起來。

　　我倒了兩杯開水，一杯給他。

　　「那麼，又為什麼要買摩托車？」

　　「騎啊！」他臉上又浮現了那份「多此一問」的表情：「噗──泊！泊！泊！泊！」

　　小黑雙手用勁，抓住看不見的車把，眯著眼，歪著嘴，兩道粗眉拉得一高一低；一縮脖子，左肩微傾：

　　「刷──轉了一個彎！卡──開足油門！刷──你一口氣也喘不來，呼吸停止了！只有速度！刷──好過癮！」

　　他由喉嚨迸出一串模糊的低吼，聽起來不像摩托車聲，倒有點像汽車或噴射機。

　　車聲中斷，小黑睜開眼睛：

　　「你會騎摩托車嗎？」

　　我搖搖頭，不願告訴他，連試一試的念頭也從未有過，看看報上那些騎士喪生的新聞已夠令人心寒。

　　「看了《第三集中營》沒有？」

　　我立刻點頭。

　　「記得吧？那裡頭，史蒂夫‧麥昆騎著機車，噗的一下，一蹦跳過鐵絲網。好過癮！能這麼神氣一回，死了也甘心！」他一口氣喝完那杯水。

　　小黑左手用力往床沿一拍，抿緊嘴，下巴一翹。

　　「我拚了老命也要買一部！最慢明年。等我拿到那筆兩千五的工錢，再添個五百，湊整三千可以標一個會，我認三份，到過年時，就能滾成四千五。另外，我想辦法再掙一點。然後……」

　　我忽然受不了他那份咄咄逼人的認真模樣，和「老子說要做，就做得到」的自信，禁不住攔口打斷他的話：

「然後，買車子，後座帶個女孩子，招搖過市。對不對？」

他唇角的一絲笑陡然飛走，眼皮倏然掛下，揚高聲音說：

「才不呢。去他媽的女孩子！」

小黑歪著頭，向我投來一個徵詢的眼光：

「女孩子沒有機器聽話。女孩子像泥鰍，抓不住！」說完哈哈大笑。

他把手一揮：

「不管你怎麼說都無所謂。反正，我有一天要有部摩托車。這是我唯一的夢想。」說著，人一溜，又躺回床上，枕著胳膊，閉上眼，黧黑而沒洗乾淨的臉，浮現一個沉入夢境的笑，安詳、滿足。

我心頭竟激起一陣羨慕之情。儘管已經二十多了，小黑看起來好小好小，是天下最幸福的那種人；單純無知的兒童，整個世界都在他們掌心中。

他一定也對馮師母提過買摩托車的事，因為幾天後，她對我搖頭，說她愈來愈不明白現在的年輕人心裡打什麼主意。辛辛苦苦，做得要死賺來的錢，不做正經打算，居然要買什麼機車。也不說積幾個錢，娶太太，成家立業。

「這孩子！」師母歎口氣，把頭搖得快斷了：「時代真的不一樣了！」

久久，很少再看到小黑。偶爾在街上碰面，也匆匆忙忙打個招呼就過去了，沒有多談。只見他頭髮更長了，下巴變尖了，顴骨聳起來，眼眶凹下去。他弄了一輛腳踏車，騎起來滿車零件匡匡作響，老遠就能聽到。

那時已經很冷了，他換了件夾克，忽藍忽紅。我說他到底換了「屬於自己的顏色」。彬美說他還是老顏色，紅的。最後弄清楚，只有嘉克說對了。他說，那小子最會作怪，穿了件可以兩面穿的夾克。

禮拜天我起遲了，快十點鐘才去吃早點，不想在豆漿店遇到小黑。紅夾克灰了一層，眼珠布滿血絲，無精打彩的，我問他怎麼回事。他說，賺錢！

「現在我什麼都幹了，只要給我錢。」

「你不知道，我那三千塊被人倒了。那操他媽的混蛋聽說帶個女人，人家的姨太太，跑到東部去了。我不怕錢要不回來，台灣就是這點兒大。可是，一切又要從頭來。你知道，一輛最起碼的摩托車也要一萬多。」

「何苦呢？小黑，」我放下燒餅油條，勸他說：「你幹麼要這麼急呢？慢慢來嘛。把身體拖垮下來，有了摩托車，你也別想騎——對了，你為什麼不分期付款買？」

「我不要！」小黑唏哩嘩啦喝完豆漿，手背嘴上一抹，站起來，要走了：

「分期付款。那是說，錢沒付清，東西還不能算你的。而我要完完全全屬於我的東西！」

——我彷彿和著豆漿喝下了一隻蒼蠅。

真希望我是個百萬富翁！這樣我便能不費力地買一輛機車送給小黑，雖然我知道他不會要。

五月裡，嘉克和彬美申請學校都有了結果。彬美弄到加州大學的免學費。威斯康辛答應給嘉克獎學金，一學期八百。兩個人樂得什麼似的，只差沒去買鞭炮慶祝。彬美決定先走，嘉克服完兵役隨後就去。

既然連獎學金也有了著落，對畢業考嘉克可不如往日那般賣命了。我念得焦頭爛額，他倒悠哉悠哉。還剩最後兩門，他也不管三七二十一地跑去看他的電影。

開了幾天夜車，我倦得要死，沒撐到十一點便抱著書，和衣睡過去。嘉克回來，我被他開門的聲音吵醒。

「小黑那小子真的瘋了！」他一面脫上衣、鬆領帶，一面說，他出去時，看到小黑騎著一輛摩托車，在小街上來來回回地馳得飛快。那輛車，奇形怪狀，擋風玻璃上還畫了一顆紅心，一個裸女。

「也許他買了輛二手貨。」我說。

幾天後，我自己也看到了那輛機車。

我們班上，在系主任的明智決定下，廢棄了傳統的謝師宴，只以寫信來表示我們對教授的感激。事情傳出後，報紙還寫短評讚揚，也有別的學校跟著響應，學我們的榜樣。

可是，沒了謝師宴，到底不十分像要畢業的氣氛。班上幾個人議決，畢業典禮前夕，同學們來次聚餐，不管如何，這是最後一次了。

餐會席設一家西餐館子，吃自助餐。那天，彬美特意穿上新裁的旗袍，又仔細修飾一番，磨磨蹭蹭的，叫嘉克和我等了好半天。三人坐車到中山北路，已遲了二十來分。

剛下車，就看見對面街口聚了些人，人人脖子拉得直直，仰頭往上望。上面，四層樓外，一個人在表演空中飛人。

嘉克是愛看偵探、西部動作片的料子，碰上這等驚險場面，豈肯白白放過。於是，我們也加入看熱鬧的人群。

那人在牆上寫字。沒搭架子，攔腰綁了根粗繩，一端拉上五樓陽台，又直垂樓底，一個小伙子緊緊拉著。

那個不怕死的傢伙，左手攀住繩子，兩腳抵住牆壁，挪出右手，握把刷子，一筆一筆地塗著。「國際畫廊」四個大字，已寫完三個，正在「廊」字上下工夫。

想是顏料用盡，那人把刷子往腰際一插，雙手抓牢繩子，一步一步地沿嵌著光滑的瓷磚的牆壁游走，四樓窗口，另一個人，手伸得長長，提著一小桶顏料等他。

已近黃昏，有點風，一陣又一陣地把繩子吹得繃繃響，把那人頭髮颳得一起一落，褲管灌滿了風，不住往上掀。下邊的人，一個個張口結舌，屏息靜觀，只有讓心跳得像幫浦，頸子仰著發痠的份兒。

「要是繩子斷了怎麼辦？」彬美拂住心口說。

我擔心的倒不是繩子。而是怕那雙長長的，瘦得幾乎沒有臀部的腿會乍然撐不住，挫了下去。看一個人穩在半空中，要上不上，要下不下，比看他掉下來更難過。

嘉克拿下眼鏡，神經兮兮地擦了一遍又一遍，戴上去，四周一望，輕呼一聲：

「那不是小黑的摩托車嗎？」

聽到小黑的名字，那拉繩子的男孩子，猛然轉頭望我們一眼，一額角汗，兩眼發直地衝著我一咧嘴巴。我認得他，阿土，小黑的伙伴之一，我上次去他們「狗窩」，小黑不在，他在，我們還聊了幾句的。

再抬頭，那個攀在窗口弄顏料的人，不正穿了那件要把整棟樓燒起來的紅襯衫嗎？

怪的是，知道他是小黑後，我竟不再擔心。我記起他有一雙多麼有力的大手，記起他告訴我，他被人喊小黑的原因。

「阿土，這是怎麼搞的啊？」

「噓！別跟我說話！」阿土頭也不回地嚷。

他是對的。我閉了口。

然而，沒一分鐘，阿土終究忍不住，開口說：

「這個人，誰也拿他沒辦法。不是說有了新規定，招牌英文字不可以比中文字大嗎？人家要把英文字換成中文。他就搶著要接，說什麼刷去幾個英文字，再寫四個字，就賺五百塊錢，是天上掉下來的運道。要他搭架子，他又嫌麻煩，說沒有為四個字搭架子的道理。我拗不過他。他這個人，說要怎麼幹就硬要怎麼幹，誰也攔不住……」

「快別說話了！」彬美叫起來：「拉好你的繩子！等下人摔死了，你怎麼辦？」

阿土丟給她一個白眼。

彬美趕緊掩住口，然後又說，她再也受不了，要走了，再說我們已經遲了不只半個鐘頭了。

拐過街角，嘉克掏出手帕擦汗：

「這小子真是活得不耐煩了，這麼要錢不要命！」

彬美開了口，又要頂他，我趕快給她使個眼色，總算沒發作。

吃過飯出來，彬美一路惦記著小黑不知怎麼樣了。

小黑自然沒有跌死。至少，第二天報上沒這條新聞。而且，他又來找我了。

那是我離開台北前夕，嘉克已捲了鋪蓋滾回台中。我與芸康去看電影，宵夜，送她回家，一個人摸回住處，已過午夜。

脫了衣服，洗過臉，正待熄燈上床。有人敲門。是小黑。很破例地穿了件純白運動衫，把一張臉襯得黑亮。

他說，幾個朋友從南部來玩，「狗窩」怎麼也擠不下，希望能在我這兒過一夜。

「沒問題，進來吧，你可以睡嘉克的床。」小黑不要被子，不像我，這種大熱天還要封得像蒸籠。我拿張毯子給他，疊起來當枕頭。

「嗨，我那天看到你的精采表演了！」

「什麼表演？」

「空中飛人，還看到你那輛美女摩托車。」

「哦，」小黑笑了，眼睛一亮，神采飛揚的：「沒什麼。有人送你五百塊，你總不能不要吧。車子也不是我的，已經還人了。」

他點上一根菸：

「剛剛上哪裡風流？我十一點來過一回，房東說你明天走。」

我告訴他，我下禮拜一入營，剛剛陪芸康看電影去，我們已決定年底訂婚。

「咻！」他吹了一聲長長的口哨。

「說正經的，你自己呢？小黑，」我突然變得像老太婆，一心想做好事：「你自己難道沒想到這一層嗎？家到底是很重要的。要嘛就趁早，一轉眼，我們都會變得七老八老了。」我簡直不知所云。

小黑還是嘻皮笑臉。

「那句話怎麼說的呢？女孩子像泥鰍？」

他絞起眉，吸了一口又一口菸，把自己囚在那團白濛濛的霧裡，眼光透過重霧，落在窗外的夜黑……

那不是個新鮮的故事。但小黑說起時，我這個沒經歷過情感波折的人，也不了解那是多麼沉重的打擊。

在台南，他幫一個家具店畫招牌，出出入入的，認識了店主的女兒，兩人要好了。女方家裡反對，嫌他沒有錢，沒有固定的事。小黑進電器行做，多少也為了讓她家人知道他不是不肯定下來，他可以從頭苦幹。他母親請人去提親，被一口回絕了。

「幹，我那時真想提把刀子，去把她父親捅了。」他說：「可是，我回頭一想，也用不著，只要她肯跟我，我們可以走。不想她翻來覆去就是那句話：她不願傷父母的心。」

於是，小黑把她丟在一家冰店，一個人走了。沒多久，電器行的差事也丟了。

「我第一次出海回來，人家告訴我，她嫁到嘉義去了。才兩個多月的工夫。昨天還在對你說，非你不嫁，今天已變成別人家的老婆。女孩子啊！」

「沒再見面？」

「去年清明，我回家時，在火車上碰見她。她在嘉義上車，抱個小孩，沒地方坐，我站起來，把位置讓給她。她要跟我講話，我沒理她，走到另一個車廂。還有什麼可談？幹！」

「所以，女孩子像泥鰍？」

小黑把菸蒂往外拋，一滴火紅殞失在漆黑中，輕輕一聳肩膀。

「或許我不該這樣說她。人都是一樣的，像魚，抓不住！我對自己也信不過。我怎麼知道，我明天會變得怎樣？——不要說人，就是狗，天天跟你走，說不定有一天看到一條母狗朝牠搖尾巴，你叫破嗓子，也叫不回來了。這個世界，你什麼也不能相信，除了自己的一雙手！」

他微微攤開手，左拇指有一痕新創，想是那天繩子搓傷的。

「你忘了，還有一樣東西。」

「什麼？」

「摩托車。」

小黑淡淡一笑，揮揮手，說不談了。

「睡吧！明天你還要坐半天車呢。」

他自己說睡就睡，踢掉拖鞋，爬上床，翻個身，面朝牆壁，不一會兒，便響起均勻的鼻息。

倒把我一個人留下來，對著天花板，想了好多事。

「隨你說，反正，我有一天要有摩托車，這是我唯一的夢。」

那也許是很踏實的夢。儘管馮師母說那不切實際。可是，做人總要抓住一點東西，才活得下去。像嘉克、彬美一心一意想出國，芸康「有一天，能拋開一切，到陽光下，舒舒服服地打一場高爾夫球」的願望，或者像馮老師看武俠小說，抽菸斗，師母打毛線，養雞，靠幾張藍藍的航空郵簡，把日子打發過去。

小黑買了摩托車以後，是否會發現事情真的如想像中那般的美好，那是另一回事。重要的是，他有一個可達成的夢，他知道他要什麼，還肯拚了命，付出代價去實現它。

比起他，我不知道自己是幸或不幸，我沒有轟轟烈烈、曲折動人的生活；更糟的是，我迷迷糊糊得過且過，隨遇而安，到底為什麼活著也弄不清楚。唉！我嘆口氣，衷心希望軍中生活會使我改變，變得更堅強些。

入伍沒兩個月，部隊奉調金門。新的環境，新的人物，新的生活，使我逐漸淡忘了小黑和他的摩托車。

年底，我得到一週假期，回台北跟芸康訂婚，順便回學校領畢業證書，看馮老師。

聽說我訂婚了，馮家二老都很高興。師母還巴巴翻出他們二兒子復活節在紐約結婚的照片給我看。一面說，這一來，只剩下小女兒還未找到對象，不過她並不擔心。在美國，出色的中國留學生多的是。

不知怎麼搞的，我聽了不十分自在，沒頭沒腦地問她是不是還在養雞。

「不養了，」師母說：「吃力不討好！中秋前後，一場雞瘟，三十隻死了二十來隻，剩下的，宰了吃啦。再說，再也沒那份閒工夫啦……」

馮老師接著說，大女兒兩個月前又生了個女兒，美國生活太緊張，一下子照顧不來三個小傢伙，決定過了聖誕，把嬰孩送回來，請外公外婆撫養。

「這一生拖兒帶女，好容易一個個長大滾蛋，想不到臨老又來這個小禍水，只怕以後沒清靜日子過了！」

馮師母立刻瞪他一眼，怪他說什麼「小禍水」。

但，兩個人額上笑得皺成一堆的紋路，卻寫清了他們對這「小禍水」即將帶來的麻煩，是多麼地歡迎惟恐不及。

突然，師母問我：

「記得小黑嗎？回台南鄉下去了，你們畢業沒好久，他也走了，聽說他父親病得厲害。」她的口氣淡淡的：「還記得他要買部機車呢。」

聽說彬美在加大另有新交，一退伍，嘉克忙忙辦好手續，八月底就走了。我則真的拿起教鞭，吃粉筆灰，誤人子弟。芸康在一家貿易行做事。

週末陪芸康看電影，在中華路口，一個人喊住我。回頭一看，居然是一年多沒見的小黑，或許是一身油汙的關係，看起來老了些，頭髮還是亂七八糟，髮腳倒修得乾乾淨淨。

我向他介紹芸康，他說有一回芸康來我們學校找我，他見過的。

「我現在在這家汽車修理廠做，不東跑西跑做散工了。」

「摩托車呢？」

「啊！」他咧嘴一笑，依然是那口參差的白牙，依然是昔日的小黑！

「快了。也真不容易。去年夏天，我父親死了。家裡一切靠我，我說服母親把地租出去，等我弟弟長大，再讓他幹吧！我妹妹進大學了，中興，她要上進，做人家大哥的，只有高興的份兒……」

我們趕時間，沒能多談，我寫了住址給他，要他來玩。

他一直沒來。

大半年過去，我和芸康結了婚，生命似乎步入軌道。本來就不怎麼活躍的我，婚後變得更不想動，常常下了班回家，電視機前一坐，一晚上就過去了。芸康說我變成老夫子了，我也覺得自己越來越像馮老師，只差沒去買根菸斗。芸康可仍念念不忘她的高爾夫球，雖然她根本不會打。我總說，有一天我們一定會去。

六月裡，一個大清早，似醒未醒之際，遠遠聽得一輛摩托車泊泊泊駛近，戛然而止，過陣子，門鈴鬼咬一口似地吼起來。

「要死了，這麼早，有誰會來？」芸康推推我。

我揉著眼睛，走過去，打開窗簾。

樓下，馬路中央，立著穿紅襯衫的小黑，一輛晶紅的摩托車像匹小馬停在他身邊，連同院裡草坪上的露珠，映著旭陽，閃閃發亮。

我飛奔下樓，開門讓他進來。

「小黑，你終於買了！」我興奮地按住他肩膀。

他不說話，光是傻呵呵地笑。這樣的笑容，我只有在上個月，同事老黃當了爸爸時，才看過的。

我感染了他一臉煥發的笑，半天，才又說：

「真叫人開心，不是嗎？」

好蠢的一句話。我曉得我不必再說什麼，小黑明白我真正為他開心。

我們一道吃早點，天南地北瞎扯，我告訴他，彬美來信說她要結婚了，不過新郎不是嘉克。馮家夫婦為美國回來的小外孫忙得沒工夫養雞。

吃過飯，小黑說他送我到學校。一路風馳電掣，世界在車旁飛近，旋轉起來。我不安地說：「哎，慢點，小黑，慢點。」

小黑把油門開到最大，把車子駛得像匹馬，笑得像個鬼。強勁的風，將他的頭髮一根根拉直起來，拂到我臉上。

我想起幼時騎竹馬，胯下夾著一根竹子，口裡喊著「馬來了！馬來了！馬兒快跑！」跑遍一條大街的往事。慢慢地沉醉在那份由高速度所帶來的近乎窒息的快感之中。

到了學校，我舒過一口氣，要他以後常來玩。雖然我們之間的話題，一直僅限於他對摩托車的熱愛，現在他宿願已償，而我相信，我們仍舊可以聊得很好的。

小黑滿口答應，卻沒來過。

禮拜天，芸康上街，看上一隻皮包，又覺得太貴，沒買。回來念了幾天，到星期四，忍不住了，死乞活賴地拖著我，一定要我去看那隻皮包，幫她作最後決定。

　　從百貨公司出來，天飄著毛毛細雨。芸康買了皮包，興致勃勃地要淋雨散步回去。

　　路過那家汽車修理廠，我進去找小黑。

　　「小黑？」一個胖敦敦的，老板模樣的中年人，衝著我皺眉頭。

　　「你不知道嗎？死了！都快一個月啦。這個人！我早說過，一個人迷跑車迷到這般田地，遲早會出事的。收了工，老是一個人三更半夜的偷偷開上麥克阿瑟公路……，就這樣，誰知道怎麼回事，衝下山谷，躺了一夜，才被人發現……。」

　　有個人，有個人有那麼件紅得像火的襯衫……

鄭清文

三腳馬[*]

○

　　我從臺北坐了三個鐘頭的車，到外莊找我工專時的同學賴國霖。最近我們開了一次同學會，難得自畢業以後二十多年第一次再見到他。在會上，大家做自我介紹的時候，才知道他回到故鄉開一家木刻工廠，專門製銷各種木刻品。

　　他的工廠規模相當的大，佔地有兩百多坪，前落兼做店面。我來這裏，主要是想找些馬匹的作品。我收集馬匹多年，已收集了大大小小兩千多件，有木頭的，也有石頭的。今年是馬年，我預備利用這個機會多收集一些。

　　他已給我看了許多木刻。也許因為大量生產的關係，那些作品都過於規格化。我們正走動觀看，突然牆角有一隻奇特的馬引起了我的注目。那隻馬低着頭，好像在吃草，也好像不是。牠的臉上有一抹陰暗的表情，好像很痛苦，也好像很羞慚的樣子。我收集了那麼多的馬，就從來沒有看過這樣的表情，就是繪畫，恐怕也找不到。

　　我把它拿起來仔細的看了一下，才發現那隻馬竟跛了一條腿。這使我感到非常驚奇和惋惜。從馬身上的線條看，牠比另外的馬都來得生動有力，尤其是臉部的表情，絕對不是其他的作品所可以比擬的。牠是素面的，沒有上漆，甚至於沒有用砂紙磨過，還可以看到刀鏤的痕跡。從牠被放在不顯眼的地方看來，可以推測牠沒有受到重視。賴國霖看到我拿在手裏把玩，不忍釋手，就告訴我說：

---

*　選自鄭清文，《三腳馬》，台北：麥田，1998年，頁169-205。

「那是一個怪人刻的。他喜歡刻一些殘廢的馬，我們去他家收購，有時隻數不夠，他就把殘廢的加了進去，他說不能賣，等他多出來，把殘廢的換回去，就像當做零錢找來找去。」

「你店內有沒有他刻的？我是說普通的馬。」

「有，這就是。」他隨手拿一隻給我看。「你覺得怎麼樣？」

「這就奇怪了。跟其他的差不多。也許你們使用模子的關係。不過，牠的眼睛，和其他的不一樣。你看一般的馬的眼睛是看側面的，他的馬是看前面的。還有，這些鬃毛，尾部和大腿也不一樣。但完全不能和那一隻跛腳的比。你看，這是動的、活的馬，而且有表情。要表現動物的表情，實在太難了。」

「他的馬，都是經過我們再修整過的。我們都說他太懶，連砂紙都不磨一下。為了這，我們還扣他的工錢呢。」

「那個人的作品多不多？」

「我也說不出來，看他把東西亂堆在一起，我們也不知道什麼是作品，什麼不是。不過，我們所要的，卻越來越少，以前，我們一個禮拜要去收一次，現在就要兩三個禮拜，甚至一個月才去一次。他放着正經的工作不做，一個人躲在那裏，刻一些奇奇怪怪的東西。」

「他真的不賣？我是說，像那些跛腳馬？」

「我也不知道。誰知道這個怪人心裏想着什麼。」

「你是不是可以帶我去看他？」

「去看他？做什麼？」

「我想看看有什麼特別的東西。」

「特別的東西？」

「就是跛腳馬之類的奇奇怪怪的東西。」

賴國霖用機車載我去，我們在彎彎曲曲的山路上駛了有半個鐘頭。當我們駛到坡頂，就停了下來，由高處望下看，看到山巒間有一塊比較平坦的地方，大概只有一二十戶民家散落其間，有的相鄰，有的隔開一些距離。

「那就是深埔村。」賴國霖說，又開了機車，駛下山坡。

那是一間非常簡陋的土塊厝，所砌的土塊都已蝕損，裏頭的稻草已鬆開，像尺蠖翹出來。這一間土塊厝算是邊房，正廳也是土塊厝，只是在表層多塗上石灰，看起來比較新淨。

門是半掩着。賴國霖輕推了一下，一走進去，我就聞到木料的香味。因為外面陽光強烈，突然走進到幽暗的房間，眼前什麼都看不見。我們在裏面站了一下，才漸漸看到在竹格子的小窗底下坐着一個六十多歲的老人。白多於黑的頭髮剪得很短，鬍髭也已有五六分長。

「國霖嗎？」

「是的，吉祥叔，我給你帶來一位客人。」

「客人？從哪裏來的？」他望着我看了一下。

「臺北。」

「臺北市嗎？」

「是的。」賴國霖說。

當我的眼睛已習慣，我就把四周掃視一下。在窗下有一尺高的工作枱，放着木槌和各種雕刻刀。老人坐在地上一塊扁平的小板上，雙腳微曲，往前伸，雙腿間放一隻還不知是何物的木塊，地上全是木片。牆角橫豎地堆着一些作品。

「你的朋友是臺北來的？」我還沒有看清楚那些作品，老人又開口了。

「是的，他是我的同學，在臺北唸書時的同學。」

「你知道臺北的近郊有一個叫舊鎮的地方？」

「我是舊鎮的人，我在那裏住了三十年，一直到十幾年前才搬到臺北。」

「你住在舊鎮什麼地方？」

「警察分局對面。」

「警察分局，是不是以前的郡役所？」

「是的。」

「從你的歲數和住的地方看來，你應該認得我。」他說，慢慢轉向我。

「我認識你？」

「還認不出來？」他指着自己的鼻樑說。從眉間到鼻樑上有一道白斑，好像是一種皮膚病。

「是不是……」

「你認得了？我就是白鼻狸。你是誰的兒子？」

我告訴他父親的名字，也告訴他父親以前開木器店。

「我記得他。我以前曾經打過他。」

「我知道。父親曾經告訴過我。」

「你父親還在嗎？」

「不，已去世了。」

「他有沒有講過我什麼？」

「……」

「你說，我不會介意。」

「我父親說，三腳的比四腳的更可惡。」

他沉默了片刻，然後從工作枱上拿起一個四五寸大的像框。「你認識她嗎？」

「不認識。」

「她是我的查某人。」

「我好像記得她的姐姐和妹妹都當過老師。」

「對，對的。」

「這一位呢？」我指着左下角一張兩寸大，已發黃的照片。

「這是我的第一張照片。我第一次到臺北時照的，寄回來給我母親的。」

照片上是剃着光頭。我注意看着他的鼻樑上，却找不到那一道白色斑。他好像已覺察到。

「那是照相師修過的。為了這，他還多拿了我五錢。」

「你是說，很小就已有了？」

「嗯，很小，很小……」

一

「烏腳矕，白鼻狸……」

一行五人，以阿狗為首，各人拿着陀螺，半走半跑，往墓仔埔前進。阿祥比那五個人中最小的阿河還矮了半個頭，也在後面緊緊地跟着。

「烏腳矕，白鼻狸，轉去，不要跟屎尾。」殿後的阿金大聲說，把手裏的陀螺猛打下去。

「我也有……」阿祥說。天氣很冷，說話時會冒出白煙。

「有什麼？有蘭鳥？」阿成說。

「我也有干樂。」

「什麼干樂？自己刻的？比蘭核還小！」阿進說。

「我阿舅說，要買一顆這麼大的給我。」阿祥說，用手比了一個碗口。

「買來再講。」阿金說。

「我阿舅住在臺北。」

「臺北有什麼稀罕。」

「轉去，不轉去，拿你來脫褲。」

阿祥一手捏着陀螺，一手拉着褲頭。他的褲頭繫着一條布繩子。他太小，沒有辦法像大人，把褲頭一摺一塞就可以繫牢。

「轉去。」阿金回頭推了他一把。他倒退了一步。阿金是阿福伯的最小兒子。第一次叫他「白鼻狸」的就是他。

有一次阿福伯在山上捉了一隻白鼻狸，放在鐵絲籠裏，準備拿到外面去賣。牠的毛黃裏帶黑，鼻樑是一條長長的白斑，通到淺紅色的圓圓的鼻尖。牠的一隻腳被圈套挾斷了，走起路，一跛一跛的。

「你也是白鼻狸。」阿金突然指着他的鼻子說。

這以後，大家都叫他白鼻狸，好像已忘掉了他的名字。

他怔怔地望着五個人，看他們彎進竹屏背後。

他舉起手，把手裏的陀螺打下去，但沒有打好，陀螺橫轉起來。

「幹！死干樂！」阿祥罵了一聲。

他撿起，把繩子纏好，順着原路折回來，看路邊有一壺茶，就蹲下去猛灌了兩碗。

他回到阿福伯的菜圃邊。本來，在這四面環山的一點耕地，是一片貧瘠的赤仁土，居民都種植着甘薯、樹薯或花生，只有阿福伯經常到外面，聽了人家的意見，闢了不到半分地的一小坵，改種了一些蔬菜。

他感到下腹脹脹的，但還不夠。他站在菜圃邊等着。那些捲心白菜已種下一個月了吧，菜心開始曲捲，種在邊緣的，已有三棵的葉子轉黃了。如果不是阿金，也不會有人叫他白鼻狸了。他想着。

冷風迎面吹過來，在竹屏上呼嘯。他略微縮着身子。小腹更加鼓脹起來了。他看看四周，知道沒有人，就趕快拉起褲管，用力把小腹一擠。尿水冒着煙向第四棵白菜灌了下去。尿水灌着菜葉，和菜心。他用力擠，集中在一棵白菜上。尿也在土上冒泡，但很快地消失在土裏。他感到滿身舒暢，萬一有人看到，他就說在灌肥。

「咿哎！」突然有人大喊一聲，從竹屏後猛衝了出來。

阿祥顫了一下，還沒有看清楚是誰，尿已收進去了。

衝出來的，却是阿狗和阿金他們五個人。他實在不能相信。他們怎麼能繞了一個大圈子，躲到這邊的竹屏來了？

「我知道一定是你這隻白鼻狸。」

「我怎麼了？」

「你灌尿。」

「我灌肥呀。替你們灌肥還不好？」

「難道你不知道灌燒尿，會鹹死菜。你看看那三棵。」

「那不是我弄的。」

「不是你，還會有誰？」

「真的不是我。」

「白鼻狸偷吃果子，還會說是牠吃的？我們抓白鼻狸來剝皮，把他的褲子脫下來。」阿金說，雙手把他抱住。

「不要，不要。」他掙扎着，手亂揮，腳亂踢。

阿進抓住他捏着陀螺的手。阿河阿成拉了他的腳。只有阿狗站在一邊笑着。

阿金把他的褲子往下一拉，褲頭滑出布繩子，好像竹筍脫殼，褲頭鬆開，褲也掉了下來。

「哈、哈、哈！」阿金拉掉他的褲子，往空中一撒褲子順着風飄了一下，飄落在地上。

「哈、哈、哈！」大家也跟着大笑起來。

阿祥猛掙着身子。風很冷，吹着他的屁股和下肢，但他不顧一切，拿起陀螺，對準阿金背部猛砸過去。

「哎！」阿金叫了一聲，伸手到背部一摸，手指已染了血。

「娘的！」阿金回頭過來，用拳頭往他的臉上猛揮過來。

他的牙齒撞了一下，咬到了自己的舌頭。嘴裏鹹鹹的，他知道已流血了。

二

天空碧藍如洗，太陽猛烈地照着，一望過去，起起伏伏的山巒，盡是鬱綠的相思樹，在無風的太陽底下，靜靜地佇立着。

阿祥已走了兩個小時的路。赤仁土的山路只有一兩公尺寬，沿着一條小溪蜿蜒而下。這是通往外界的唯一一條路。每當雨後，水牛走過，就在路上留下許多腳印，經太陽晒乾，就變得尖銳刺腳。

阿祥打着赤腳，邊走邊跑，裹着書本和便當的包袱巾從右肩到左腰部打斜地繫着。

他在山路上又行走了一段，然後下坡到溪邊，踏上舖在水中的石頭。水位較低的時候，隔着半步的距離舖着的石頭便露出水面，人可以踩踏過去，一到下雨天水位漲高，有些地方也深過腰部，聽說在暴風雨的季節，溪水猛漲，曾有人想硬涉過去，却被溪水沖走了。

有人迎面而來，是阿福伯。在鄉下，住在路程兩三個小時內的人，都算鄰居。

「阿福伯。」他叫了一聲，有點不好意思。他一路上一直怕見到熟人。他正在溪中央，要躲也來不及。

「阿祥，你上街了。」

阿福伯並沒有問他為什麼不上學。鄉下沒有禮拜幾的觀念，也不重視上學不上學。他一腳踩進水中，讓阿福伯過去。水很涼，他覺得很舒服。乾脆就兩腳都站到水裏。腳底有點滑。是長在石頭上的青苔。他站穩了腳，把手也伸進水裏浸一下，連心裏都感到涼爽。

如果阿福伯碰到父親，告訴他說在路上碰到了自己，父親追問起來該怎麼辦？他站上來，回頭看看阿福伯。但他更怕那位新來的日本老師井上先生。井上先生白白胖胖，和又黑又乾的村人都不一樣。井上先生來的第二天，就叫學生把桌椅全部搬到後面，騰出空地來，叫大家跪下去，用竹棍子在每一個人頭上敲了一下。井上先生看看他的鼻子，又加了一棒。

「馬鹿野郎，青番，無教育，捧庫拉……」

井上先生一邊喊一邊打。全班學生沒有一個人知道為什麼被打，這一件事發生之後，隔天就有十分之一的學生不再來上課。

「讀書有什麼用？」有人說。

「我才不去跪他。我只跪我祖公。」

阿祥挨打的機會要比其他的同學多，在一兩個禮拜中，至少要被打一次。每次被打，腦袋上都腫起來，像長着一個瘤。為什麼呢？他實在想不出道理，也許是因為鼻上那一道白斑。

他實在不想讀下去。但每次都想到阿舅。阿祥所以能到一個鐘頭路程的內埔去讀書，完全是阿舅竭力說服父親的。

「你要認真讀書，讀完了來臺北。」

阿祥知道他今天一定會挨打。本來，他是不會遲到的。他走到半路，在路邊樹上看到一隻奇怪的鳥。牠的樣子像水鴨，但鼻上卻有一塊紅肉冠，有點像蕃鴨，但小得多。他不知道這叫什麼鳥。他追了一程，結果連跑帶衝趕到學校，還是沒有趕上。

井上先生揮動着竹棍子的樣子一直在他眼前晃動。還有那棍子敲在頭上的清脆聲音。他跪在地上等着，要來就快一點來，但又怕它真的來。一棍打下去，眼淚都擠了出來。

他在學校——說得正確一點只是分教場，附近徘徊了一下。忽然又想起阿舅住在臺北，要坐火車去。他到現在連火車都沒有看過。聽說，火車走在鐵軌上，那是要到外莊才能看到的。

他走過了中埔，太陽已相當的高，也相當的熱。他走到樹蔭下，把包袱巾解下，取出便當。飯是夠的，佐餐的只有三片蘿蔔乾和一小撮豆豉。有時，父母到街上才買一點鹹魚回來。不到幾分鐘，他把所有的東西都裝進肚子。太陽已快到中天了。從家裏走到內埔的分校要一個多小時，由內埔到中埔也要一個多小時，由中埔到外莊也要一個多小時，加起來也要四個小時多。

他的心又開始蹦蹦地跳着。這和想到井上先生的棍子的時候是差不多的，不過他早已把井上先生的事忘掉了。

他不知道火車什麼樣子，也不知道鐵軌什麼樣子。阿舅雖然曾經在稻埕上畫給他看過，但他還是沒有正確的輪廓和確實的感覺。

他也曾經要求父母帶他出去。但他們都說他太小。

他爬過一個小山崙。忽然看到山凹下去。他站在崙頂。在兩堵山壁之間，他看到了鐵路。那就是鐵路嗎？他以為要到外莊才能看到，他知道這裏離外莊不遠，却還不到外莊。

兩條鐵軌向兩邊延伸。他不知道哪一邊是通往臺北的。那一邊都是一樣的吧。他凝然望着。他的視線順着鐵路來回地移動着。一邊，在遠處，他看到了一個山洞。

他攀下山坡。鐵軌是舖在許多木頭上，木頭上有煤屑、有鐵銹。他蹲下去看看鐵軌的上面銀亮而平滑，在太陽下不停地閃着光。他用手去摸它，好像上次偷摸土地公的臉一般。

「嗚——嗚——嗚——」從山洞那邊傳來汽笛的聲音。

他猛醒過來，起立退到山邊。火車從他面前急擦過去。他什麼都看不清楚。火車過去之後，才覺得車上有人看着他，對他笑着。

他拔腳追了過去。火車就在他面前。他追着，追着。

三

　　小學一畢業，阿祥就到臺北阿舅所開的食堂幫忙。他先學掃地、洗碗筷、擦桌子，然後端菜，招呼客人。後來，他也學會騎腳踏車送麵飯。他學得很快，尤其他很會認路。雖然他第一次到大都市來，時間又不很長，却比那些來得更久、年紀更大的孩子更管用。

　　阿舅很高興，有時也叫他去採購或跑銀行。他很快就成為阿舅最得力的助手。

　　有一天，已是深夜十一以後，他送麵到榮町一家布店，有四五個店員正在玩四色牌。

　　「麵來了，有燒沒？」一個店員說。

　　「白鼻的。」另一個叫他。「湯那會這麼少？你偷飲了？」

　　他騎車子送來，難免盪出了一些湯。而且麵泡久了，也會吸湯。

　　「對，他真像白鼻狸。喂，少年家呀，聽說你是從內山來的，那邊一定有很多的白鼻狸吧。」另一個幫腔說。

　　「趕快洗牌了，不去睬他嚛。」

　　「喂，是你老爸白鼻，還是你老母白鼻？」

　　「不要講笑，講笑也要有程度。」另一個說。

　　阿祥用雙手把麵一碗一碗端起來放在桌上。他很用力，手在發抖。他怕把湯再盪了出來。他把提麵箱的蓋子蓋好。當他再騎上腳踏車的時候眼淚已流了出來。他一腳踩在地上，用手背把眼淚擦掉。為什麼？為什麼每一個人都叫他白鼻呢？他想離開故鄉，也是因為在那裏每一個人都叫他白鼻狸。來到城市裏，認識的人不多，但只要一熟，就又叫他白鼻。

　　這幾個人他並不熟，却這樣叫他，而且還侮辱他的父母。他沒有直接回到店裏。他到公園邊的派出所去報案，說有人賭博。

　　警察要他帶路。因為送食物去過派出所，他和警察也認識。警察把那些人抓去拘留。雖然他只到門口，沒有跟警察進去，他們也猜想他去報案的。他們在牢裏叫飯的時候，把他臭罵了一頓。

他又去報告。警察警告他們，如再這樣就不放他們出去。

這時候，他更清楚地覺得，人分成兩種，一種是欺負人的，一種是受人欺負的。井上先生是前一種，自己是第二種。但現在，他親眼看到那幾個店員由第一種變成第二種，而自己又好像從第二種變成了第一種。

那些店員釋放出來以後，曾經到店裏找過阿舅和他聲言要報復。但他不怕他。警察曾經說他是好國民，好日本國民，以後有什麼事和他們多多連絡。

有一次，阿祥在晚上送麵的時候，從巷子裏跑出幾個人，把他連車帶人推倒在地上，痛打他一頓，等他爬起來，碗和箱都破了，輪圈也已扭彎。他又跑去報案，警察來了，那些人也早已沒有踪影了。

他回來店裏，阿舅很不高興。

「我對你講過，我們生意人，應該規規矩矩做生意，其他的事全不必管。你却不聽。最好，你先回鄉下去，也比較安全，等一些時候，我再寫信叫你來。」

阿祥並沒有回鄉下。他跑到派出所訴苦。他們看他聰明，就留下來做工友。因為他是臺灣人，有語言上的方便，又因為送飯麵的關係，對附近的地形和居民都很熟悉，他們有時也帶他出去辦案，有時也叫他自己打聽一些消息。在名義上，他是工友，却兼有線民的身分。

在這一段時間，他感觸最深的是隔開拘留所的那一道木格子。不管是誰，一進那裏，就銳氣全消，變得那麼柔順，不管是知識分子，或者是有錢的商人，都會趴在格子上求他給他們一杯水。

有時，他也看到警察把犯人提出來，帶到後面的浴室，用水龍頭沖着他們，像鼠籠裏的老鼠一般，沖得全身透濕，連腳都發軟。有時，警察還把橡皮管插進犯人的嘴裏，用手捏住犯人的鼻子，把水不停的灌進去。犯人一邊哀叫，一邊把水不停地吞，等肚子都脹了，警察叫他趴在地上用腳蹬着，教他把水吐出來。

目前，他只是一個工友，只是一個未成年的孩子，但只因他站在木格子的外邊，裏面的人都要用哀求的眼睛望着他。在裏面的人，從來沒有叫他白鼻的。

　　當然，他是要站在木格子的這一邊的。但他不是要做一輩子的工友，也不是一輩子的線民。他要把這木格子擴大到整個社會。他要做警察，只有這樣，所有的人才會尊敬他，才會畏懼他。

　　他把這種決心告訴那些警察。他們教他讀什麼書，怎麼讀，也教他如何參加考試。他第一次沒有考取，第二次却順利地通過，而且名列前茅。

四

　　曾吉祥和吳玉蘭坐在石階。石階有二十多級，每級寬二尺，高八寸，長有二十多尺，上面是通往慈祐宮的寬大的通道，下面就是大水河的水面，石階本身就是河堤的一部分，也算是碼頭。

　　烏黑的天空上點綴着稀疏的星星，從四周照出來的探照燈時明時滅，有時獨自尋索，有時在天空上交會在一起。

　　日本已向美國宣戰，預防是必要的。

　　「不行，阿爸說結婚不能用日本的儀式。」吳玉蘭微低着頭，眼睛注視着大水河的流水。水影隨着探照燈的明滅而閃爍不定。

　　「妳老爸真頑固。」

　　「不能說他頑固。他說，我們有我們的儀式。」

　　「妳是受過教育的人，不能像那種無教育的人。」

　　「阿爸也讀過書，只是讀不同的書。他曾經說過。讓我們姐妹讀書最沒有用，讀一些奇奇怪怪的東西，講起話來，沒有一句聽得懂。」

　　「部長桑勸我這樣做。他勸我，其實這就是命令。」

　　「我姐夫也說我們應該用自己的儀式。他還到過內地讀書呢。」

　　「妳不要再提到他。他是可疑的人物。他需要我保護，將來也需要我救他。本來，親戚裏有他這樣的人，對我很不利。他們將不會信任我。至少不會像以前那樣信任我。這一次，我決定要用日本人的儀式，有一半也是為了妳有這樣的親戚。」

　　「不過阿爸說，不照我們的方式，就不准我們。」

「不准，就……」曾吉祥倏地站了起來。

「曾桑。」吳玉蘭也站了起來。

「妳自己怎麼想呢？」

「……」

「妳的決定很重要。在臺灣，還沒有這種例子。寶貴就寶貴在第一次。妳可能還不知道。政府正在計劃推廣皇民化運動。以後，不但要按照日本的儀式結婚，還要拜他們的神，還要改姓名。譬如說，我姓曾，可以改成曾我，曾我兄弟的曾我。妳們姓吳，日本人也有，不過很少，而且讀法不同。要徹底皇民化，最好也要改個姓。日本現在已把南洋的許多地方佔領過來，以後我們都要去南洋，那地方太大了，我們要去做指導者。」

「我姐夫說，日本會……」

「不要說。妳要說什麼，我已知道。妳一說出來就犯罪。我就不能不捉人。我不能捉妳，因為我必須保護妳，但妳的親戚，我就無能為力了。我有責任保護國家。任何人造謠就是危害國家。日本一定會打勝仗的。部長桑說得對，我們應該做模範，開風氣，我們要看許許多多的人追隨在我們的後面。」

「……」

「妳怎麼說？」

「我答應過您的話，一定會做到的。」

兩個月前，他們一起在宿舍後面的網球場打球。雖然是公共球場，由於運動的性質和意識的問題，只有一些日本人、警察、老師和讀中學以上的男女學生，這些屬於所謂優秀分子才能使用。

兩個人打完球之後，她就到他宿舍休息，順便看看他的球拍。以前，她雖然也去過，却都是和其他的朋友一起去。

他打網球是在訓練所受訓時學習的。他學過柔道、劍道和網球。柔道、劍道是護身術，也是晉升的手段。他已是黑帶。網球却是社交活動的重要一環。他在臺北做工友的時候，就已把這看在眼裏了。

她的球技雖然不出色，他却喜歡她的體態。自從和她打球之後，她的影子就一直在腦際出現。她穿着白色的短衣，白色的短褲。白色的襪子、白色的布鞋，纏着白色的髮帶，手拿着球拍，微蹲着身子的體態，還有那嬌甜的聲音。這些都是家庭和教育的結果。

從教育而言，她比他高。她雖然不是有名的高女，却也是私立的女學校畢業的。和他只有小學畢業完全不能相比。

今天，她也穿着一身的白，只是頭髮有些散亂。她把白色髮帶取下來，用手把頭髮往後攏一攏。她和他坐得那麼近。但兩個人之間却有那麼大的距離。要消滅這種距離，只有一個辦法，就是征服她。而現在却是一個最難得的機會。

他一下子撲過去。

「您要我，應該好好的商量。您再碰我，我只有一死。」她低沉地說。

「原諒我。」他跪在榻榻米上，雙手托前，頭一直低到可以觸着榻榻米。「我很愛妳。請妳答應我。」

「……」

「玉蘭桑……」

「您父母也贊成用日本儀式？」

「他們鄉下人，不會有什麼意見，就是有什麼意見，我也可以說服他們，萬一說服不了，我還是要用這種儀式。」他的聲音很堅決，也有點高昂。

他說完，視線由吳玉蘭身上慢慢轉開，看着大水河的對岸，再轉向天空。幾道探照燈依然交迭在天上尋索。在大水河的下游那邊便是臺北市。他依稀看到總督府的高塔。

「噗通。」河裏遠處傳來渾重的聲音，有人擲了石頭。

「噗通。」「噗通。」石頭越擲越近，一直擲到石階下的水面。

「誰！」曾吉祥大聲叫了起來。

「不理他們。」

「顯然是故意的。」

「今天，就是故意的，也不理他們。」

「噓！」從堤頂那邊傳來吹口哨的聲音。

「查脯帶查某！」是小孩子的聲音。

「噓！」

「噗通。」

「咿唷，查脯帶查某。」

「白鼻的。」

「畜生！」曾吉祥倏地站起來。

「曾桑，拜託您。」

「好吧，不過……」

「我可以答應。」

「您父母呢？」

「我會盡力勸他們。」

五

「日本輸了。」

「日本輸了。」

開始，大家都竊竊私語，還有點不敢相信。大家都知道日本雖然不會打到一兵一卒，雖然日本的報紙一再說着沖繩玉碎，雖然米國已在廣島和長崎投了兩顆原子彈，雖然大家都知道日本遲早要投降，但大家都沒有料到是今天。

今天，大家都似乎感到有點異樣。早上，天空一片晴朗，卻寧靜得出奇。已沒有警報，也沒有飛機的聲音。

郡役所裏，大家顯得很緊張，精神有點恍惚。

有人把收音機放在郡役所前庭，到了中午時分，郡守以下每一個人都跪在地上聆聽天皇陛下的玉音。收音機的效果並不好，雜音太多，而且天皇陛下的聲音在顫抖，顯得已泣不成聲了。

開始，大家只是默默地跪着，然後有人跟着飲泣。每一個人都緊張地握着拳頭，頭越垂越低。有人用手搥地。

曾吉祥也跪在人羣之中，他不知道是悲還是苦。他只是楞楞地跪着。這件事好像與他無關，也好像有切身的關係。

玉音播放完畢，大家還向收音機行禮，久久無法站立起來。

「日本輸了。」

這一句話變成有分量了。他看到郡守起來。街長、課長、主任、巡查部長繼續起來。有些人垂頭喪氣，但也有些人好像已有了決心，臉上露出堅決的表情。

「日本輸了。」他走到街上，已有人大聲地說。

「日本輸了？」回到家裏，妻迎面出來，幫他脫下衣服。

「輸了。」

「以後怎麼辦？」

「我也不知道。」一輩子裏，他沒有這樣徬徨過。

「米國兵會把每一個人都殺死？」

「妳相信？」

「我當然不相信。」

「那妳還問？」

「日本人真會宣傳。就是現在，我還想着從沖繩的絕崖縱身自殺的女學生，我是指那些姬百合。」

「妳想那些幹嗎？」

「我是說，如果您……」

「我怎麼樣？」

「如果您下一聲命令，我什麼都不怕。」

「馬鹿，我們不同，我們不是日本人。」

「我知道不是日本人，但您是日本警察呀。」

「我把這制服丟掉就行了。」

「可以丟嗎？」

「日本已沒有國家了，難道還會管我？」

「可是……」

「郡守還命令我們本島人維持治安。」

「玉蘭，玉蘭。」有人在外面喊着。

「姐姐，請進來。」

「妳姐夫說，曾桑要趕快逃。」

「為什麼？」

「妳看現在民眾還平靜，因為事情來得太突然，大家不知道怎麼做。也許明天，也許一個禮拜之後，一旦有人發難，說不定還會打死人呢。」

「那我們母子怎麼辦？」

「孩子可以暫時放在我家。」

但曾吉祥還不相信民眾會怎樣。他說他有義務維持舊鎮的治安。

到第二天，舊鎮也開始有了情況。

開始是巡查部長的自殺。在播放玉音當天，內地就有幾個日本的大官自殺。自殺好像會傳染，報紙上幾乎天天都有報導。部長雖然只是一個小官，但在舊鎮却是一件大事。

舊鎮本來是平靜的小鎮，鎮民都安分守己。但報復之風很快地傳到了舊鎮。

據說，最先發難的是一個鑲牙師的兒子。鑲牙師沒有執照，接近密醫。這個鑲牙師在戰時因為一位開業牙科醫師的密告，被抓去拘留。一旦終戰，他兒子在中學學過柔道，就去找牙醫算帳，在公眾面前把對方摔在地上。然後，這個兒子又去找抓過父親的琉球籍警察。

這時，民眾一下子覺醒過來，大家喊着「冤有頭，債有主」，各自尋找仇人報復。

有些警察被拉在廟前跪着，向代表着我們的神陪罪。有個屠夫，在戰時因私宰被警察抓去拘留灌水，這時候却拿着宰豬的尖刀抵着兩個警察的背部從海山頭走到草店尾，押着他們遊街示眾。他很得意，比誰都得意。

臺灣人的警察，大部分是辦事務的，與民眾沒有什麼瓜葛，都能相安無事。只有一個姓賴的，被大家拖到慈祐宮前面的廣場。

「打死他！」有人喊着。

「打死這走狗！」有人應着。

「饒我，饒我。」他跪在地上，不停地叩頭哀求，他的妻子也跪在旁邊。

「打死他！」又有人喊着。

「狗，三腳，死好。」有人踢他。

「死狗呀，打死你！」又有人拿着棍子棒他。

「哎唷，哎唷！」

姓賴的警察，只是第二號罪人。他被打斷了一條腿。

「把姓曾的，把白鼻狸抓出來。」但沒有一個人知道白鼻狸逃到哪裏去。

當民眾來敲門的時候，曾吉祥迅速地逃到屋頂上。當天晚上，他悄悄地逃出了舊鎮，却沒有機會帶走他的妻子。

但大家並沒有放棄他。大家把他家裏的一些傢具打壞之後，扣住了玉蘭。

「人，我也不知道跑到哪裏。除此之外，你們有什麼要求，我都可以辦，你們打死我，我也不會有怨言。」

大家決定要她在慈祐宮廟前演戲，一連三天，在這三天內，她要準備香烟，讓鎮民無限制取吸。

那時，被日本禁止已久的子弟戲開始復出，爆竹的聲音已替代了炸彈的聲音，大家都可以再聽到鑼聲和鼓聲。民眾開始在各廟寺行香，答謝眾神賜給平安。

在慈祐宮的對面，靠着河堤邊的地方搭着戲臺，戲棚的前簷上用紅紙寫着「民族罪人曾吉祥敬奉」幾個大字。在戲棚前和廟前之間，用平底籮一籮一籮放滿香烟，輝煌的燈光，把這一條通道照得有如白天。每一籮香烟上面，都掛着紅旗，同樣寫着「民族罪人曾吉祥敬奉」幾個大字。他的妻子玉蘭就跪在廟上向全鎮民謝罪。

「來呀，來去吃白鼻仔烟！」鎮民相互招呼，熙熙攘攘前往慈祐宮。「來呀，來去看白鼻仔戲！」

雖然大家沒有抓到他，心裏不無遺憾，但聊勝於無，時間一過，也把這一件事淡忘掉了。

六

「當時你幾歲？」曾吉祥老人問我。

「十二歲吧。」我略微想了一下。

「你還記得那麼清楚？」

「這是一件大事情。」

「已三十三年了？」

「嗯，三十三年了。」

「唉，舊鎮，舊鎮……」

「你沒有再回去過？」

「回去？怎麼回去？」他略微抬起頭來看我，而後又低下了。我很清楚地看到他的鼻子，雖然歲月使他的整個臉都已老化，卻無法消除鼻部那道不同的顏色。

「唉，舊鎮，舊鎮是我的夢魘。」他又嘆了一口氣說，他的眼睛望着牆壁，但他的視線卻好像已穿過牆壁看到牆外的一點，遙遠的一點。

「我不知道什麼叫夢魘。也許舊鎮的經驗便是我的夢魘吧。我一直想忘掉舊鎮，卻不能夠。雖然，我離開舊鎮已那麼久，我一閉起眼睛，就會看到那些善良，有時也是愚蠢的人的臉孔。我也記得你的父親，那個子矮小、雙腳向外彎的善良的木匠，鎮上的人都以伯叔稱呼他。他已不在了？」

「嗯，不在了。」

「我因為要他做一個書桌，他遲疑了一下，我就打了他一個嘴巴。他年紀比我大。但我還是打他。我的背上背荷着一個國家。我當時這麼想着。我還記得他看我的眼神。那眼睛充滿着憎惡和忿恨。但，我覺得權威比仇恨還要強大。

「我也記得那個叫柴扒鳳的女人。她應該是你們的鄰居。在領配給豬肉的時候插了隊，我就叫她跪在大家面前，頭上還頂着一木桶的水。既然是配給，每個人都可以買到。卻有人一定要插隊。這本來是一件小事，我也可以裝着不知，但我曾經聽日本人指着這一點，貪小便宜不惜破壞秩序的這一點，指責臺灣人的愚蠢和無教育。以前，日本老師以這樣的眼光看我，我却很快學會以同樣的眼光看自己的同胞。

「我也記得那個叫阿灶的屠夫。有人密告他豬肉裏灌了水。他不承認，我就叫他吃水。現在，我還聽得到他哀叫和求饒的聲音。

「那是一場惡夢，沒有終止的惡夢。我有極強的記憶力和敏銳的推斷力。我以這做本錢，完成了自己，以王者的姿態君臨舊鎮。我自以為是虎、是獅子。但骨子裏，我却是貓、是狗。我學會借重日本人的力量。

「我自認為是王爺，但舊鎮的人却把我看做瘟神。我知道他們在避開我。但也有人逢迎我，正如我逢迎日本人一般。玉蘭也曾經勸過我不能過分，因為舊鎮是一個小鎮，她家又是個舊家，推算起來，幾乎有三分之一的鎮民不是她家的親戚便是朋友。但我如何能放手呢？人在權威的絕頂，自然會沉醉其中，而忘掉了自己。

「然而，有一天，日本打敗了。老實說，就是日本人自己也有預感，只是沒有人想到會來得那麼快。因為事情來得太突然，我還沒有來得及想怎麼辦的時候，玉蘭的姐夫，那位律師就叫我逃匿。

「我不聽他的話。我以為我還可以繼續領導鎮民，一直到有一天忽然發現這些馴鹿已變成了猛虎。在倉皇中，我一個人逃出了舊鎮，回到鄉下來。這是唯一可以逃避的地方。真沒有想到父親竟不收留我。他說我不再是他的兒子。我知道因為結婚的儀式開罪了他。我實在沒有想到一個鄉下人有這種氣節。幸好母親苦苦央求，他才把這個放農具的小倉庫騰出來給我暫住。父親有一點田地，但他不讓我耕種。其實，我也無法耕種。母親偷偷地送東西來給我吃。

「我在默默地等着玉蘭來團聚，或者情勢平靜下來，我可以去找她。真想不到，經過不到兩個月，她竟因為患了傷寒，獨自走了。當這消息傳到了這裏，我實在不能相信。

「我還記得，當時她家周圍還圍着，大家都說傳染病遠遠地繞過。」

「這時候，我忽然感到我是世界上最孤獨的人。在這世界上，再也沒有什麼可以替代她的了。現在，我還能記得她打球的姿勢。戰爭剛結束的時候，她曾經表示過，如果我自殺，她會毫不猶豫地跟着我。我也好像可以看到她一個人跪在廟前向民眾贖罪的情形。

「聽說，在面對着狂暴的民眾，她是那麼鎮靜，那麼勇敢。她以一個弱女子，為了我這個人，擔負了民族罪人的重負。民眾罵她，她向民眾求恕，但不是為了她自己。有人唾她，她也不去拭擦。我是一個男人，卻讓自己的女人出醜受辱。

「難道她不會有怨言嗎？我連見她最後一面也不能夠。她就是有怨言，又如何伸訴呢？我不知道她是怎樣瞑目的。

「我何幸得到這樣一個女人呢？我的罪孽太深，所以必須得到她而又喪失她？在所有的人，包括我的親人都厭棄我的時候，只有她一個人默默地承受着，而我還沒有機會表示感激和愧疚之情，她就默默地走了。

「她一死，我的整個心也死了。其實，要死應該早一點死。在日本投降的時候，我就應該死。許多日本人都自殺殉國。我卻沒有這分勇氣。我卻說我不是日本人。我是一個民族的罪人，我應該以死來謝罪。但我沒有，我反而逃到這深山來。你看我這個人有多可恥，我逃到這裏來，讓她替我向國民謝罪，而我卻還在心裏想着有一天當情勢平靜下來的時候，我還可以回去當警察呢。

「但玉蘭的死，使我的想法完全改變了。從那一天開始，世上再沒有曾吉祥這個人了。其實，在日本投降的那一天，他就應該不復存在了。他的人民，他的親戚朋友，他的父母都已唾棄他了，只是他恬不知恥地留了下來而已。」

「唉，玉蘭。」他又拿起那張照片仔細地看着。「你真的認不出她？」他的手在發抖，他的眼神還有一點木然，看來還是乾涸的。

「我知道她。可能當時年紀太小，實在認不出來。」

「不認得她的人，何止是你一個人！以你的年齡還不認得她，可能全舊鎮，已沒有幾個人認得她的吧。剛才你還說，舊鎮擴展很快，你回去，在街上已不容易碰到熟人了。我知道人家會很快地把她忘掉的。」

「你沒有替她刻個像？」

「我試過，但不能刻。她雖然是我的妻，雖然曾經那麼近，我却不能刻。她離開我太遠了。她的身體，我曾經摸過，但那不是屬於我的。她的心雖然曾經屬於我，我却捉摸不到。她的臉，她那臨去的臉，是帶着什麼表情呢？到現在還沒有人告訴我。

「我知道她只有一個心願。就是死在我的身邊，埋在我的身邊。聽說她的父母都已先後去世，聽說舊鎮都已改變了，我却一直沒有再去過。我不敢去。開始，我怕那些人記恨於我，而後，我又怕我的不純沾污她的土地。我沒有臉再見到她的親人。我也想把她的骨灰帶到這個地方來的，但我怕她在生的時候沒有來過，會不會太生疏。

「她的兒子也已長大成人。我說她的兒子，因為我沒有資格。目前，他已離開舊鎮到臺北去。本來，我想事情平靜過去，就把他們接到身邊來，沒有想到她猝然撒手而去，把他留給她姐姐撫育成人。他也曾經來看過我，叫我去和他同住。但我不敢面對着他，看着他比什麼都痛苦。他有一點像玉蘭。我希望他能像其他的人一般唾棄我。

「我想應該把我和玉蘭的事告訴他。但我不能夠開口。在沒有人的時候，我可以和玉蘭說話，但如果她真的出現，我怕一句話也說不出來的吧。我無法刻玉蘭，這也是一個原因吧。」

「你刻那些馬，是一種自責？」

「當時，臺灣人稱日本是狗，是四腳，替日本人做事的走狗，是三腳。」

「你為什麼只刻馬？而不刻其他的動物？」

「因為他們要的是馬。我刻着，刻着，突然間，好像在那些馬身上看到了自己，所以就試着把自己刻上去。」

我把地上、牆角的馬一隻一隻拿起來，雖然每一隻的姿勢都不一樣，却都有一個共同的特點。牠們的表情和姿態都充滿着痛苦和愧怍。

「你打算如何處理牠們？」

「我也不知道。」他遲疑了一下。「也許，有一天，我會把牠們全部燒掉。」

「燒掉？」

「因為牠們和別人無關。」他無力地說。

「你能不能賣一隻給我？」我鼓起勇氣說。其實，我心裏想着，只要我付得起，我想全部買下來。

「賣給你？」他又遲疑了一下，把臉慢慢轉向我。「好吧，你挑一隻吧。這三十三年來，我沒有見過舊鎮的人。我一直想見舊鎮的人，也一直怕見到。」

「但，我也已離開舊鎮了。」

「至少，你知道舊鎮曾經有一個叫白鼻狸的警察。」

我挑了一隻。牠三腳跪地，用一隻前腳硬撐着身體的重量。牠的頭部微微扭歪，嘴巴張開，鼻孔張得特別大，好像在喘氣，也好像在嘶叫，牠的鬃毛散亂。我再仔細一看，有一隻後腿已折斷，無力地拖着。

「這一隻，就送給你吧。」他遲疑了一下說。

「為什麼？」

「我心裏一直怕挑到這一隻。怕來的事，往往來得早。有一天晚上，我夢見玉蘭回來。我已好久沒有夢見過她了。我怕已把她忘了。我看到她，跪在我面前哭着。我也哭了。我一直以為不再會有眼淚了。但那天晚上，我哭得連枕頭都濕了。早上，我一起來，就決心把所有的工作推開，一心刻着一隻馬。就是你手裏的這一隻。看馬要看眼睛，你看看牠的眼睛吧。」

我先看馬，再看他。他那乾涸無神的眼睛突然濕潤起來。

我趕快把頭轉開，把手裏的馬輕輕地放了回去，拉着賴國霖默默地退出來。

——一九七九年

作者簡介

余光中（1928-2017），曾任國立中山大學英文系特聘教授。作為知名詩人與多產作家，余光中一生在兩岸三地發表了超過七十卷的詩歌、散文、文學評鑑與翻譯，並在港台文學界獲得許多重大獎項。1991年余光中獲得香港翻譯學會頒發榮譽會士，並在1990至1998年擔任中華民國筆會會長。2000年時，余光中的詩集被收列於二十世紀必讀的一百本中國文學榜單中。2017年他在高雄辭世，享耆壽九十歲。

白萩（1937-2023），本名何錦榮，曾在1956年獲得中國文藝協會第一屆新詩獎。身為笠詩社與《笠》詩刊創辦人之一的白萩在一生中發表了許多作品，包括詩集《風的薔薇》、《香頌》、《天空象徵》、《詩廣場》與《現代詩散論》等等。2023年白萩辭世，享壽八十七歲。

陶忘機，自由作家、譯者。於華盛頓大學取得中文比較文學博士學位，如今是美國加利福尼亞明德大學蒙特雷國際研究學院教授。陶忘機翻譯了許多台灣現代詩歌、小說、以及佛教文學，其中包括中華民國筆會前主編齊邦媛教授的暢銷書《巨流河》。

洛夫（1928-2018)，本名莫洛夫，《創世紀》詩刊的創辦人之一，並曾擔任多年的總編輯一職。他畢業於讀淡江文理學院英文系，曾任東吳大學外文系副教授。洛夫曾榮獲國家文藝獎等多項獎項，並獲選為「台灣當代十大詩人」。洛夫出版過多部詩集、散文集與譯著，代表作曾被譯成英、法、日、韓、荷蘭、瑞典等外國語文。1999年，詩集《魔歌》被選為三十部台灣文學經典之一。2001年，洛夫發表了三千行長詩《漂木》，允為移居加拿大後最重要的代表作。2018年3月19日，洛夫在三軍總醫院病逝，享耆壽九十一歲。

白　靈，1951年生，本名莊祖煌，出生於台北萬華區。美國史蒂文斯理工學院化工碩士，曾主編詩刊，並任教於臺北科技大學，現已退休。白靈曾獲國家文藝獎等許多文學獎項，並且出版了多部詩集，包括《沒有一朵雲需要國界》、《愛與死的間隙》、《白靈截句》以及《流動的臉：白靈‧新世紀詩選》。

殷張蘭熙（1920-2017），原籍湖北枝江，畢業於華西聯合大學外文系，曾任東吳大學外文系副教授三年，並於1996年赴劍橋出席哈佛大學研討會。翻譯的中文短篇故事以及詩歌皆出版於《新聲》、《綠藻與鹹蛋》、《象牙球與其地》以及《黑色的淚》。殷張蘭熙的創作文類主要為詩，曾在1971年出版詩集《葉落》。除此之外，她還翻譯了陳若曦《尹縣長》等，曾擔任中華民國筆會英文季刊主編等職，是筆會的靈魂人物。殷張蘭熙於2017年12月22日離世，享耆壽98歲。

商　禽（1930-2010），本名羅顯烆，出生於中國四川，1949年隨部隊赴台。詩作量少質精，著有兩部詩集《夢或者黎明》跟《用腳思想——詩及素描》及增訂本《夢或者黎明及其他》，另有詩選集《商禽‧世紀詩選》及《商禽詩全集》。

馬悅然（1924-2019），瑞典漢學家、瑞典學院院士、諾貝爾文學獎評審委員。歷任斯德哥爾摩大學東方語言學院中文系漢學教授和系主任。馬悅然在中國語言學領域發表了許多作品，也曾翻譯過古今中外的中國經典文學包括《水滸傳》、《西遊記》，和沈從文的作品。作為諾貝爾文學獎評審委員中唯一的漢學家，馬悅然也見證了莫言獲得2012年的諾貝爾文學獎。2019年10月17日，馬悅然在家中安然離世。

羅　門（1928-2017），本名韓仁存，中國海南省文昌市人。著作有十五本詩集、七本散文集，以及羅門創作大系十卷等。曾獲中山文藝獎等榮耀，1965年並以詩作〈麥堅利堡〉獲菲律賓總統金牌獎，作品曾被翻譯成英文、法文、日文、韓文等。2017年1月18日，羅門在北投道生院老人長期照顧中心逝世。

梅　新（1937-1997），本名章益新，另有筆名魚川。1937出生於浙江縉雲，自軍中開始現代詩創作，1956年加入由紀弦創立的「現代派」。他在編輯工作上貢獻卓著，曾參與催生籌劃《中外文學》、《國文天地》、《聯合文學》等雜誌，規劃《中國現代文學大系》、《中國現代文學年選》、《詩學》等出版品，1982年並促成了《現代詩》復刊。在主編《中央日報》副刊十年間，曾四度榮獲新聞局金鼎獎副刊編輯獎。著有《再生的樹》、《梅新詩選》、《履歷表》等書。

向　明，1928年生，本名董平，湖南長沙人。藍星詩社資深同仁。曾任《藍星詩刊》主編、臺灣詩學季刊社社長、年度詩選主編。曾獲文藝獎章、中山文藝獎、國家文藝獎等，著有詩集、詩話集、散文集、童話逾五十部，作品被譯成英、法、德、比、日、韓、斯洛伐克、馬來西亞等國文字。年過95仍筆耕不輟，最新著作為《野草說法：向明寫詩讀詩》。

葉維廉，1937年出生於中國廣東，在香港長大。畢業於台灣大學外文系、台灣師範大學英語研究所。1963年赴美國愛荷華大學攻讀碩士，1967年獲普林斯頓大學哲學博士。他是加州大學聖地亞哥校區比較文學榮譽教授，著有《龐德的國泰集》、《中國現代小說的風貌》、《飲之太和》、《比較詩學》等論著，與多部中文詩集和散文集。

陳義芝，1953年生於台灣花蓮。詩人，國立高雄師範大學中國文學博士，曾任《聯合報》副刊主任，國立臺灣師範大學國文學系教授。2010至2014年間擔任中華民國筆會秘書長，2019至2022年間曾任筆會副會長。主要著作有詩集《邊界》、《無盡之歌》與散文集《歌聲越過山丘》等。所獲文學獎項，包括時報文學推薦獎和中山文藝獎。

梁欣榮，祖籍廣東，生於香港，17歲移居台灣，就讀於台大外文系。美國德克薩斯州A&M大學英美文學博士，曾任國立臺灣大學外國語文學系系主任及研究所所長，臺灣大學國際事務處副處長及國際華語研習所所長，並曾於外交部教授寫作與翻譯。2006至2023年間，擔任中華民國筆會英文季刊主編。著有《魯拜新詮》與《魯拜拾遺》等。

陳育虹，1952年生於台灣高雄。文藻外語學院英文系畢業，旅居加拿大溫哥華十餘年，現定居台北。她以《索隱》獲2004《臺灣詩選》「年度詩獎」，以《之間》、《閃神》獲2017「聯合報文學大獎」，2022年並榮獲「瑞典蟬獎」（Cikada Prize）。另有譯作凱洛·安·達菲詩集《痴迷》、艾特伍詩選《吞火》、爾伯特詩集《烈火》等。

鴻　鴻，本名閻鴻亞，1964年生於台灣台南。著有詩集、短篇小說、散文集以及劇場評論。鴻鴻是衛生紙詩刊的主編，同時也在2009年創立黑眼睛跨劇團，成為劇團創辦人之一。鴻鴻迄今擔任約四十齣戲劇、舞蹈及歌劇之導演，亦從2004年起擔任台北詩歌節之策展人。著有詩集《土製炸彈》、《仁愛路犁田》、《樂天島》、《跳浪》等。

許悔之，本名許有吉，1966年生，台灣桃園人。國立台北工專（現改制為國立台北科技大學）化工科畢業。曾獲多種文學獎項及雜誌編輯金鼎獎。曾任《自由時報》副刊主編、《聯合文學》雜誌及出版社總編輯。現為有鹿文化社長，從事文學、藝術創作。著有《有鹿哀愁》、《創作的型錄》、《但願心如大海》、《我的強迫症》、《不要溫馴地踱入，那夜憂傷：許悔之詩文選》等多部詩集、散文集。2007年出版日譯詩集《鹿の哀しみ》。

范德培，生於德國特里爾，父母是荷蘭與德國人。於里爾大學學習中文及日文後，從國立成功大學中文系畢業，並在輔仁大學翻譯所修得碩士學位。范德培從1989年起在台灣居住，現職自由工作者。

楊　牧（1940-2020），本名王靖獻。1940年（昭和15年）於花蓮出生。早年筆名「葉珊」。美國愛荷華大學創作碩士、美國柏克萊加州大學比較文學博士。曾任西雅圖華盛頓大學教授、中央研究院中國文哲研究所創所所長，國立東華大學人文社會科學學院創院院長。曾獲時報文學獎、中山文藝獎、吳三連文藝獎、國家文藝獎、聯合報讀書人最佳書獎、花蹤世界華文文學獎、紐曼華語文學獎、瑞典蟬獎等。他著有散文、詩集、戲劇、評論、翻譯等逾五十部，並與瘂弦等人共同創辦洪範書店。2020年3月13日，楊牧病逝於臺北國泰醫院，享壽八十一歲。

羅智成，1955年生於臺北。台大哲學系畢業，美國威斯康辛大學東亞所碩士、博士班肄業。擔任過《中國時報》人間副刊編輯和撰述委員、《中時晚報》副刊主任及副總編輯，並創辦過多所電台、雜誌、出版社。著有《畫冊》、《光之書》、《傾斜之書》、《寶寶之書》、《擲地無聲書》、《黑色鑲金》等詩集，散文或評論《亞熱帶習作》、《文明初啟》、《南方朝廷備忘錄》、《知識也是一種美感經驗》等。最新作品為詩集《預言又止》。

林文月（1922-2023），臺灣彰化縣人，誕生於上海日本租界，啟蒙教育為日文，至小學六年級返歸臺灣，始接受中文教育。她自大學時期即從事中、日文學翻譯工作。1958年至1993年在國立臺灣大學中文系任教時，專攻六朝文學、中日比較文學，並曾教授現代散文等課。曾獲中國時報文學獎、國家文藝獎散文獎及翻譯獎，也是臺北文學獎與第三十一屆行政院文化獎得主。其作品多以散文與日本古典文學譯著為主，包括《飲膳札記》和紫式部《源氏物語》等。

齊邦媛，1924年生於遼寧鐵嶺，是享譽國際的教育家、學者與作者，同時是國立臺灣大學外文系的榮譽教授。齊邦媛不僅是美國密芝根大學與印第安納大學的傅爾布萊特計畫學者，更曾任1985年柏林自由大學的客座教授與台灣第一本現代中國文學選集--《中華現代文學大系》的主編。她的文學評論集有《千年之淚》與《一生中的一天》，自傳《巨流河》被譽為文學巨作。1992至1999年間，齊邦媛擔任中華民國筆會英文季刊主編一職。

白先勇，1936年出生中國廣西。臺大外文系畢業，愛荷華大學碩士，後任教於加州大學聖芭芭拉分校東亞語言文化系。白先勇是小說家、散文家、評論家、戲劇家，著作極豐，如《臺北人》、《孽子》、《樹猶如此》等。1960年他創立《現代文學》雜誌，推動文運，影響深遠。他從加州大學退休後，投入愛滋防治的公益活動和崑曲藝術的復興事業，製作青春版《牡丹亭》巡迴各地，獲得廣大迴響。他也從「現代文學傳燈人」，成為「傳統戲曲傳教士」。

戴德巍，曾在汶萊達魯薩蘭大學擔任助理教授，主要教導語音學與文法。妻子**陳艷玲**是土生土長的台灣人，目前也是一名譯者。

廖玉蕙，1950年生，臺中潭子人。東吳大學中國文學博士，台北教育大學語創系退休教授。曾獲吳三連散文獎、吳魯芹散文獎、台中文學貢獻獎、中山文藝獎等。她的創作以散文為主，著有《大食人間煙火》、《彼年春天──廖玉蕙的台語散文》、《像我這樣的老師》、《五十歲的公主》、《教授別急！──廖玉蕙幽默散文集》等五十餘部，並編選《廖玉蕙老師的經典文學》等二十餘種語文教材。

湯麗明，國立臺灣大學外國語文學系學士、輔仁大學翻譯學研究所碩士。已於國立高雄第一科技大學退休，現職教師與自由口筆譯者。

龍應台，1952年生，高雄大寮的自來水廠裡出生，南部的漁村農村長大。留學美國九年，旅居歐洲十三年，任教於香港九年；台北市首任文化局長、中華民國首任文化部長。2014年12月1日辭官，2017年移居台灣屏東潮州鎮，開始鄉居，行走於鳳梨田、香蕉園、大山大海之間，與果農、漁民、獵人、原住民為伍。2021年開始在太平洋畔、台東山中生活。

石岱崙是加拿大多倫多大學的台灣小說與電影博士，論文研究主題則圍繞在跨族裔愛情上。石岱崙現在正在研究中文與原住民語言，特別是賽德克語。他曾在阿爾伯塔大學和國立台灣大學教授翻譯課程，現任職於香港嶺南大學。

隱　地，1937年生於上海，1947年來臺；政工幹校畢業後，先後擔任過《青溪雜誌》、《新文藝月刊》、《書評書目》等雜誌的主編，1975年創辦爾雅出版社，擔任發行人。曾先後發起與編輯出版「年度小說選」、「年度詩選」、「年度文學批評選」等。持續寫作超過七十年，著有《漲潮日》、《一日神》、《法式裸睡》、《隱地極短篇》等，涵蓋小說、散文、詩等各種文類。近作為日記書寫「雷聲三部曲」。

吳敏嘉，生於台灣，在紐西蘭、泰國與韓國長大。從國立臺灣大學外國語文學系以及輔仁大學翻譯學研究所畢業的吳敏嘉，目前是臺大外文系的助理教授和專業的會議口譯，如今也有涉略文學翻譯。她是現任中華民國筆會英文季刊《譯之華》的主編之一。

王文興（1939-2023），福建人，1946年移居台灣，為美國愛荷華大學藝術學碩士，退休前為國立台灣大學外文系教授。王文興發表了文學評論、散文和小說，並以獨特且具實驗性的文字，以及鮮明的藝術風格聞名。在王文興出版的小說中，《家變》和《背海的人》引起了讀者最廣泛的討論。他最後一部長篇小說《剪翼史》在2016年出版。2007年，他被國立台灣大學授予榮譽博士學位，2011年獲得法國榮譽軍團騎士勳章。2023年9月27日，王文興安詳辭世，享壽84歲。

陳竺筠，南京人。國立台灣大學文學碩士，曾任國立臺灣大學外文系副教授，2005年與先生王文興同時自臺灣大學退休。

林懷民，1947年生於嘉義新港。雲門舞集創辦人兼藝術總監，台北藝術大學舞蹈系創辦人，曾在台灣學習中國戲曲，在紐約學習現代舞，在日本和韓國學習古典宮廷舞。他是國際知名的編舞家，曾獲得許多獎項，包括國家文化藝術基金會頒發的兩次國家藝術獎、香港演藝學院頒發的榮譽院士獎和紐約市文化局頒發的終身成就獎。文字出版品有《蟬》、《跟雲門去流浪》、《摩訶婆羅達》、《激流與倒影》等。

胡耀恆，1936年生於中國湖北，台灣大學外文系畢業，美國貝勒大學碩士、印第安納大學戲劇系及比較文學系博士。曾任美國密西根州立大學教授、夏威夷大學副教授、澳洲墨爾本大學教授。回台任教於台灣大學外文系、世新大學英語系。1995年創立台灣大學戲劇研究所及大學部，現為台大外文系及戲劇系名譽教授。著作有《西方戲劇史》，翻譯劇本《伊底帕斯王》、《阿格曼儂》、《酒神的女信徒》等。

鄭清文（1932-2017），新北市（原台北縣）人，出生於桃園。國立台灣大學商學系畢業，任職華南銀行四十多年。鄭清文為戰後第二代重要小說家，自1958年起，共發表了223篇短篇小說、3本長篇小說、59篇短篇童話、1篇長篇童話、詩3首、457篇評論與隨筆，以及37篇翻譯作品。他曾獲鹽分地帶台灣文學貢獻獎、吳三連文藝獎、國家文藝獎等獎項，以及「桐山環太平洋書卷獎」。2017年11月4日，鄭清文辭世，享壽85歲。

鄭永康，輔仁大學翻譯學碩士班畢業，曾榮獲1997、1998以及1999年的梁實秋文學大師獎翻譯獎。現職自由譯者、撰稿人、編輯，同時也在輔仁大學翻譯碩士班授課。

The First Issue of *The Chinese PEN*

For many years it has been the hope of the Chinese Center, International P.E.N., to bring out some kind of publication, be it a quarterly or an annual magazine. There has always been difficulties that seemed to be insurmountable: lack of financial resources, a working staff who would and could devote their time and energies to bringing such a project to fruition, and the finding of adequate translators to work with the materials available.

It was not until the hosting of the Third Asian Writers' Conference in Taipei in 1970 that this hope gathered momentum, spurred on by the feeling of having achieved some success in introducing the literary achievements that have occurred in the Republic of China within the last twenty years or so. All the more it was realized how little the western world knew about what was going on, is still going on, here in Taiwan. That there is a constant sprouting up of new talents whose works should be introduced to the outside world. Even if some of these works may not become masterpieces of world literature, at least they have their importance in opening up a door to a better understanding of the life and thoughts of the people here in the Republic of China.

With this aim in mind, our Chinese P.E.N. Center has finally surmounted the various difficulties. We have collected some financial support and together with members who willingly contribute of their time and energies, we have come out with this first issue of our long hoped for quarterly.

It is our hope that in the issues to come, we can present to our counterparts all over the world, a picture of what is being produced here by our present generation of writers. We hope to introduce some of the achievements in the various aspects of the literary field: essays, fiction, poetry, criticism.

Today the East and West must meet. May this quarterly be a bridge towards such a meeting.

Late President: LIN Yutang 林語堂
Chinese Center, International P.E.N.

PEN CHARTER

The PEN Charter is based on resolutions passed at its International Congresses and may be summarized as follows:

PEN affirms that——

1. Literature knows no frontiers and must remain common currency among people in spite of political or international upheavals.

2. In all circumstances, and particularly in time of war, works of art, the patrimony of humanity at large, should be left untouched by national or political passion.

3. Members of PEN should at all times use what influence they have in favour of good understanding and mutual respect between nations; they pledge themselves to do their utmost to dispel race, class and national hatreds, and to champion the ideal of one humanity living in peace in one world.

4. PEN stands for the principle of unhampered transmission of thought within each nation and between all nations, and members pledge themselves to oppose any form of suppression of freedom of expression in the country and community to which they belong, as well as throughout the world wherever this is possible. PEN declares for a free press and opposes arbitrary censorship in time of peace. It believes that the necessary advance of the world towards a more highly organized political and economic order renders a free criticism of governments, administrations and institutions imperative. And since freedom implies voluntary restraint, members pledge themselves to oppose such evils of a free press as mendacious publication, deliberate falsehood and distortion of facts for political and personal ends.

Membership of PEN is open to all qualified writers, editors and translators who subscribe to these aims, without regard to nationality, language, ethnic origin, colour or religion.

中華民國筆會大事紀要

1928～1930年	1921年國際筆會於倫敦成立後，胡適、徐志摩、林語堂等文化界人士倡議中國成立分會。根據高平叔著《蔡元培年譜》，蔡曾口述筆會於1928年在上海成立。唯因無其他佐證資料，未能視為定論。1930年11月16日中國筆會正式加入國際筆會，首任會長為曾任北大校長之蔡元培。
1957～1958年	「中華民國筆會」（英文名：Chinese P.E.N. Center）在台成立，張道藩為會長（1957-1958）。 1958年「中華民國筆會」經國際筆會正式通過，羅家倫為復會後第一任會長（1958-1969），會址設於羅氏任館長之國史館內。
1959年	「中華民國筆會」恢復派遣代表出席「國際筆會」會議。
1970年	林語堂獲選為第二任會長（1969-1973），王藍為秘書長。
1972 年9月	英文《中華民國筆會季刊》創刊。發行者：Chinese Center, International P.E.N.。 發行人陳裕清，主編殷張蘭熙（1972-1992），編輯顧問王藍、姚朋。
1973年	陳裕清獲選為第三任會長（1973-1978），姚朋為秘書長。
1975 年	《中華民國筆會季刊》發行者改為：The Taipei Chinese Center, International P.E.N. 林語堂膺選國際筆會副會長

1978 年6月	筆會及季刊地址改為：台北市光復南路180巷33-4號5樓。 姚朋獲選為第四任會長（1978-1985），殷張蘭熙為副會長。
1985年	殷張蘭熙獲選為第五任會長（1985-1991），王藍、余光中為副會長。
1990年	五月於葡萄牙舉行「國際筆會」第55屆世界大會，殷張蘭熙獲選為「國際筆會」副會長（Vice President），為終身殊榮。 9月8日於內政部正式登記成立社團法人，余光中獲選為第一屆會長（1990-1994），高天恩為秘書長。
1992 年9月	《中華民國筆會季刊》創刊二十週年。 改由齊邦媛主編（1992-1999），殷張蘭熙擔任發行人。 編輯：王慶麟、彭鏡禧、高天恩、陳長房。
1995年	余光中獲選連任為第二屆會長（1995-1999），高天恩為秘書長（1995）。按：前屆當選證書之任期至1994年9月，但1995年3月25日方完成第二屆改選。
1995 年9月	宋美璍加入季刊編輯（1995-1999），與齊邦媛女士同任主編，姜保真任秘書長（1995-1996）。
1996年9月	高天恩任秘書長。
1997年7月	筆會及季刊地址改為：台北市溫州街68巷4號4樓
1999 年3月	朱炎獲選為第三屆會長（1999-2003），歐茵西為秘書長；宋美璍辭季刊主編，由彭鏡禧接任（1999-2000）。
1999 年9月	齊邦媛辭季刊主編。

2000 年7月	彭鏡禧辭季刊主編，張惠娟接任（2000-2001）。
2001年9月	張惠娟辭季刊主編，高天恩接任（2001-2006）。
2003 年1月	朱炎先生連任為第四屆會長（2003-2006），歐茵西女士任秘書長。
2006 年12月	彭鏡禧獲選為第五屆會長（2006-2010），歐茵西任秘書長；高天恩辭季刊主編，梁欣榮接任（2006-2022）。
2010 年12月	彭鏡禧連任為第六屆會長（2010-2014），陳義芝任秘書長。
2014 年12月	黃碧端獲選為第七屆會長（2014-2018），林水福為秘書長（2014-2015）。
2015年6月	林水福辭秘書長。
2016年1月	吳淑英任副秘書長，同年7月底辭副秘書長。
2017年8月	周昭翡任秘書長（2017-2019）。
2019年1月	高天恩獲選為第八屆會長（2019-2022），梁孫傑為秘書長（2019-2021）。
2021年1月	梁孫傑辭秘書長，吳鈞堯任秘書長（2021-2022）。
2022年9月	吳敏嘉及胡宗文加入季刊編輯，同任副主編。
2022年12月	廖咸浩獲選為第九屆會長（2022-），楊宗翰為秘書長。
2023年1月	吳敏嘉及胡宗文同任主編（2023-）。梁欣榮任名譽主編（2023-）。

Editor-in-chief
Sebastian Hsian-hao Liao 廖咸浩

Executive Editor
Sarah Jen-hui Hsiang 項人慧

Administrative Editor
Shih-ying Chang 張詩瑩

Proofreading/Copy Editors
Feimei Su 蘇斐玫
May Li-ming Tang 湯麗明

Assistants
Amanda Choo 朱旻
Huai-ling Huang 黃淮芩
Tzu- chia Tseng 曾子嘉
Rou-pin Wang 王柔蘋

Artistic Director
Jung-ling Huo 霍榮齡

Cover Design
Lee Wei-han 李偉涵

Calligraphy
Sebastian Hsian-hao Liao 廖咸浩

Design
Hsiao Fan Sun 孫筱凡

Editorial Consultants
Daniel T. Hu 胡宗文
Te-ping Feng 封德屏
Michelle Min-chia Wu 吳敏嘉
Tsung-han Yang 楊宗翰

Published by the Taipei Chinese Center, PEN International, with grants from
Hotel Royal Group 老爺酒店集團   PEGATRON Corporation 和碩聯合科技股份有限公司

PEGATRON
和 碩 聯 合 科 技

心繫今古,筆匯東西 : 中華民國筆會季刊五十周年精選集 = Bridging
past and present, east and west : celebrating 50 years of translating
Chinese literature from Taiwan at the Taipei Chinese PEN / 廖咸浩主編.
-- 二版一刷. -- 臺北市 : 中華民國筆會出版 : 正港資訊發行, 2023.12

面 ； 公分

ISBN 978-986-86674-6-4(平裝)

1.CST: 中華民國筆會 2.CST: 文集

863.3   112020989

心繫今古，筆匯東西：中華民國筆會季刊五十周年精選集

Bridging Past and Present, East and West—Celebrating 50 Years of Translating Chinese Literature
from Taiwan at the Taipei Chinese PEN

主　　　　編	廖咸浩
執 行 編 輯	項人慧
助 理 編 輯	張詩瑩
核 稿 編 輯	湯麗明、蘇斐玟
助　　　　理	王柔蘋、朱旻、黃淮苓、曾子嘉
藝 術 總 監	霍榮齡
封 面 設 計	李偉涵
封 面 題 字	廖咸浩
設 計 排 版	孫筱凡
出 版 者	中華民國筆會
發 行 者	中華民國筆會
	中華民國臺灣臺北市溫州街68巷4號4樓
	Tel: (886-2) 2369-3609 Fax: (886-2) 2369-9948
E m a i l	taipen@seed.net.tw
網　　　　址	http://www.taipen.org
排 版 印 刷	東豪印刷事業有限公司
零　　　　售	唐山書店（臺北市大安區羅斯福路3段333巷9號B1）
	Tel: (02) 2363-3072
經　　　　銷	正港資訊（臺北市大安區溫州街64號B1）
	Tel: (02) 2366-1376
網 路 書 店	http://www.tsbooks.com.tw/
E m a i l	tonsan@ms37.hinet.net
出 版 日 期	2023年12月二版一刷
定　　　　價	380元
I S B N	978-986-86674-6-4